Long-Term Profit Planning

Long-Term Profit Planning

Ernest H. Weinwurm
George F. Weinwurm

An AMA Research Book

American Management Association, Inc.

© American Management Association, Inc., 1971.
All rights reserved. Printed in the United States of
America.

This publication may not be reproduced, stored in a
retrieval system, or transmitted in whole or in part, in
any form or by any means, electronic, mechanical,
photocopying, recording, or otherwise, without the
prior written permission of the Association.

International standard book number: 0-8144-5256-6
Library of Congress catalog card number: 71-150292

First printing

About This Book

MANAGERS are devoting a considerable portion of their time to satisfying the evident need for profit planning, and quite a few have made considerable progress in this regard. Yet few managers contacted in the field research for this book did not express considerable dissatisfaction with the degree to which they had been able to convert their intentions into operational realities.

Various surveys in recent years have suggested that forward-looking managements now rely on some sort of formal planning procedures for both the short and the long term. At the same time, the extensive field survey undertaken for this research indicates that comparatively few companies have implemented the comprehensive planning system necessary for meaningful long-term profit planning.

The field of planning—and long-term profit planning in particular—is very much in a state of flux. The reader should keep in mind that this study reflects conditions as they were found to be in the summer and fall of 1968, except as companies have updated case study and exhibit material. The transitory nature of a study in this field can be gauged from several replies the authors received from planning executives who had been sent draft material for review. Here are two:

> In general, the text appears to reflect adequately the situation at the time we talked, about a year ago. I am sure you recognize that the entire process of planning is in constant evolution, so that it will come

as no surprise that most of what you report has been superseded by new processes and new people.

A major problem with your write-up of . . . our planning process is its heavy dependence on the program that was suggested by our planning cycle memorandum, most of which was never implemented because of the subsequent creation of the Planning Committee. Thus we have never made use of the "Total Mission Approach" nor have we ever developed a "Strategic Plan." The management conferences have been shifted in tone and greatly de-emphasized, so now they can scarcely be considered as "intrinsic parts of the planning process."

Of course, material known to be out of date is not used in this report except where it is judged to be of value to other companies that are perhaps less advanced than the company that no longer uses it. In all cases, the material included in the report represents accepted and proved practices.

This study describes the state of the art of long-term profit planning. It is based on interviews with 59 companies from coast to coast and 23 responses to a mailed questionnaire. (Questionnaires were mailed to 51 companies which the researchers anticipated would have valuable experience to report but which were not located in cities where interviews were planned.) Information was collected from 81 companies between April and November 1968. Each company whose long-term profit planning practices are described in the study or whose forms are used was contacted again in July or August of 1970 to ascertain that the descriptions of its practices were still accurate. The kinds of industries and how many companies in each category were involved are—

Food products	11
Machinery manufacturing	7
Airlines	5
Chemical and oil	8
Office equipment	6
Electronics	6
Retailers	4
Electric utilities	3
Aerospace	4
Automobile manufacturers	2
Steel	2
Insurance	2
Paper manufacturers	2
Publications	2
Other	17
Total	81

About This Book

Procedural statements, reporting forms, speeches, and personal observations were gathered in the course of this study. This material was carefully screened and a selection representative of good practices appears throughout the study. Naturally, the contributions of individual companies varied substantially and, as a result, certain companies are mentioned more often than others. In some instances, where the collected materials were considered inadequate, the authors have relied on their personal experiences in the field.

Much important information collected during this survey is presented in the form of case studies in an attempt to make the narrative as realistic as possible. The cases in Chapters 13 to 16 reflect the specific information received from company executives; it has been reviewed and approved by them as to accuracy. On the other hand, those cases incorporated in preceding chapters represent a composite of data received from a number of companies. In order to distinguish the composite cases from the specific ones in the latter chapters, the composite cases are identified by "neutral" capital letters. The use of composite cases is to illustrate and emphasize particular issues that were discussed in that particular chapter.

The authors of this study are Dr. Ernest H. Weinwurm and George F. Weinwurm. Dr. Ernest H. Weinwurm is a consultant to industrial organizations. He recently retired from his position as a professor of accounting at De Paul University in Chicago. He received his LL.D. from the University of Vienna and his M.B.A. from New York University. Dr. Weinwurm is active in many professional associations and is a past president of the Chicago chapters of The Institute of Management Sciences and the Budget Executives Institute and a life member of the Planning Executives Institute. He has contributed to many management publications and coauthored *Managerial Budgeting*, published in 1964, and *Business Information and Accounting Systems*, published in 1967. He is a member of the editorial boards of *Management International* and *The Engineering Economist*.

At the time of this study George F. Weinwurm was with System Development Corporation; he is now a vice-president of the Security Pacific National Bank, Los Angeles. He received his B.S.M.E. from New York University and his M.B.A. from the University of Southern California. He has published widely on various aspects of management information systems and the management of computer projects. He has chaired sessions of national and international meetings of the Association of Computing Machinery and The Institute of Management Sciences and has spoken at meetings of the American Management Association and at local chapters of The Institute of Management Sciences. He is a member of the editorial review board of the *Journal of Systems Management*.

The authors would like to thank the many executives who have been so generous with their time, their experience, and their materials. They have made this study possible. It is hoped that the results will justify their efforts by contributing to increased management understanding of and involvement in the highly important process of long-term profit planning. They also give special thanks to Ernest C. Miller, who at the time was research program director in AMA's Research and Information Service. He contributed substantially to the planning and execution of the study and with JoAnn Sperling, AMA research associate, readied the final manuscript for publication; through his continuing guidance and assistance, he made an essential contribution. The opinions and conclusions expressed in the study are solely those of the authors and the executives interviewed; neither Mr. Miller nor AMA necessarily agrees with these opinions and conclusions.

Contents

1 **Long-Term Profit Planning: The State of the Art**   1

Terminology—Organization and Staffing—Operating the Long-Term Profit Plan—Functional Planning—Presenting the Long-Term Profit Plan

2 **Why Management Needs Long-Term Profit Planning**   14

Short-Term Versus Long-Term Planning—Why Profit Planning

3 **Long-Term Profit Planning—Prerequisites and Concepts**   19

The Statement of Objectives—From Objectives to Action Plans—Problems of Terminology

4 **The Long-Term Profit Plan**   25

Operating Problems in the Transition to Long-Term Planning—The Comprehensive Nature of the Long-Term Profit

5 **Staffing and Organizing for Long-Term Profit Planning**   31

A Glance at the Present Situation—The Size of the Long-Term Profit Planning Staff—Job Descriptions for Long-Term Profit Planning—Decentralization in Planning—The Use of Planning Committees

6 **Data Requirements for Long-Term Profit Planning**   39

Availability of Necessary Data—The Human Mind as a Forecasting Device—Scientific Techniques for Developing Future Data—Installing the Long-Term Profit Plan

7	**Launching the Long-Term Profit Planning Effort**	49

Launching JKL Manufacturing Corporation's Long-Term Profit Plan—Top Management Provides the Ground Rules for Long-Term Profit Planning—The Importance of Profitability—Communication Regarding Long-Term Profit Planning

8	**Planning and Controlling Capital Investments and Management Manpower**	64

The Impact of Investment Planning on Long-Term Profit Planning—Modern Evaluation Techniques Can Help in Analyzing Long-Term Investment Projects—The Importance of Innovations in Long-Term Planning—Capital Investment: Plans and Reports of an Automobile Manufacturer—Management Manpower Planning

9	**Sales, Distribution Expense, and Product Planning**	77

The Importance of Forecasting in Sales Planning—Planning for Distribution Expenses—Product Planning for Present and New Products—The Product Life Cycle—Technological Forecasting in Product and Profit Planning—Technological Forecasting in Realistic Sales Planning

10	**Production, Material, Labor, and Manufacturing–Overhead Planning**	91

Production Planning—Planning for an Adequate Supply of Materials—The Long-Term Labor Plan—Planning for Overhead Costs

11	**General and Administrative Expenses, Cash, and Financial Planning**	101

Long-Term Profit Plan and General and Administrative Expenses—Cash Planning—The Long-Term Financial Plan—Final Step Toward the Long-Term Profit Plan—Resources That Support the Profit Plan—Psychological Factors in Long-Term Profit Planning

12	**Presenting the Long-Term Profit Plan**	112

The Long-Term Profit Plan for Top Management—Analysis of Long-Term Profit Plan Data—Review and Approval of Plans

13	**Food Manufacturing and Wholesaling Companies: Selected Examples**	117

Foremost-McKesson, Inc., San Francisco—The F. & M. Schaefer Brewing Co., New York—Nestlé Company, Inc., White Plains, New York—A Food Company

14	**Retail Merchandising Companies: Selected Examples**	123

A Department Store Group—Jewel Companies, Inc., Melrose Park, Illinois—Montgomery Ward & Co., Inc., Chicago—Sears, Roebuck and Co., Chicago

15	**Manufacturing Companies: Selected Examples**	133
	An Electronics Manufacturer—Continental Can Company, Inc., New York—Miehle-Goss-Dexter, Inc., Chicago—Texas Instruments Incorporated, Dallas—Xerox Corporation, Stamford, Connecticut	
16	**A Process Company: Standard Oil Company (Indiana)**	154
	The Corporate Planning Philosophy—The Planning Organization—The Planning and Control Cycle—Discussion	
Exhibits		163
Bibliography		255

1

Long-Term Profit Planning: The State of the Art

W<small>HY</small> do companies engage in long-term profit planning? These are the benefits mentioned by one or another of the 82 companies contacted in the course of the research:

- The process helps the company's managers reach agreement on the directions in which we should be moving and our basic objectives.
- We find that the more effective control of our business that has resulted from our planning process has increased our profitability.
- Most noticeable has been the increased incentive throughout the company to achieve our objectives.
- We find that our long-term profit planning program forces our divisions to think consciously about the future.
- We're just more efficient, that's all.
- Our long-term profit plan provides us with a basis for evaluating alternatives.
- Having a long-term profit plan forces us to use an orderly planning procedure.

- Our management is now forced to think about the future.
- Having goals gives us something against which we can compare our progress and alerts us when some corrective action might be necessary.
- The different functions of our business are now better coordinated and focused on common objectives.
- We are now better disciplined in our thinking about the future.
- We have been stimulated to take actions that might otherwise have been deferred.
- Our attention is now focused on future opportunities.
- Our long-term profit plan is a major communication device between the corporate and divisional levels.
- Our planning process helps our management avoid unpleasant surprises.
- Planning develops a climate for future thinking.
- Now we can make reasonable long-term cash-flow projections.

From comments like these a message comes through loud and clear: with long-term profit planning, companies have a better chance to *make* the future, rather than waiting for the future to unfold.

But many companies that have established long-term profit plans are far from satisfied with their present practices. Here are a few shortcomings in their present planning processes:

- There is no integrated analysis of our total investment package.
- Our planning is not as flexible as it should be.
- Our long-term planning does not enable us to evaluate fully alternative uses of funds.
- We just don't evaluate critically the plans proposed by our subsidiaries.
- Since we don't document our plans adequately, people question their credibility.
- Management just doesn't give enough time to planning.
- There is insufficient continuity in our planning.

- We've had trouble in identifying the truly important issues.
- The forecasts we've been using haven't been sufficiently reliable.
- Our plans have put too much emphasis on historical data.
- We concentrate too much on present product lines.
- Our managers are reluctant to set goals for five years ahead.
- We have never reached agreement on the amount of detailed justification that should be required in support of a strategy.
- Those who review our plans don't know the questions to ask and the ways they should probe.
- Our plans concentrate too much on numbers and not enough on broader statements of direction.
- There's too much duplication of effort in the preparation of our short- and long-term plans.
- These really aren't long-term plans because we give much too much attention to the current year.

It is clear that these companies do not want to do away with their long-term profit planning programs—they want to make them better. Making them better primarily involves getting management to spend more time on *long-term* planning so that flexible, soundly based plans can be prepared that will inspire managerial commitment and will focus on the period a number of years ahead rather than on tomorrow or next year. And most companies that feel that their planning programs are not completely as they would like them to be plan to do something about them. These corrective efforts involve small changes year after year until the problems and objections are removed. These companies are making planning a continuous process, are working to improve their forecasting, are concentrating on developing criteria for sound plans, are working on the information requirements for their plans, and are educating their managers in the spirit and practices of planning.

Among the 82 companies there is general agreement that long-term profit planning is an important management tool. But since its use is very recent, its techniques have not yet been fully worked out. Few of the companies engaged in long-term profit planning expressed complete satisfaction with their accomplishments up to this time. In the circumstances, it is impossible to ascertain and recommend any standardized practices.

While businessmen have always engaged in informal planning, the need for formal, organized, and comprehensive long-term planning has been recognized only recently. Formal long-term planning has become necessary because of the increasing size and complexity of businesses. There is, therefore, considerable agreement that long-term profit planning is an important addition to management's bag of tools, because it makes possible the coordination of the many necessary activities of these large and complex enterprises.

Short-term planning or budgeting, which has been widely used during the last half century, is not sufficient for management's present longer-term horizons. It has had to be supplemented by a longer-term management tool. Long-term profit planning, the final step of the long-term plan, is designed to focus management's attention at all levels on long-term profitability as the ultimate objective of all its activities.

Long-term profit plans are presented in the form of commonly used financial statements and are of great importance to the finance function. However, long-term profit planning encompasses all business activities and, therefore, uses the planning efforts of all functions of the organization. As a summary in financial terms of the impact of the company's planning, a long-term profit plan is of great value to top management.

Terminology

Profit-planning terminology is a source of considerable difficulty. Inconsistencies in the use of terms appear to be an unavoidable result of the still unsettled state of this new field. Most companies engaged in long-term profit planning, however, are careful to define the terms they use. In general, terms used in military planning have been widely adopted for business planning: the term *strategic planning* has a meaning similar to long-term planning of objectives and goals; *tactics* represents the equivalent of the short-term operating plan; and *missions* refers to the activities required for a comprehensive program.

A *statement of a company's objectives,* the basis for all corporate planning, is prepared by top management and guides those involved in the planning effort. The objectives must be sufficiently specific to serve this purpose; if they are too broad they can become meaningless. In our use of the term, objectives are expected to remain unchanged for a considerable period of time and therefore represent a stable part of the plan. *Goals* identify nearer-term accomplishments necessary if the objectives are to be realized and thus are a more flexible part of the plan. Goals are modified as required by changing internal and external conditions; they are reviewed and revised from time to time, usually once a year. They are prepared at and for the top management level in broad terms with little, if any, detail. *Operating plans* are the short-term part of the long-term plan (the budget), usually covering the first year. An operating plan is prepared in considerable detail. It serves as both a planning device and a control device, especially for the lower levels of management, which therefore usually participate in its preparation.

Some companies make these conceptual distinctions in their planning, but our survey indicates that they are in the minority.

A long-term profit plan enables management to consider anticipated changes in conditions that might affect managerial decisions. This is especially important for capital investments, research and development projects, or marketing strategies.

Organization and Staffing

While the short-term operating plan is usually developed by the finance function, long-term planning is increasingly a separate function, often under a vice-president who has direct channels to top management. Short-term planning is sometimes included as part of this long-term planning function.

The extent to which planning activities are centralized or decentralized differs for short-term and long-term planning. Divisional management generally is involved in all phases of planning. However, only in the case of short-term planning is decentralization extended to the lowest management levels (foreman, office supervisors, and so forth). Some companies centralize all planning at the corporate level, especially long-term planning. Our field research indicates that any kind of organization can be successful under specific conditions. Whether there should be a separate corporate planning staff is controversial. There are advantages in having a small, highly competent staff available. But there are objections that such a staff could become too powerful and dominate divisional and lower levels.

Whether different qualifications are important in personnel assigned to short-term and long-term planning is a concern of the survey participants; this concern is eased somewhat by a trend toward combining the two activities, which naturally requires that the same people work on both short- and long-term planning. A major problem in achieving effective long-term planning is the difficulty of staffing the activity with well-qualified people. Inadequate educational facilities and opportunities to gain practical experience are principal causes for the lack of sufficient training among present personnel. Many individuals engaged in planning seem to have lacked the necessary background when first assigned and received their training on the job. No immediate improvement in the number of qualified planning people available can be expected. Managements might well avoid starting long-term profit planning until at least a few well-trained personnel are available. Outside consultants can be helpful but are expensive if used for extended periods. Postponement of the program until trained personnel are available will help the company avoid costly false starts.

Job descriptions of personnel engaged in long-term profit planning differ markedly from company to company. The same is true for the education and experience requirements for long-term profit-planning personnel as indicated in job-offering advertisements. Regardless of these differences, the proper selection of the planning department manager is of critical importance. In addition to being an expert in his field, he must be able to deal with executives of the company whose interests may differ widely from those he represents.

Operating the Long-Term Profit Plan

Adequate communication between top management and the lower levels is essential to effective long-term profit planning but difficult to accomplish in practice. The objectives and goals of top management must be fully explained to the lower levels. But excessive influence from the top may stifle the lower levels. Joint meetings of top executives with divisional managers and their staffs for frank discussions and development of future plans are usually desirable and have been found very effective in some cases.

Before management starts to develop long-term profit plans, it is wise to ascertain whether the necessary trained people and data are available. Our survey found a number of companies that suffered from a neglect of these essential prerequisites. The data are of two kinds: historical data derived from existing records (frequently not accumulated in the necessary detail) and future-directed data (planning *is* primarily concerned with the future). Historical data serve as a starting point and, assuming that "the past will be repeated in the future," may be valuable as indicators.

Adequate forecasting techniques are essential for long-term profit planning. Experience is and will continue to be an important aspect of forecasting, but such judgment is being supplemented by the use of mathematical techniques, including probability. Subjective probabilities, as a formalization of individual judgments, are coming into increasing use. The difficulties of getting useful forecast data were frequently mentioned by the executives interviewed; use of the new mathematical techniques such as mathematical models, correlation analyses, and simulation techniques is still infrequent.

The long-term profit plan results from a number of carefully designed steps. Some companies have developed elaborate procedures, which are not always followed in practice. A survey of whether the necessary people and data are available is usually the first step; required staff and data not currently available can be identified and their cost and the probable time-lags before they can be made available can be determined.

Selection of the planning manager is usually the next step. If possible, an insider familiar with company conditions is usually appointed. (Our survey indicates that the job is too often given to a person with insufficient knowledge.) The manager usually assumes full responsibility for installation and operation of the planning program. He develops the organization structure for the long-term profit planning operation, develops a workable budget, and selects his staff assistants. Quality is more important than quantity in planning and selecting the planning staff. To keep the planning staff as small as possible, temporary assignments of specialists from other functions are sometimes arranged. These men can subsequently provide liaison between the long-term profit planning staff and the planning of their own functions.

Starting a new activity is difficult. The difficulties of the planning manager's position must be appreciated if disappointments are to be avoided; to find a person with *all* the necessary qualifications will be extremely difficult, if not impossible. Strong support by top management is essential if the planning is to succeed, for considerable opposition from other executives in the company must be anticipated. The planning manager must have a direct channel to top management in order to be fully informed of its thinking and future intentions. He serves as the principal channel of communication between top management and the divisions.

Numerical data are essential for the completion of the long-term profit plan. Each function presents its unique problems that require the joint efforts of the corporate and functional planners to resolve. Economical techniques for the accumulation of the data are necessary. The profit plan will alert functional executives to the importance of financial considerations in general and profitability in particular. The profit plan serves as a constant reminder of the interrelationship of all company functions and exposes the areas of potential conflict between specialized interests. Management in turn must be familiar with the special functional planning problems and their potential impact on the long-term profit plan. These points were emphasized by many of the executives interviewed.

Functional Planning

Investment planning is typically long term and therefore affects a number of profit-plan periods. New techniques have been developed to assist management in evaluating investment proposals and their effect on long-term profitability. Especially important are considerations of the time factor and the return on investment—techniques used by a substantial number of the companies interviewed. Each of these techniques has its advantages and shortcomings, and each may have different results. Management must carefully appraise the significance of these differences.

The cost of capital and the risk involved in a project are other important factors considered in investment planning. The investment-planning process usually insures a careful analysis of all factors relevant for appraising whether an investment is worthwhile. Our survey uncovered a variety of approaches for ensuring the most advantageous allocation of the available funds for achieving maximum profitability over the long run.

Presenting the results of capital investment planning usually involves the use of special techniques. These presentations are designed to serve three principal purposes: to describe and justify investment projects; to report their progress toward completion; and to compare the original proposals with the actual performance (the so-called post-audit) in order to test the accuracy of the original estimates on which management decisions were based.

Planning the supply of management personnel over the longer term—more and more considered a form of capital investment—is also important in a company's long-term profit planning. Shortages of managers often are the principal stumbling blocks in plans for growth and increased profits, particularly because of the long training periods required to develop effective managers. Long-term planning of management needs is essential to assure a long-term profit plan of value for management decision making.

The sales plan is another key component of the long-term profit plan. Sales-forecasting techniques have been developed on a broad scale and are widely used. Forecasting relates to "expected" events; planning reflects the "intentions" of the planners. The resulting figures can differ substantially. The difficulties encountered in forecasting make computation of highly precise figures impossible; the best that can usually be expected is a range of probable values. This makes forecasting hazardous, a fact fully appreciated by the executives interviewed in our survey.

Planning of distribution expenses, including, of course, advertising and sales promotion, is closely related to sales planning. Many of these expenses are not related to sales volume, however, but have to be fixed by management decisions. They can substantially affect the long-term profit plan. Strong efforts are usually made to assure the closest possible correlation between such expenses and their effects on sales volume.

A product plan is the third basic requirement of the long-term profit plan. Product planning is done both for current products and for products to be produced in the future. The job is simpler for current products since data on past sales are available, but possible changes in demand must be kept in mind. No sales data are, of course, available for future products: market research studies are valuable to suggest probable sales volume, but these studies don't provide a completely secure basis for the planning effort. And the risks surrounding the future become increasingly significant with the lengthening of the planning period. The "product life cycle" concept is central to product planning. The resulting "aging curve" for a product has a definite impact on estimates of its future profitability, and it is usually the aging of products that stimulates new product development. The need to develop a steady flow of new products to maintain growth and increase profits has gradually been accepted by management. The timing element is important, though, to avoid unwanted fluctuations of production, sales, and profits.

Technological forecasting has become a highly important tool of product planning. Technological forecasting is also very helpful in sales planning, particularly as it exposes emerging technologies that may affect the sales of present products. Though judgment will always be an important factor in forecasting future developments in technology, these forecasts can be improved significantly, for example, if qualified scientists and engineers contribute their professional opinions in a systematic way. Thus the Delphi method—one approach to technological forecasting that has received much publicity—obtains the opinions of independently working top scientists, engineers, and executives as to future developments and the probability of their occurrence. The ideas that appear most probable are carefully analyzed, and the anticipated time when they will become a reality is estimated. Basic considerations in evaluating possible developments are desirability, feasibility, and timing.

Technological innovation is a highly important factor in long-term profit planning. Sound long-term plans almost always consider the prospects of new inventions that may occur during the more distant planning periods, and such careful attention to possible innovations is an important factor in successful long-term planning.

Careful production planning is essential for minimum cost production and thus influences the long-term profit plan to a significant extent. An important aspect of production planning is the effort to maintain a stable level of production and thereby avoid the capacity, labor, and lost-sales costs often associated with unstable levels. Production planning on a long-term basis makes possible timely consideration of alternative strategies to reconcile conflicting influences of production, demand, finance, and so forth. A wise balancing of the interests of each function is often one outgrowth of the long-term profit planning process. But the field research did not uncover many companies giving adequate attention to this important matter.

Planning for the supply of materials can be a key part of long-term profit planning whenever a company depends on specific materials that either are in short supply or are supplied by a limited number of sources. For such companies the whole long-term plan depends on the availability of materials at acceptable prices. A particularly difficult profit planning situation exists for companies that depend on a fluctuating supply of agricultural products that have to be accepted and brought to the market regardless of their impact on profitability.

A labor plan is an essential and sometimes a decisive part of a production plan. In view of our national policy of full employment, a policy shared by most companies, considerations of the labor supply loom large in long-term planning. Labor-supply considerations often affect, for example, decisions on locating plants. Differentials in labor rates can have a significant effect on the long-term profit plan, as can poor planning that leads to substantial overtime payments.

Provisions for workers' training in needed skills are an important part of the labor plan, and training expenses can affect the long-term profit plan substantially. Carefully designed manning tables are valuable in forecasting the requirements for individual job classifications. The long-term labor plan can also make a contribution to contract negotiations by forecasting the long-term effects of new agreements on costs and profits and by forecasting the need for labor, especially when a reduction of the labor force can be expected.

A long-term plan for cash requirements is a highly important part of the planning program, though it is not directly linked to the long-term profit plan. Many executives, we found, did not give it the necessary attention. Yet careful planning of the long-term sources and applications of funds can make a significant contribution to long-term profitability.

Planning for nonmanufacturing expenses is based mainly on specific management decisions. Many of these expenses can be reduced and/or postponed in order to meet the goals of the long-term profit plan. The survey indicates that formal planning for these expenses is not yet common.

The financial plan converts the various functional plans into monetary terms; the long-term profit plan is also presented to management in monetary terms. Both the financial and the long-term profit plan are represented by pro forma financial statements. The financial plan, moreover, indicates the planned approach to the financing of the whole planning program; it lists the monetary resources that will have to support the long-term profit plan. The financial plan reflects managerial goals for the years ahead in broad terms; it represents the final step in the development of the long-term profit plan. The financial plan requires the corporate planners to cooperate closely with corporate and divisional financial executives in determining future financial requirements and their impact on the long-term profit plan. In certain instances, financial planning is the only kind of planning in use; it may include some informal profit planning. Also, it may represent the beginnings of a broader planning program.

Management has two alternative approaches to the development of long-term profit plans: It may take a somewhat passive attitude and await the completion of the profit plan and then evaluate whether the plan moves the company sufficiently toward attainment of its objectives; or management may take the lead and announce its intentions at the outset as a guide to the company's planners. The choice will reflect the basic management philosophy. Our survey indicates a definite preference for the second alternative, though the first is used by some companies.

Presenting the Long-Term Profit Plan

The long-term profit plan is usually presented to management in terms of the "pyramid concept." This concept provides that only data needed for making decisions are forwarded to management. The guiding principle usually is to present a *minimum* quantity of information containing a *maximum* amount of relevant information.

The use of pro forma statements seems to be preferred by managements for two reasons: businessmen are familiar with this form of presentation, and comparison with historical data is made easier. Pro forma statements, of course, reflect estimates subject to uncertainty, not facts.

Long-term profit plans are usually prepared annually; plans for the first year—and sometimes several more years—are usually given by quarters, especially if there are significant differences among the quarterly data. The first year of the long-term plan usually serves as the short-term plan (budget). When the first year of the long-term profit plan is the budget for the year, management receives regular reports of actual compared with planned results, summary reports, and flash reports as necessary. Summary reports present selected figures that are indicative of trends. Flash reports emphasize the time factor; that is, data of particular relevance are sent to management as soon as they are available, even though they may not be completely accurate. For top management's needs speed takes precedence over complete accuracy—reasonable approximations are useful.

The mode of presentation of long-term profit plans usually reflects management's preferences and needs. These may differ for particular executives. Some executives prefer verbal presentations, some tabular, some graphic, and so forth. To the extent feasible, long-term profit planners try to adjust to the preferences of their executives.

* * *

Certain general conclusions can be drawn about the state of the art in long-range planning:

- No generally accepted rules and forms for long-term profit planning have been developed as yet by U.S. companies; there is a lack of uniformity in the approaches used by the companies contacted for the research, even for companies in the same industry.

- Planning is concerned with the uncertain future; long-term planning data are estimates with a certain probability of occurrence, not historical data of which management can be reasonably certain.

- People and data are the most important factors in developing a long-term profit plan. They must be available in the required quantities and qualities for a company to be able to develop a successful long-term profit plan.

- The present shortage of personnel qualified to develop and implement long-term profit plans has made it difficult for many companies to make much progress in their planning.

- Long-term profit plans require a large volume of data; their accumulation can be time consuming and expensive.

- Management must understand the concepts and techniques for planning for the different functions of a business in order to be able to evaluate the impact of these functional plans on the long-term profit plan.
- Long-term profit planning presentations and reports are usually prepared in terms of the needs of management.

2

Why Management Needs Long-Term Profit Planning

WE all plan. To reach our personal goals, we need to decide how to pursue them. Every mature person realizes sooner or later that to act without a plan—that is, aimlessly or randomly—is a prescription for disappointment and perhaps disaster.

But there are profound differences between the informal planning on which we tend to rely as individuals and the formalized planning introduced by many businesses during recent years. The casual approach to planning is likely to be as ineffectual as no planning at all when attention shifts from individuals to institutions. Formal planning, in fact, is necessary to our way of life. Modern industrialized society is both the most dynamic and the most interdependent the world has ever seen. Its most conspicuous element is the managed institution. Managed institutions cannot survive in this sort of society, much less flourish, without *managed planning*—that is, planning that is as organized, as deliberate, as intensive, and as carefully controlled as the primary functions of these institutions.

The need for managed planning is most apparent in organizations where managers are held to explicit, objective, and competitive standards of performance. Business organizations are, of course, the most prominent examples, but certainly not the only examples, of organizations with such standards. Throughout the known history of economic enterprise, businessmen who contemplated a new facility, a new product or service, or a new territory have necessarily engaged in some sort of formal planning. The acquisition of outside capital also usually required some sort of plan that reflected the use to be made of the funds and the resources likely to be available for their repayment. Developing new facilities, products, services, or territories and seeking outside capital are, however, relatively infrequent events for the average businessman. Consequently, while formal planning has been a familiar part of the business scene for a long time, it has usually been done by having employees from various parts of the organization contribute to the preparation of a "plan" and, upon its completion, return to their regular assignments.

Since the end of World War II the inadequacies of this ad hoc, case-by-case approach to planning have been generally acknowledged, and this approach has been gradually superseded by a much more ambitious and sophisticated planning concept. The new concept rests mainly on three related propositions. To be effective,

1. Planning must be institutionalized as a permanent function similar to marketing, production, personnel, and the other established business functions. Moreover, it must be performed by trained specialists.

2. Planning must be done comprehensively; that is, it must encompass all a company's activities regardless of what they are or where they are performed.

3. Planning must be integrative; that is, it must serve to coordinate and harmonize planning throughout an organization, so that the result is meaningful for the company as a whole as well as for its various subdivisions.[1]

Short-Term Versus Long-Term Planning

Numerous surveys have indicated that comprehensive planning has become accepted as a necessary part of managerial decision-making processes by a majority of forward-looking companies. These companies, however, do not plan using some widely accepted and generally applicable notion of what planning involves and how it is to be done. On the

---

[1] Consider, for instance, President Kennedy's charge to the National Aeronautics and Space Administration to land an American on the moon before 1970. Some of the *managerial* dividends of this enormous national effort are described in "The Unexpected Payoff of Project Apollo," *Fortune*, July 1969.

contrary, our survey clearly shows the very significant variations from company to company in the depth and scope of planning, especially with regard to the relationship between the near term and the long term. This diversity in approaches to planning seems to be related to the fact that most formalized planning has developed from financial budgeting.

Less than half a century ago it was considered highly risky to adopt a formal procedure for anticipating the future as much as a year in advance. And although short-term planning has since then come into wide use, long-term planning is still a relatively recent addition to the manager's kit bag. In rough terms, about four out of five of the companies contacted in the field research indicate that they have been engaged in short-term planning since before 1960, and a substantial portion since before 1950; in contrast, about four out of five of the companies contacted have been engaged in long-term planning since 1960 and about three out of ten since 1965.

About half of the companies differentiate between long- and short-term planning. Companies that do differentiate consider the short-term plan to be a part of the long-term plan or consider the long-term plan to be the primary basis for the long-term profit plan. Regardless of whether management formally differentiates between short- and long-term plans, a strong majority of the companies indicate that their short- and long-term plans are consistent with each other. Large companies have been among the earlier users of long-term planning; until recently only a few of the smaller companies engaged in long-term planning. While annual budgets have become commonplace, companies still vary widely in the extent of their commitment to a time frame for planning that exceeds the requirements imposed by the short-term budgeting process. For instance:

- "Every year we prepare a three-year plan which is distinct from the annual budget. We hold our managers to the budget and not to the plan, which we consider an informational and coordinative device."

- "We have a ten-year planning exercise, which is essentially unlimited in scope. . . . The result is a ten-year plan and ten-year management forecasts, which in turn result in one-year operating budgets."

- "We work on three sets of planning premises. One is selected as the most likely and is developed into a five-year plan, from which our annual budget is worked out."

- "We plan the next year in detail, and the following ones more broadly."

In part, this variation reflects the nature of each company's environment—that is, the degree to which the future seems predictable to its management. This predictability of the future in turn is greatly influenced by the techniques of long-term forecasting that are at hand. Most managements are cognizant of the deficiencies of the short-term view; but they are equally aware that the methodology of long-term planning is still in an early stage of development. Companies realize that the extent to which long-term planning is appropriate for them is not necessarily determined by its use by other organizations. A company's long-term planning horizon seems to be predominantly a function of its management style and its success in applying existing techniques to the environmental factors management deems most important.

Why Profit Planning

Alexander B. Trowbridge, former president of the American Management Association, has stated the need for long-term planning succinctly:

> The world of corporate management has increasingly come to the conclusion, after seeing the wastage from constant "fire fighting," that a systematic process of long-range planning can avert the crisis before it develops. This process goes from the general to the specific. . . . Gaps between objectives and capabilities are analyzed and plans set for closing the distances. Alternative options are reviewed and selections made. . . . The process is continuous, with regular review of progress and updating of plans as events shape their path.[2]

Our subject, however, is not planning in general, either short-term or long-term, but long-term profit planning. What is the relationship between long-term profit planning and these other ways of looking at the problem of anticipating and preparing for the future? Are these different approaches independent and distinct? Are they mutually supportive and synergistic? Or, does one subsume the others?

The research reported herein indicates that valid planning cannot exist without a substantial foundation of management information; further, long-term profit planning cannot have any meaningful effect on

---

[2] Alexander B. Trowbridge, "The President's Scratchpad: Brinkmanship—Is It Inevitable?" *Management News* (August 1969).

management's decision-making processes unless it is a part of a comprehensive and integrative planning system. Profit planning, whether in a short-term or a long-term frame, is above all a way of organizing the planning processes (and the products of planning) so they are focused on the profit to be derived from the resources for which management is responsible. Profit planning is not an independent form of planning. It serves the essential purpose of concentrating attention on profit goals and of making the relationship of each part of the plan to those goals as conspicuous as possible. Exhibits 1 and 2 illustrate the scope of the long-term plans in schematic form. Exhibit 1, "A Framework for Business Planning" developed by Stanford Research Institute, depicts the three basic plans that together compose a planning system (the process of creating the plan) and the special-purpose and functional plans usually included. Exhibit 2, "The Annual Corporate Planning Process" of United Air Lines, focuses on the flow of planning and on technical aspects.

Exhibit 3 presents an example of the way one company, Sylvania Electric Products Inc., explains the concepts, purposes, and practices of long-term planning to its organization.

NOTE. Exhibits are grouped at the back of the book.

3

Long-Term Profit Planning—Prerequisites and Concepts

T<small>HE</small> long-term profit plan is the culmination of the planning effort. Numerous factors must be considered if it is to be the essential decision-making tool for management. Executives often identify the long-term profit plan with the financial aspects of planning. This is not surprising, for profit is a term commonly used in finance and profit is the final measure of the income statement. But it would be a mistake to confound a formal with a factual condition. Although presented in financial-accounting format, the long-term profit plan is not a part of the accounting system. Its scope is far wider and it contains information not usually found in the accounting system. The long-term profit plan incorporates all the activities of the organization. Many of these activities are measured not in financial-accounting terms but by other means such as number of units, weight, time, and so forth.

Business executives concerned with long-term profit planning are often surprised to learn of the many factors that need to be taken into account in developing the plan, many apparently outside the immediate area of long-term profit planning. Often these executives have initially questioned the necessity for dealing with the fundamental prerequisites for sound plans; in the end, however, they usually come to appreciate their importance.

The initial step management must take to achieve a useful long-term profit plan is to develop and issue a statement of the company's objectives. These objectives guide the work of the various functions and parts of the organization.

The Statement of Objectives

There is substantial agreement among planning experts that a set of guidelines or objectives, to be developed and announced by management, is an essential prerequisite for successfully launching long-term profit planning. Without such a formal statement each planner in the organization will use his own guidelines, and these may be neither the same as management's nor the same as those used by other planners.

Why, then, are there so many corporate planning programs without such a formal statement of objectives? One planning executive interviewed offered this interesting explanation:

"We have been trying for years to get our president to release a statement of objectives for our company. We have prepared numerous drafts for review by our top management. Those they finally accepted turned out to be so general as to be virtually meaningless, something like praising motherhood or the flag at a Fourth of July oration. Of course, such a statement would neither help us nor help the line executives and their staffs in doing their planning.

"In fact, though, statements of objectives don't have to be very specific. For they are designed to remain unchanged for an extended period unless there are major changes such as a merger or the introduction of a completely new line of activity. Nevertheless, we find that top executives don't like to be tied down to any extent. They want a free hand and under no circumstances do they wish to appear to have made a mistake in the past.

"In my opinion, this is the heart of the problem. You should have the courage to admit that you may be wrong in your decisions once in a while and then have the courage to change or modify them. Even highly effective executives appear to refuse to accept what seems logical and reasonable. But we live with it and do the best we can in the circumstances."

Among the companies contacted for this research approximately four out of five had statements of objectives, most for the company as a whole. Some companies had objectives both for the whole company and for its major functions. The companies that have objectives for the whole company or their integrated product divisions set objectives for such items as market share, return on investment, growth of sales, product-line expansion, earnings per share, sales-to-earnings ratio, return on assets, profit contribution, and company image. Illustrative objectives that are set for the marketing function include sales volume, profit contribution, a rating in the first quartile of the industry in sales, and return on gross sales.

Exhibits 4 and 5 illustrate the approaches of several different companies in presenting their corporate objectives. Although these statements are basically similar in their purposes, there are significant variations in format and language, which deserve attention.

From Objectives to Action Plans

The statement of objectives represents a relatively stable part of the planning process; it is expected to serve as a guide for an extended period of time. How these objectives will be attained will vary depending on conditions. Programs for accomplishing objectives, therefore, constitute the relatively flexible portion of the plan, and make up what is often called the action plan. Action plans may be divided into two parts. *Goals* comprise the first part. They are the responsibility of line management and its staffs, and they indicate in general terms how the objectives will be realized during a particular period, say three years. The second part is operating plans. *Operating plans* describe the details of what is to be done for a limited period, usually a single year, in such a manner that they are usually used to evaluate and control performance.

As an illustration, let us assume that the ABC Corporation [1] has as its objective a profit of 5 percent of annual net sales after taxes. (This is understood as a continuing objective, an average figure that will vary from year to year.) This objective has been set by top management. Each division of the company will use it as the starting point for developing its goals for each of the next five years. The goals for each of the five years will hopefully meet this objective each year. Most of this planning work will be done by the divisional managements and their staffs. A detailed operating plan that meets these goals is then worked out for the first year of the five-year period. This involves operating management enlisting the cooperation of the lower-level managers (foremen, supervisors, and so forth), who will be expected to use the plan to guide their

---

[1] Fictional names (consecutive letters) are used when the descriptions of company practices are composites of the experiences of a number of companies.

current activities and who know that their actual performance will be evaluated in accordance with this operating plan. Here, then, is how this company divides the long-term planning responsibility.

Concept	Responsibility	Period
Objectives	Top management	Indefinite
Goals	Operating management	To a specified date
Detailed operating plans	Operating and supervisory management	One year

Exhibit 6 illustrates how one company states its goals, goals describing interim accomplishments necessary to achieve longer-term objectives.

Problems of Terminology

At present there is no standardized terminology in the field of long-term profit planning, to a large extent because the field is still in an early stage of development. Military planning, however, is well established and has had an important influence on the terms used in business planning. Most widely adopted by business planners are the terms *strategy, tactics,* and *missions: Strategy* is related to the broad objectives of a company; *tactics* refers to shorter-term decisions within the framework of established strategies; and *missions* refers to the broad lines of activity of a particular enterprise. In the military, a mission is a joint project in which several branches of the armed forces are involved.

Perhaps the thinking of other students of planning will help in clarifying planning terms. Dr. George Steiner, a professor in the Graduate School of Business at UCLA, states that business planning starts with the company creed and philosophical statements, which include its missions. These are followed by long-term objectives and short-term goals and targets.[2] Strategic planning is

> . . . the process of determining the major objectives of an organization and the policies and strategies that will govern the acquisition, use, and disposition of resources to achieve those objectives. Objectives in the strategic planning process include missions and purposes, if they have not been determined previously, and the specific objectives that are sought by a firm. Although the strategic objectives are usually long-range, they can be short-range. Policies are broad guides to action, and strategies are the means to deploy resources. . . .

[2] George A. Steiner, *Top Management Planning* (New York: The Macmillan Company, 1969), pp. 141 ff.

> ... strategic planning includes every type of activity of concern to [the] ... enterprise. ... The characteristics of strategic planning differ greatly from those of medium-range programming and short-range planning ... strategic planning covers different periods of time for different subjects. ...
>
> Medium-range programming is the process in which detailed, coordinated, and comprehensive plans are made for selected functions of a business to deploy resources to reach objectives by following policies and strategies laid down in the strategic planning process. All medium-range programs and plans for a company cover the same period of time, usually five years. ...
>
> Short-term budgets and detailed functional plans include such matters as short-range targets for salesmen, budgets for material purchases. ... If the medium-range programs are detailed and the timing of the overall planning cycle coincides with the required dates for budget-making, short-term plans may be the same as the first year of the medium-range programs. The detail of medium-range programs is not usually deep enough for current operations, hence, a separate set of short-range plans is usually required.[3]

Professor Robert N. Anthony, Graduate School of Business, Harvard University, defines strategic planning as

> ... the process of deciding on objectives of the organization, on changes in these objectives, on the resources used to attain these objectives, and on the policies that are to govern the acquisition, use, and disposition of these resources.[4]
>
> Our definition of strategic planning combines two types of planning that often are viewed as quite distinct from each other: (1) choosing objectives and (2) planning how to achieve these objectives. ...
>
> Strategic planning does *not* correspond to what some call long-range planning. Strategic decisions do have long-range consequences, and often, but not always, a relatively long time is required to put a strategic decision into effect. ...
>
> The long-range, short-range distinction has more validity in relation to the duration of the consequences of decisions. Strategic decisions tend to have long-range effects; often they are irreversible in the short run.[5]

[3] Ibid., Chapter 2, pp. 34–35.
[4] Robert N. Anthony, *Planning and Control Systems: A Framework for Analysis*, Studies in Management Control (Boston: Harvard Business School, Division of Research, 1965), p. 24.
[5] Ibid., pp. 26–27.

According to Dr. Russell Ackoff,[6] a professor in the Wharton School at the University of Pennsylvania, strategic planning is different from tactical planning in three main ways: the time element involved, how much of the organization is being planned for, and the level of goals involved. The longer the range of planning, the more strategic it is; if the time period involved is at least three years, and preferably five, the planning is strategic.

Tactical planning accepts a set of goals established by a higher management and seeks ways of obtaining them, whereas strategic planning tends to be oriented more toward ends. A strategic plan should involve five essential parts that should be developed simultaneously: objectives and goals; operating policies; resources—requirements and provisions; organizational structure; and controls.

Most of the companies contacted for this research do not use these more sophisticated planning terms; they generally stick to the simpler terms discussed earlier in the chapter. However, the more precise planning terms are used by some of the companies contacted. For those used by one large industrial corporation, see Exhibit 7.

[6] Russell L. Ackoff, "The Meaning of Strategic Planning," *The McKinsey Quarterly*, Summer 1966, pp. 50 ff.

4

The Long-Term Profit Plan

LONG-TERM plans often exist more in form than in substance. Instructions had been given and procedures had been prepared—sometimes in elaborate form—but they failed to reach the lower levels of the organization. How to make planning a way of life throughout a company is one of the most important, but most difficult, problems facing managements that believe in long-term profit planning. Even companies with considerable experience in operating long-term plans are aware of other continuing problems. These problems are simply a reflection of the complexity of planning, and much additional research and experience will be required before satisfactory solutions will be found. Some of the major problems and issues will be examined to provide interested executives with a realistic picture of the present situation and to make them aware of possible pitfalls.

One important reason for adopting long-term planning is that short-term decisions are meaningful only if they are made with a view to their impact on the more distant future. It follows that without a reasonable picture of what the future will probably be or might be, it will be impossible to arrive at appropriate short-term decisions.[1] A substantial number of the companies interviewed appear to accept this approach. Their

---

[1] This has been emphasized strongly by Peter F. Drucker for many years, most recently in his book *The Age of Discontinuity* (New York: Harper & Row, 1968).

annual planning begins with their long-term plan, into which they then fit their short-term plan. They accomplish this by covering the long-term plan review in the first part of the fiscal year and then completing their short-term plan later in the fiscal year. Since this system seems to work, it will probably be widely adopted.

The long-term plan is a prerequisite for the long-term profit plan. Enlightened managements have recognized the shortcomings of the age-old drive for the "fast buck"; today, they are looking for profitability over the long run. This, however, requires a knowledge of what the "long run" is going to be. Some companies use the concept of a one-year profit plan; this practice results from uncertainties regarding forecasting for longer periods. It appears, however, that this practice fails to take advantage of the opportunities of long-term planning. It seems to reflect a defeatist attitude, which is not justified by experience. Exhibits 8, 9, and 10 present a variety of approaches to long-term planning and its relation to long-term profit planning. Although these companies emphasize different issues, they are in fundamental accord as to the basic factors that characterize long-term planning.

Operating Problems in the Transition to Long-Term Planning

Since short-term planning (budgeting) represented the initial application of the planning concept to business operations for many companies, it was only natural for them to start with the short-term plan when the need for long-term planning became apparent. However, for many other companies, the long-term plan has been given precedence, with the short-term plan forming the initial period of the long-term plan. From an organizational point of view, short-term planning originally developed within the finance function under the supervision of the corporate controller. Our survey indicates this is still a widely used approach. However, there is a growing trend to consider all kinds of planning as a separate, independent function, often under a vice-president who reports directly to the chief operating executive. In such cases this vice-president would have charge of both short-term and long-term planning.

In some instances long-term planning was first used in connection with an activity such as capital investment or research and development planning. When this was the case, the planning work was done as a part of the function without coordination with the company's other planning activities. Such planning is still done, but there seems to be a general trend toward more comprehensive planning, perhaps because of the increasing recognition of the importance of long-term profit planning.

Another interesting question involves the qualifications of personnel engaged in planning: Should those who do short-term and long-term planning have the same or different qualifications? Some practitioners say the short-term planner (the budgeteer) should be a practical person who prefers to concentrate on issues that can be readily measured and controlled. According to this concept, the short-term planner should have the attributes of an accountant; indeed, many budget men have been recruited from accountancy. On the other hand, these practitioners say, the long-term planner should be concerned with the broader aspects of the enterprise; he should be interested less in detailed figures than in overall trends. However, our survey substantiates references in the literature that indicate a preference for minimizing the differences between short- and long-term planning; greater emphasis is being placed on the problems common to all planning. In an increasing number of companies, all planning activities, short- and long-term, are carried out by the same people. It is not unusual to find all these different approaches used in the same industry—an indication that there is as yet no agreement about the best organization of planning work.

Executives in companies contacted gave many examples of problems they had encountered in going from functional and short-term planning to long-term planning. An executive in a large manufacturing company explained:

"We always had to plan for the replacement of our equipment a number of years in advance, for we had to wait several years for delivery of new equipment. But this was mainly a problem for our engineers. Our engineers did not work closely with our finance people because finance didn't look much beyond one year in their own planning, which was mainly related to budget. Sometimes our market research people planned ahead for a number of years. But, in any case, our costs would be determined from year to year and incorporated in the budget—just as the Congress appropriates—on an annual basis."

Another executive pointed out his company's difficulties in moving from functional plans to a comprehensive long-term plan:

"Our functional executives who have been operating their own planning programs are unwilling to submerge their planning efforts in a company-wide effort. They're afraid they may lose much of their independence. There is widespread opposition to the establishment of a corporate program, and it has been difficult to overcome. We anticipate it will take much time and effort before we will have a comprehensive long-term planning program that works."

Still another director of planning mentioned problems in connection with mergers.

"We have absorbed many, many companies over the years. In some cases these companies used planning programs superior to ours; in others they had never done formal planning. When the companies had never planned, our problems were simpler: we started from scratch and gradually helped them introduce planning. But we faced a dilemma when their planning programs were better than ours. Should we force the planning director of the merged companies to accept a less developed program than his, or, perhaps better, should we try to use his program to upgrade our own? Everything, of course, depends on the circumstances. There is no general rule to follow."

The Comprehensive Nature of the Long-Term Profit

To be of greatest benefit to management, the long-term profit plan must include *all* activities of the company. In practice, this will often be quite difficult to accomplish, as there may be many obstacles.

Systems analysis has been proposed in recent years as an effective means for achieving a comprehensive long-term profit plan. Everyone favors systems analysis in principle, yet the difficulties in its application are considerable. It is not a simple matter—if it is possible at all—to consider every aspect of a complex situation. Even if this can be accomplished, it may require an inordinate amount of time and money. Fortunately, two techniques—operations research and the computer—often keep the work within manageable bounds. Use of these techniques has made systems analysis practical for long-term profit planning.

Only a small number of major companies have introduced systems analysis and related techniques, but managements are slowly beginning to appreciate their importance for long-term profit planning and other decision making. Computers are used rather widely, however. Roughly three out of four of the companies contacted in the research use computers in some aspect of their long-term profit planning. These companies report using computers in forecasting, making budget comparisons, extending sales for computing a dollar-sales forecast, compiling product gross margins, making sales analyses, compiling general management information for planning purposes, developing probability distributions for use in analyzing items in the profit-and-loss statement, and developing a long-term planning model for evaluating planning alternatives and possible acquisitions.

An important early application of systems analysis was made in the

U.S. Department of Defense. The technique has since been applied in other government agencies under the name of cost/effectiveness and Planning–Programming–Budgeting–System (PPBS). The essence of the approach is a method for including all relevant factors in decision making. Specifically included are the qualitative factors that cannot be expressed in quantitative, numerical terms and are too often excluded in decision making. Such qualitative factors are of great importance to business, since they include many human activities so significant in management decisions.

The number of companies using systems analysis in planning seems to be comparatively small, and most of those companies are large. But the impact of systems analysis—along with operations research and the computer—on long-term profit planning is undeniable. Many companies are exploring the use of these techniques whenever suitable occasions arise. With the increasing availability of computer services, such experimentation will become easier.

A few cases perhaps will illustrate the potential of systems analysis in solving intricate and apparently insoluble problems. One case is from the airlines industry. There has been a substantial increase in airline traffic during recent years. This increase was by no means unexpected; on the contrary, the airlines had ordered an increasing number of aircraft, and once these became available they scheduled more flights so the planes could make a contribution to the companies' profits. However, in doing this, they failed to consider adequately the available airport capacity. Existing airports, especially at major transfer points, have been unable to accommodate all the scheduled flights, especially under unfavorable weather conditions. The result has been lengthy delays, equally costly to the airlines and their customers.

Indeed, airline profits declined in the face of expanding patronage. If an analysis of the whole system had been undertaken—including planes, airports, approaches to the airports from the central city and suburbs, available airspace, and other pertinent considerations—existing limitations would have become apparent in time and remedial action could have been taken. But there was no comprehensive long-term planning; everyone looked merely at his own particular sector of the business without giving consideration to other closely related sectors.

A similar situation developed in the securities industry in 1968 when business suddenly increased substantially. The industry's attention had been focused on the selling side of the business—new offices were opened, and many new salesmen were hired. But the industry completely failed to realize that increased sales volume would also affect their "back offices," where transactions are handled and recorded. The result was chaos. Many firms finally had to restrict their selling activities, and the stock exchanges had to reduce trading hours so brokers could manage the flood of paper. The exchanges and some of the leading brokerage houses hired systems analysts to help them clear up the mess in their record keeping and securities delivery.

These two cases illustrate how long-term profit plans may fail when situations that could easily have been anticipated are overlooked or neglected by planners. Large planned profits too often exist only on paper; they will rarely be attained when important factors have not been taken into account.

5

Staffing and Organizing for Long-Term Profit Planning

AMONG the prerequisites for making the long-term profit plan a success, none is more important than the people involved in its operations. Special attention must be given to the selection of the people who will introduce and operate the long-term profit plan. Considering the scarcity of well-qualified people, the present situation is, in general, unsatisfactory. Too often, because of lack of experience and training in long-term profit planning, those assigned to the task are not really qualified. Most are eager to do a good job, but the lack of adequate educational facilities and the difficulties encountered in acquiring the essential practical experience—there are comparatively few organizations that could serve as a training ground—have prevented them from preparing themselves adequately. Some companies elaborately outline the responsibilities of managers of the various planning functions. These statements, however, are of little value if the people who fill the positions are inadequate.

A Glance at the Present Situation

A few examples will illustrate the shortcomings in the qualifications of some of the people engaged in long-term profit planning. Such shortcomings reflect the present early stage in the development of the new planning techniques. There is no doubt that these problems will be straightened out in due time.

The attitudes of the top managers of the ABC Corporation, a billion-dollar service organization, vary widely in respect to long-term profit planning. The company's president, however, has shown a strong interest in developing a planning program and has issued the appropriate orders. In the past there has been considerable planning in specific areas such as engineering, marketing, and finance; a budget program with a staff of 20 people, administered by the finance function, has also been in use for a number of years.

The manager of the long-term planning department of the ABC Corporation cheerfully explained that he had little to tell since he was in the position only a couple of months and was still trying to get his feet on the ground. He went on:

"My principal job right now is to recruit a competent staff. The organization plan provides for several groups, each headed by a director and staffed by several analysts. The intention is to keep the department as small as possible. The directors I have selected so far and I have attended a number of professional society meetings on long-term profit planning, including some offered by the American Management Association; we have also visited a number of companies that operate long-term profit programs. We were particularly impressed by one of these, which has been used successfully by a company in our industry for a number of years.[1]

"I am trying to get the best-qualified men in the company to work for me, even though they haven't had any special training. Under present circumstances the best we can do is learn on the job."

When questioned on the possibility of recruiting outside experts, he replied:

"The number of real experts is very limited and all of these, of course, hold good and well-paid positions. To lure them away would require offers of substantial salary increases which would tend to upset our present pay scales. We do retain outside consultants from time to time, but this can be expensive. Management is reluctant to authorize it on a large scale."

The DEF Corporation, a large, diversified manufacturer of industrial

[1] The manager of long-term profit planning of this company was subsequently interviewed. He had operated his department for the last eight years. To the best of his knowledge, his was the only company in the industry currently operating a meaningful long-term profit plan.

and consumer products, started its long-term planning program a couple of years ago. The planning group, with one exception, consists of young men with a minimum of experience. In fact, the manager of long-term planning, who has an accounting background, pointed out:

"I prefer to hire young men who are recent graduates from prominent business schools to serve as my principal assistants and as planning managers in the operating divisions. I think these assignments provide an excellent training ground for higher level executive positions. The advantages of this practice appear to outweigh greatly the disadvantages resulting from lack of experience."

One of these young divisional planning managers, however, commented, "Lack of experience is a major handicap in my work. I am without any assistance; one man who has been promised to me has not yet shown up." On the other hand, the one divisional planning manager with considerable experience has a staff of seven and, not surprisingly, his group is doing much better work than the other divisional planning groups.

The GHI Corporation, a large producer of consumer goods, has planned in several functional areas for a number of years. After the company expanded substantially through growth and acquisitions, management decided it was time to install a comprehensive long-term profit plan. The company controller, only a few years away from retirement, was assigned to develop the planning program. He had no special qualifications for the job. The program is still in a preliminary stage.

The key problem appears to be that a company that has failed to develop any long-term profit plan in the past suddenly decides it needs one, and then immediately proceeds to implement this decision without considering whether the necessary trained personnel are available. The men who are given the assignment cannot be blamed: long-range planning is certainly a challenge, and they can't very well claim ignorance and thus reject the assignment. Sufficient patience is needed to accept the unavoidable time lag between decision and implementation. Sound long-term profit planning programs are not easily started without the presence of at least a few individuals who know what needs to be done.

At some future time, after improved educational programs in long-term profit planning become available, it will be possible to hire well-qualified people at reasonable salaries. But with the present scarcity of well-trained personnel, staff training must come first. Only when a trained staff is in place should a company attempt to install a program, even if this means a delay of perhaps a year. In practice, the delay will not be significant, for trained employees will be able to proceed much faster and more successfully than those who have to learn on the job. Companies that accept this approach will avoid unnecessary expense and the disappointments that come when expected results are not realized.

The Size of the Long-Term Profit Planning Staff

Most long-term planners accept the principle that planning staffs should be kept as small as possible. Application of this principle depends on the organization of the company, especially whether it is centralized or decentralized. If the company is centralized, emphasis is placed on the corporate staff, which therefore will be larger than in a decentralized approach where most of the work would be done in divisions. In the extreme case of decentralization there is no corporate staff at all and all planning work is done by the divisional staffs, especially in the larger divisions; smaller divisions may use only part-time help for their periodic planning work.

Our survey indicates that the corporate professional (exempt) long-term profit planning staff rarely exceeds ten persons and in most instances these groups have fewer than ten. For example, approximately nine out of ten of the companies contacted in the field research indicate that they have ten or fewer exempt employees on their staffs; about six out of ten indicate that five or fewer professional employees are engaged full time in long-term profit planning. As mentioned earlier, there may be separate staffs for short-term and long-term planning, or the two assignments may be combined. Additional temporary and part-time help may be recruited from other functions as needed whenever the workload exceeds the capacity of the full-time staff.

Job Descriptions for Long-Term Profit Planning

Job descriptions for long-term profit planning vary widely in the companies surveyed. More important than formal descriptions, however, are actual practices. A lengthy period of observation would be required to ascertain actual practices and their relationships to the job descriptions, but field research indicates that there are substantial differences between form and practice. In all likelihood these are at least partly the result of necessary flexibility in the practical application of formal job descriptions. Exhibits 11, 12, 13, and 14 present job descriptions for long-term profit planning from companies with considerable experience in the activity; it can be assumed that these job descriptions substantially reflect actual practices.

Exhibit 15 provides a picture of the qualifications expected in a profit planner. Men who have these qualifications seem hard to find. E. Kirby Warren, a professor in the Graduate School of Business at Columbia University, sets forth his view of the planning task and the kind of a man needed for it:

> Many companies in recent years have appointed someone to a position which is typically called vice-president or director of long-range planning. . . . The men who bear [this title] . . . typically make very little direct contribution to the development of plans. . . . Where they have been used most successfully, they have been regarded primarily as architects and overseers whose major task is the development of a sound planning process rather than actual planning. In addition, it falls on them to help reshape line executives' attitudes toward long-range planning and create an environment in which to minimize the potentially negative impact. . . .
>
> The men who are to play a more direct role in the design and administration of the planning process [should] be selected with a clear notion of the intellectual and political difficulties they must be equipped to face.
>
> The ideal choice for such a post should be a man who is both philosopher and realist, theoretician and practical politician, soothsayer and salesman and, as one planner points out, he probably should be able to walk on water. . . . More often, because of misconceptions about the nature and purpose of planning, men selected for this key job have been poor ones.

Although until recently most of the men selected for the job of long-range planner have been former controllers, Professor Warren disqualifies them for this position since there are "more or less basic conflicts between [the] need for the controller to be guardian of corporate resources . . . and the need for a planning designer who can gain the confidence of line and staff participants in planning." Another mistake, in his opinion, is to select men "not because they possessed the necessary talents, but because they had the potential for some other job . . . and would gain valuable experience. . . . It is most dangerous to mix executive development with an attempt to get this vital and often misunderstood activity off the ground."[2]

---

[2] E. Kirby Warren, *Long Range Planning: The Executive Viewpoint* (Englewood Cliffs, N.J.: Prentice-Hall, 1966), pp. 42, 43–44, 46.

Decentralization in Planning

Almost all managements consider the extent to which long-term profit planning will be centralized or decentralized. In most instances, long-term profit planning is centralized at the corporate level, even though it depends heavily on the contributions of the divisional managements. On the other hand, short-term planning tends to be decentralized to the lowest management levels (foremen, office supervisor, and so forth). Since the short-term plan guides each supervisor in his operations and provides a means of measuring and controlling his performance, his participation and cooperation are considered essential for the success of the planning effort. The objective is to have each supervisor accept the short-term profit plan as a personal commitment so he will carry it out to the best of his ability.

On the other hand, long-term profit planning does not immediately affect lower management levels. Lower-level managers may be told about management's broad future intentions and objectives, but usually they are not personally involved. The long-term profit plan serves primarily as a management tool. Moreover, contrary to the requirements of the short-term plan, the long-term plan is not usually worked out in detail; its contents are usually approximations, with the usual margins for error. Also, the specific items usually change whenever new information becomes available. (The short-term profit plan, in contrast, is usually less subject to change: it must be firm to be effective.) Who participates in the development of the long-term plan depends mainly on the significance of particular functions to the company's future rather than on the size of the functions' staffs or budgets. For example, the manager of a small research group may be important to the growth of the company and will therefore take part in long-term profit planning, while managers in charge of more routine activities will not. The selection of the participants in a company's long-term profit planning is usually made with care and consideration of all the relevant factors, rather than in a routine fashion.

Whether in fact there should be a corporate planning staff is an important issue for many companies, one closely related to the issue of centralization versus decentralization. Is it necessary to go below the corporate level in developing and maintaining the long-term profit plan—to enlist lower management levels? This question is especially important in the large, multidivisional companies. The present trend seems to be toward decentralization, often described as "making each division a separate business." The conglomerate company, which unites enterprises operating in a variety of fields, is a case in point. Our survey indicates that most companies, at the corporate level at least, accept this point of view. The lower levels in the divisions, however, face many difficult problems, and practice often differs considerably from the official corporate position.

Some companies are dead set against having a corporate staff for long-range planning. In the words of one executive:

"Once you have such a corporate staff, you shortchange the divisional management. Management no longer gets the division's position, for the division's plans have been filtered through the corporate 'sieve'; and often the plans have been changed considerably. We don't want any such filter. We want our corporate management to get the opinions of divisional management without change or interference."

What is the reason for such a vigorous stand? Obviously, whether a company should have a corporate staff is not a simple question. The corporate planning group—especially if its head has direct access to top management—must be fully conversant with top management about the future in order to prepare the information management needs for its decisions; it must analyze all the alternatives before management makes its final decisions. As a result, corporate planning staffs review divisional plans "with the eyes of management."

The unavoidable outcome is typical of large bureaucratic organizations: the divisions tend to accommodate themselves in advance to the position of the corporate staff, which they believe is the position of top management itself. When preparing their plans, the divisions usually sound out the corporate staff to try to discern the probable acceptability of their ideas. As a result the vice-president or director of planning tends to dominate the whole planning effort. Not many division managers will stand up to defend proposals rejected by the corporate planning staff. This *is* what happens, regardless of instructions that give division managers maximum leeway in preparing their plans. And this situation is more prevalent than is generally apparent.

The Use of Planning Committees

The use of committees in connection with short-term and long-term profit planning is another controversial issue. The issue can be looked at from two angles, for committees can be set up at two different organizational levels.

First, a committee—for example, a long-term profit planning committee or a budget committee—may be established at the top level: such a committee will usually consist of the president or executive vice-president as chairman, and several vice-presidents who report to the chief executive officer. Often some or all division managers are also members. The purpose of this committee is not to plan, as such, but to *advise* and support those who do the actual planning. In addition, it settles differences that cannot be decided at lower levels. Thus such a committee assists the planning director or budget manager whenever problems arise in connection with long-term profit planning activities.

Second, committees operate at lower levels and serve mainly to provide *liaison* between the corporate planners and the managers of functions whose plans have to be coordinated by the corporate planning group. The members of such committees mainly represent the functional vice-presidents; the long-term profit planning manager or budget manager often serves as chairman. The job of the committee usually is mainly one of coordination and liaison between the corporate planners and planners at lower levels. The committee also settles differences between the corporate and divisional levels and often settles differences between two divisions.

There are wide differences of opinion regarding the value of committees for planning. Committees may spend too much time in lengthy discussions and thus delay accomplishment. We found, however, that many companies are convinced of the value of committees. Exhibits 16 and 17 illustrate these different viewpoints. A variety of factors influence these arguments, and no approach can be applied in all situations. Each case must be decided on its merits.

6

Data Requirements for Long-Term Profit Planning

A LARGE volume of information is necessary for the development of long-term profit plans. Data are frequently available from existing routines; other data will have to be specially prepared. Before investing in the preparation of special data, an inventory of the existing information is usually made. This is essential for several reasons:

1. Generating new data will involve investing substantial amounts of money. Keeping costs under control, therefore, becomes highly important and deserves management's full attention. Far too often, total costs of the planning program are underestimated, leading to disappointment and, even worse, to subsequent arbitrary restrictions that jeopardize the satisfactory completion of the work.

2. Most of the data that are available relate to the past and thus must be adjusted to give them the future orientation necessary for their use in the planning program. To be significant, the adjustments must be based on the judgments of persons with the necessary knowledge and experience. Making these adjustments can involve a considerable expense.

3. The information essential for the planning program must be carefully identified and its availability ascertained. Only after this has been done is it possible to work out a realistic estimate of the scope, time

requirements, and costs of installing a long-term profit planning program. The expected benefits from the earlier completion of the program made possible by an immediate large investment in the data needed must be compared with the additional cost to be incurred. The more carefully all related factors are examined and evaluated, the closer will be the correlation between anticipations and final results.

Availability of Necessary Data

Management must review carefully the availability of data needed in long-term profit planning before proceeding with the installation of a plan. Two principal kinds of data are needed, historical and future-oriented.

Historical data can be obtained from existing records, to the extent that they meet the requirements of the profit plan. Charts of accounts, however, are commonly designed for the purposes of financial accounting; detailed revenue and expense accounts receive little attention. Yet revenue and expense data are the data most needed for the profit plan. As stated by the financial vice-president of a large international manufacturing company:

"When I joined this company about three years ago, I found the existing accounting and statistical data to be utterly inadequate for the requirements of the long-term profit plan I had been asked to install. I knew it would be foolish to proceed with the plan without having the essential historical data. It took two years to improve the existing accounting system to the point where it provided the needed information. In part, this was the result of anticipated and probably unavoidable resistance of a long-entrenched organization. As a result, we are just now in the first year of our profit plan. Fortunately, our top management had a full understanding of the situation. You won't find this too often."

The accounting system is not the only or necessarily the best source of information. Frequently statistical techniques such as sampling can be very helpful, especially in this computer age. Statistical techniques are often simpler and cheaper than accounting procedures.

Let us not forget, however, that planning is concerned with the future. Historical data look toward the past and thus their value for planning purposes is limited. Future-oriented data, however, are only infrequently available within the information system. There are some exceptions. Two examples of future-oriented data are a company with a heavy backlog of orders that makes it possible to predict sales and production for several years ahead, and a company whose expenses are based on contractual arrangements. Historical information is important in considering the future, for it indicates trends that may continue into the future, assuming that past developments will continue more or less unchanged.[1] For example, prices or wages may be expected to increase by a given average percentage figure; the same may be true for productivity and other factors.

Unavoidably, future-oriented data are usually based on estimates. How to develop these estimates is an extremely important problem, and the success with which it is handled will affect the profit plan significantly. Estimates traditionally have been based on judgment. However, for many years efforts have been made to replace these judgment-based estimates with scientifically derived data. The first such efforts were made in marketing: sales forecasts are at the very heart of all planning, and large funds have been spent to improve these forecasts. (It should be noted that forecasting refers to *anticipated* conditions, while planning indicates management's *intentions* as to the future results of business activities.) During the past two decades, a vigorous and extensive attempt has been made to introduce into managerial decision making techniques that have been proved effective in the physical sciences.

All the companies providing information for this research indicate that they prepare forecasts or estimates for the company's overall sales. About nine out of ten of these companies forecast product prices, and about the same proportion forecast labor, material, and other costs. In contrast, only about six out of ten forecast economic conditions.

In addition to these overall forecasts, about a fourth of the companies contacted develop forecasts for specific functions. Slightly more, about four out of ten, make estimates for significant functional data. To illustrate, companies forecast product sales, by product groups; manufacturing facilities needed; manufacturing costs and expenditures; research facilities needed; product improvements and new products needed; engineering development costs for products and facilities; engineering services needed by the operating divisions; requirements for recruiting and training personnel; requirements for management manpower; and needed revisions in the company's organization. But it isn't always possible or worthwhile to develop formal forecasts of information that is needed for long-term profit planning. In such cases, many companies rely on estimates based on an analysis of past experience. Companies use countless estimates, based on, for example, historical comparisons with other companies and the company's industry, ratio analysis, historical growth

---

[1] Some of the case studies in Chapters 13, 14, 15, and 16 indicate how companies deal with these trend anticipations in their long-term planning programs.

rates, market share, historical growth rates of the prices received for the company's products, and the historical trend of manufacturing costs as a percent of net sales.

The Human Mind as a Forecasting Device

Despite the availability of ever more complex machines, the human mind is still management's most effective means of forecasting the future. In some fashion, still only dimly understood, the human mind is capable of evaluating a large number of factors virtually instantaneously and of combining them to arrive at a solution or decision. Some individuals accomplish this kind of mental activity with consistent success and thus are invaluable as business managers. Managers who need information about the future but who do not possess this extraordinary ability must acquire it using other tools and techniques.

Experience is of great importance in efforts to forecast future events, especially when past factors can be expected to continue into the future with little change. Indeed, experience will always remain a principal basis for managerial decisions. But when the past nature of events does not carry over into the future, the value of experience is substantially reduced and it can become an obstacle to a realistic appraisal of the future.

However, human judgment will remain the tool of last resort in forecasting and decision making. The manager–predictor will have to use his education, experience, and familiarity with external and internal conditions *and* newly developed objective approaches in making his forecasts. In most instances, the new objective techniques will be inadequate; they will not provide the manager with all the assistance he needs; they will not furnish the quantity and quality of data needed; or the accumulation of these data would be too time consuming or expensive. The manager's contribution is to fill the gap.

Scientific Techniques for Developing Future Data

It would be premature to say that a large number of companies are using the most advanced quantitative techniques for long-term profit planning, but approximately eight out of ten companies do report using some advanced techniques, primarily in the capital-budgeting area.

The companies contacted use quantitative techniques to help them evaluate capital investments, possible acquisitions, product lines, new products, research and development expenditures, the profit performance of profit centers, and management performance in general. For capital investments, for example, slightly better than seven out of ten companies report using some quantitative technique to help them. For evaluating the performance of profit centers, roughly two out of ten report using quantitative techniques. For capital investment analysis, about four out of ten use payback, about four out of ten use discounted cash flow, about two out of ten use return on investment calculations, two out of ten or so use present value, and about the same number use average return on assets. Only about two out of ten of the companies report using probability concepts to help them in their profit planning.

Interestingly, about five out of ten companies contacted report using incremental cost/revenue calculations to help them in profit planning: they use the technique for investigating large capital investments, the expansion of facilities, and the contribution margins on new products. Breakeven analyses are made by about three out of ten companies responding, primarily in reviewing capital investments and possible new products. And operations research techniques are used by about two out of ten of these companies to prepare economic and sales forecasts, to evaluate major projects, and to develop probability distributions of sales and gross margins.

Probability concepts were originally developed to help dukes and princes win at gambling. In more recent times these concepts have been applied widely in the physical sciences. And more recently still the use of probability concepts has extended into business. Traditional probability deals with frequencies of events derived from a large number of observations. These are *objective probabilities.* Insurance illustrates the use of objective probability; the data are based on actual experience. The applications of this approach to business have been limited, however, since a large number of relevant observations is seldom available.

The lack of an objective history of the occurrence of different events has led to the development of the concept of *subjective probability.* Subjective probabilities constitute the individual businessman's evaluation of the probabilities of future events. Businessmen long have made such evaluations, but now the evaluations are formalized. Systematic procedures are used for the expression of the businessman's informed judgment as to the probability of a specific result under various conditions. The usefulness of the results will obviously depend on the ability of the businessman to estimate future events. To illustrate, let us assume that a businessman wishes to forecast sales for next year. He will assign probabilities to the possible levels of sales:

Possible Units Sales	Probability of Occurrence
150	.40
250	.50
360	.10
	1.00

The businessman assigns the highest probability to sales of 250 units, but a smaller volume is almost as probable; however, sales substantially above 250 units are unlikely.

Various benefits are claimed from the use of probability concepts. Using the formal approach permits a more complete and logical evaluation of alternatives. Moreover, this method of reasoning is explicit and can be checked by others; this makes it easier to catch weaknesses of reasoning. This method can serve as a valuable tool in the development of future data as long as its limitations are kept fully in mind. The results of our survey indicate a minority of companies, predominately the large ones, uses the probability concept.

Probability concepts are useful, also, to help counteract traditional accounting concepts of precise, definite numbers. Typical accounting preciseness has recently been questioned, even for historical financial accounting. However, there can be no doubt that it is unsatisfactory for future-oriented data for which it is impossible to arrive at definite figures. We must usually work with a range of probable conditions. To illustrate: While it would be almost impossible for a chain of stores to fix in advance the exact sales for each outlet—say $12,530 per week for store 324—the budget for the store can provide for sales of $12,000 plus or minus 5 or 10 percent, depending on local conditions, and give probability estimates that these sales will be achieved. Management can work with these reasonable approximations of the uncertain future.

Another widely used statistical technique is correlation analysis. This technique serves to relate two series of data. For example, if sales of a particular company in the past have been closely related to fluctuations of the National Income and Money in Circulation (NIMC) Index it can be assumed, with a considerable probability of being correct, that the relationship will continue in the future; so knowing the forecasts for the NIMC Index, it is possible to forecast sales. Our survey indicates a substantial number of companies are using correlation techniques at the present time.

Mathematical models are widely used as forecasting tools. Simulation, based on models and computers, makes it feasible to experiment with a business in a way similar to what military people have been accomplishing with their "sand box game," in which they move armies around and try out different tactics. When the assumptions and related data are fed into the computer, it becomes possible to determine the effects of each of these assumptions and of managerial decisions on sales, profits, and other end-result measures. Many large companies have been using simulation techniques advantageously for some years. And the growing use of computers will make it possible for an increasing number of companies to take advantage of these advanced techniques.

Installing the Long-Term Profit Plan

Management can make an important contribution to a successful implementation of the long-term profit planning concept by allowing sufficient time for all necessary steps to be completed without undue haste. Pressure for results within an arbitrarily set time schedule—which fails to permit full consideration of all pertinent factors—rarely leads to a successful implementation. A realistic picture of the problems to be faced and the work to be completed in implementing such a program is presented as the case of JKL Manufacturing Corporation. The experience of this fictitious company is a composite of the experiences of a number of companies that have recently installed long-term profit plans.

"At present we operate five plants in the West and South. We have more than 5,000 employees, including almost 1,000 engineers and research scientists. We expect our sales to reach $50 million in the near future with profits of approximately $3 million," explained James Bright, executive vice-president and former controller of the company, a well-known supplier of parts and assemblies for the aerospace industry. Mr. Bright had been one of the founders of the company some 20 years earlier. "For a number of years," he continued, "we have been working toward diversification of our activities because of the fluctuating level of sales of our principal customers. Our desire to get a better grip on our profit situation was the main reason for our decision to install a long-term profit plan.

"We looked inside the company for a man with the necessary qualifications for the job. Our efforts were unsuccessful. We had operated a one-year budget program for a few years, mainly in the financial area. The manager of budgets, a former accounting supervisor, did a fair job with his three assistants, but we did not believe he had the abilities for a more demanding position. This was the reason we had to look for outside help. We finally retained a man with experience in long-term profit planning.

"John Howling, the new man we brought in, made a careful evaluation of the information used by the budget department; he found that it was of limited value for the long-term profit plan. In particular, the nonfinancial data used were mainly based on rough estimates.

"From his earlier experience, Mr. Howling was convinced of the importance of adequate forecasting data. He suggested we initially concentrate on this area especially as far as marketing and sales data were concerned. Top management and the heads of marketing and sales failed to appreciate the difference in forecasting for the short and long term, so they had difficulty understanding the point he was making. The data used for the budget were of little value as a basis for the long term.

"Substantial deficiencies were also found in the case of expense records. Since a restructuring of the accounting system to provide data suitable for extrapolations in the future would have taken a great deal of time, we decided to use sampling techniques. In this way we could get inexpensive data adequate to indicate trends. We felt the data would be satisfactory until we obtained more compatible data from the improved accounting system. Our computer installation provided significant help in all our data collection and processing.

"Our investigations covered all parts of the organization, and we were able to spot the areas where current data collection techniques were inadequate for our project. These included cash flow and controls, investments, research and development, and several others. This review in depth of our data collecting system brought substantial savings in a variety of fields and thus led to profit-enhancing results we had not expected. Frequently, improvements were made with a minimum of effort and expense by simple changes of long-used practices.

"We had to deal with two different kinds of problem. On the one side, we had to improve the flow and availability of the data provided by the accounting system. However, many essential data are not available from this system. These data often cannot be expressed adequately in quantitative terms. Then there is no alternative but to resort to estimates and individual judgments.

"Whenever it would have been too time consuming or too expensive to obtain certain data, a decision had to be made as to their significance, whether they were really essential or whether some other information could be substituted, although it would be less valuable. Who should have authority to make such a decision? It could have been the planning director, the chief accountant, the controller, or perhaps top management. The final decision was to have the controller do it until the planning director was selected and then have it become a joint assignment. We couldn't postpone the decision. I cooperated with the chief accountant in deciding what data we would assemble and looked to the functional heads for special advice. The president and the executive vice-president helped me when needed. The main purpose was to make sure that only essential new data were developed and accumulated. When the planning director was appointed, he accepted almost all the decisions that had been made.

"The other and more complex problem was determining the nonquantitative data that could be based only on individual judgments. Who should do the estimating? It had to be a person whose judgment could be trusted. We also considered an arrangement whereby these judgments could be reviewed by other executives with ability, seniority, rank, or some combination of these. After wrestling with the problem for quite a while, we agreed Mr. Howling would select the persons who would review the judgments. Those selected would prepare a report for a committee consisting of all functional vice-presidents and top management. In cases when the report cast doubts on the original decision, the committee would discuss and reconsider it. The executive who made the original decision would be a member of the committee and thus, it was hoped, would not feel offended when his judgment was amended as a result of these discussions. This approach has worked quite satisfactorily.

"I would not suggest that our decisions on these matters should serve as a model for other companies. Personal considerations are strongly involved in such situations and each case must be decided on the basis of circumstances.

"In this context, I would like to mention another important issue. In recent years, some companies have begun to use complex mathematical techniques to support and improve their forecasting procedures. They hope thereby to reduce the effects of shortcomings resulting from unsatisfactory individual judgments. We have not yet taken advantage of these new techniques. The principal reason is that we do not have on our staff experts to handle these techniques, nor have we felt justified to hire experts or to make arrangements for some of our own people to acquire the necessary knowledge. We have had to recognize the limited resources of our company and the substantial additional costs that would have been required. We thought these funds could be used to better advantage for other important projects, such as research and development or the improvement of our marketing and distribution facilities.

"This should not be taken to indicate lack of appreciation for the benefits from these new techniques. An executive in our company has indicated interest in this new area and we are encouraging him—with free time and limited funds—to engage in the necessary studies. He will keep us informed of new developments that, in his opinion, could be applicable to our organization. His suggestions will be given careful attention. The electronic computer we installed recently, at considerable expense, will help us apply these new techniques when we feel the right time has arrived. In fact, our market research staff has the use of these techniques under study. Our executive–student is expected to acquire soon sufficient knowledge to train some of our people for work on developing an improved forecasting procedure. It seems to me that our approach is correct: we keep these activities within the framework of our resources."

7

Launching the Long-Term Profit Planning Effort

W͟H͟O pushes for long-term profit planning? In roughly eight out of ten of the companies contacted in this research, the president played either the principal or a major role in launching the long-term profit planning activity, and more often than not he played the principal role. Usually the president indicated his support of long-term profit planning through his public, personal endorsement of the concept and the company's program. This he did by face-to-face comments in support of the effort and by letters and memoranda; approximately eight out of ten of the companies that responded indicate this kind of presidential support.

Other than the obvious way of pointing out the need for formal planning, the president and his top management indicate their support for long-term profit planning through such moves as putting a qualified person in charge of the program, asking for the long-term implications of short-term objectives and plans, indicating the board's special interest in the company's progress in developing and installing a long-term profit planning program, and tying long-term profit plan performance in with incentive compensation decisions. One specific way presidents indicate the importance with which they view the activity is by having it report to them or to another officer. About three out of ten of the companies indicate that corporate long-term profit planning reports to the president, roughly 25 percent indicate that it reports to the vice-president of finance, and about 25 percent indicate that it reports to the controller. In the other companies long-term profit planning reports to the treasurer, the administrative vice-president, or other executive. In the divisions the long-term profit planning activity usually reports to the division manager in about eight out of ten companies; in the other companies it reports to the division controller.

So in the majority of cases top management appears to take the initiative. But as might be expected, our survey indicates that more often than not the original proposal to install a long-term profit planning program came from the company's staff people, who sometimes had to fight long and hard to win management's acceptance. With the growing use of long-term profit plans, however, more top executives are becoming aware of the benefits of such plans. Their discussions with other top executives who are successfully profit planning probably influence them more than the persuasiveness of their own staffs. As managers learn the benefits that usually result from comprehensive long-term profit planning, they give more careful consideration to proposals submitted by their staffs.

Launching JKL Manufacturing Corporation's Long-Term Profit Plan

Many of the problems in organizing and launching a long-term profit planning effort can be illustrated by continuing the composite case study (JKL Manufacturing Corporation) started in the last chapter. JKL first outlines the prerequisites required of a planning director. Then the man selected for the job describes how he approached his assignment and how he handled the problems he encountered in organizing his group. He calls attention to the human aspect of his work, especially the methods he used to familiarize other executives with the objective of the company's long-term profit plan. Then he discusses the techniques used to acquire the necessary data.

Mr. Bright introduced Franklin Jones, the corporate planning director. Franklin Jones was a graduate of a leading business school and had several years' experience in the installation and operation of long-term profit plans. He also had excellent references from his former employers. Mr. Bright continued:

"I am sure you would like to know how we selected Frank Jones. Mr. Howling had told us time and again that it was critical to find the right man; he also pointed out how difficult it would be. As I mentioned before, we were unable to find a qualified person among our present staff, our preferred solution. We had made a careful review of the junior executives who might be eligible. We even discovered a few who could probably be trained to assume the position at some later date, but as happens too often, their superiors were unwilling to release them. So we had to give up this possibility. We interviewed a number of persons referred by recruiting agencies, but none met our expectations. Finally, Mr. Howling heard about a man interested in changing jobs for geographic reasons. He had performed similar assignments successfully and appeared eager to come to our headquarters city. He made a very good impression on our top people who interviewed him, and in fact, I liked him almost immediately."

At this point, Franklin Jones entered the conversation.

"Things didn't look too auspicious at the beginning. As is usually the case, executives in the different functions appeared suspicious and rather unfriendly when I met them for introductory discussions. This was especially true of the budget manager, who appeared irked at not having been given the long-term profit planning assignment. In my experience, the best way to meet such a problem is head-on. I told the budget manager point-blank that he could change jobs in the company or join another company if he was unwilling to cooperate with me. As I had anticipated, this did the trick, but naturally his cooperation remained limited and reluctant.

"I had to spend a considerable amount of time getting acquainted with the operations of the company, finding out what information was available, and establishing contacts with the executives in the functions. These things took considerable time, so nothing else significant was accomplished for some months. I am still grateful to Mr. Bright for his patience and for letting me proceed at my own speed. On his advice, top management took the same attitude."

At this point, Mr. Jones emphasized his opinion that the planning director's responsibility for the installation of the long-term profit plan must be made clear at the outset.

"I didn't suggest many changes in the preliminary decisions made before my appointment. This does not mean I would have approached the project in exactly the same manner. But I felt that procedural differences were not sufficiently important to spend the time in the extended discussions that would have been required to bring about changes. In my opinion, the first thing to do was to talk with the future users of the profit plan: I felt it was especially important to serve those who would use the long-term profit plan for their decision making. Also by dealing first with the high-level executives and their staffs and developing an understanding with them, I anticipated it would reduce frictions with lower-level managers. Other procedural questions were technical matters that could always be solved in some manner. The uppermost issue for me was to know exactly what was expected of me and to develop my procedures accordingly. (This approach made a good impression on top management and got me its support.) On the basis of these discussions, I laid out a detailed plan and time schedule for the introduction and initial operation of the long-term profit plan. I carried the plan to the point where long-term profit planning would have become routine.

"A number of matters I had to take up with the controller and, in some cases, top management. They included:

1. The organization of my group, its size, prerequisites for staffing, salary schedules, and channels of responsibility.
2. The length of the period of the long-term profit plan.
3. The amount of decentralization desired.
4. Top management's objectives.
5. The cooperation that would be required from top management and other executives.
6. The interface with the present short-term plan (budget).

"Obviously, important and complex questions such as these could not be settled in one sitting. But some understanding was possible, except, perhaps, with the budget manager. I assumed that remaining differences would be straightened out as uncertainties were resolved. But I was badly mistaken. I found that the same terms did not mean the same thing to all of us. This resulted in arguments and misunderstandings. I should have insisted on formal, written arrangements. A written understanding might have eliminated a few of our troubles."

Franklin Jones feels that many misunderstandings can be avoided if the peculiar position of the planner is recognized.

"In the literature you find all kinds of ideas as to what managers of long-term profit planning should be and do. A manager of long-term profit planning needs many fine qualities, but you can hardly expect to find anyone who possesses all of them. You have to be satisfied with less. The big question is, how much less? Particularly important in determining the profit planning manager's success is his skill in human relations. I have found that success or failure in long-term profit planning depends much less on the manager's technical qualifications than on his attitudes toward the people he has to work with and whose cooperation and understanding he depends on. The more you analyze his work, the more you realize how comparatively small is his personal contribution to the final plan and how large are the contributions of others. Yet the manager's contributions are indispensable to the whole effort.

"The manager of long-term profit planning's principal task, therefore, is to influence those who are doing the main job, a job he cannot and should not do himself. This is the heart of his problem. The man who can exert this influence will be successful. It took me quite a while to realize this essential truth. I could give you any number of examples, especially from my experience during the first couple of years, but I shall mention only one highly significant instance.

"Obviously, effective long-term profit planning requires full coordination among the principal functions of the organization; production must be coordinated with marketing and sales, and all these must be coordinated with finance. They are all, in turn, dependent on effective research and development and on an adequate flow of new, low-cost products or new cost-saving techniques. This is especially important for a company like ours, which produces for other manufacturers items also made by numerous competitors. Our success in recent years has been the result of our ability often to be ahead of other companies in marketing of cost-saving devices.

"This coordination is essential for achieving the desired long-term profit. To achieve it, there must be data available for each function for several years ahead. I could not develop those data myself. Even if I had the information, it was not my job to accumulate it. It was my responsibility to convince the executives of the different functions that they should maintain sufficient coordination with their fellows so they all could develop the necessary data. All these executives gave lip service to my requests, but, in fact, each was mainly concerned with his own ideas and plans and gave scant attention to what the others were doing. It was my duty to examine the functional plans to see whether they were properly coordinated, and if I found they were not, I had to insist that these deficiencies were remedied. But how could I accomplish this essential task? This was the fundamental issue I had to solve if I were to come up with a long-term profit plan of value to management.

"Special difficulties arose in my contacts with the director of the research and development department. As I indicated, this department was particularly important in our planning, but I was unable to arrange proper coordination. The director of the department insisted he was unable to forecast his department's contribution for the period of the profit plan. In his opinion, there were too many uncertainties to permit even rough approximations. When I was unable to make any progress, I finally talked with Mr. Bright and we decided to bring the matter to the attention of the president. The president was a former director of the research and development department. Even his intervention was unsuccessful. The present director of R&D has an excellent reputation and the president did not wish to antagonize him. There was nothing I could do. Eventually, with the assistance of experts he retained, the president himself made a careful evaluation of present and planned work in the department and came up with estimates I could use for the profit plan. It often took several years to get products ready for large-scale production and marketing. This made estimating new product launchings quite difficult but not by any means impossible. The research director remains unconvinced to this day. This is the kind of human problem you have to contend with in profit planning.

"It seems to me—and I think Mr. Bright will agree—that the proper education of our executives is often the only way to solve this type of problem. Patience is indispensable when you have to explain the benefits of a long-term profit plan to some doubting executive over and over again and convince him he has to make a contribution for the benefit of the whole company. Because of our experience, we have now placed a man in charge of such educational activities. He arranges meetings with groups of executives and talks to them individually, if necessary, explaining the benefits the company obtains from long-term profit planning.

"I still have difficulties with some executives and I know it is not always their fault. I assure you I am trying my best but sometimes it seems not to be good enough. So I suggest you use care in selecting the man who will introduce your long-term profit plan. He should be a good salesman so he can convince others of the importance of the plan and the need for their contribution to make it a success."

Mr. Jones emphasizes that the size and character of the planning staff should be based on quality rather than quantity.

"Some companies get along with a single planner. I don't think this is the best arrangement. There should at least be a back-up man ready to take over if necessary. In any case, the group should be as small as possible—too small for empire building or taking over activities that can be carried out better and cheaper by other parts of the organization. The minimum staff should provide one back-up man and a secretary. Any additional personnel would depend on the workload.

"It seemed to me that we should make a distinction in our staffing decisions between the introductory and break-in period and the point when our routines would be well established. After discussions with Messrs. Bright and Howling, I decided to hire one young man on a permanent, long-term basis and two others with similar high qualifications as assistants for the introductory period. Thus the table of organization would list the group reporting to me as three full-time specialists and a secretary. One important reason we hired younger men was the shortage of fully qualified long-term profit planners. We also had to consider the possibility that our back-up man might be offered another, more attractive position. If that should happen, we would still have another man who could be trained for this challenging assignment.

"It was my responsibility to make the necessary selections. I knew it would not be easy. Every effort had to be made to select present employees and to hire outsiders only as a last resort. Initially, I wanted to avoid a formal announcement of the openings on these new jobs. I thought an informal approach would be preferable. I used the grapevine and, indeed, from it received several inquiries from young men who had been with the company for one to three years, most of them college graduates. I talked with each of these men without first looking into their personal files; I wanted my impression not to be influenced by grades and similar information. None, however, appeared outstanding intellectually or personally. When asked why they were interested in the new position, the reply from most was the higher salary. Only one man said he was looking for a more challenging assignment.

"I looked into this man's record and found he had a bachelor's degree in industrial engineering and a master's degree in business administration. His grades had been good but not outstanding. He had had another job with a large company and had made a satisfactory record. I offered him a full-time position on a temporary basis so we would have a chance to test his handling of complex problems. He was unsure at first of his ability to handle an assignment for which he had no previous preparation and experience. But he finally accepted and promised to do his best to justify my confidence in him. Dick Connor, the man I've been speaking of, still serves as my back-up man. He's done very good work.

"I decided not to hire anyone else at that time. I arranged, instead, to get part-time assistance from other departments whenever I needed it.

"About a year after we first started, after the work of the group had become known within the company, I sent a notice to all departments asking for recommendations of young men they considered qualified for my group. From among a number of people suggested, I selected a man who seems to me superior to Dick in various respects to be a full-time member of the group. He has a bachelor's degree and a master's degree and several years' experience in public accounting, and he had worked as an analyst in our controller's department. At present, he and Dick are virtually working at the same level, so I now have two qualified back-up men. I also selected two part-timers for a year's service; they took leaves of absence from their departments. This arrangement gives a number of men an opportunity to learn about long-term profit planning and then to serve as liaison with the planning department after they return to their permanent positions."

At this point, Franklin Jones turned his attention to the importance of the planning director having easy access to top management.

"Since most top managements try to limit the number of executives who report directly to them, the long-term planner is not going to have a direct channel unless he has the rank of vice-president. This will not often be the case. There was little enthusiasm for having me report directly to the president; I was to report instead to the controller. However, Mr. Bright, who was then the controller, did not want the assignment. This opened the way for me to report to the executive vice-president, now Mr. Bright."

Mr. Bright interjected a comment here:

"In my opinion, the director of profit planning is like a nonvoting member of top management: He must be fully familiar with its thinking, objectives, and ideas. I feel there is no better way to obtain this information than to let him participate in top management's deliberations.

"Frank has done an outstanding job in selecting his assistants. His two assistants know virtually as much as he does. He debates issues with them and often they come up with ideas or solutions that become the group's recommendations to management. Everyone is fully aware of Frank's abilities, and he is often called in as an adviser on a variety of problems far removed from his own field of responsibility."

In Franklin Jones's eyes, one of the planning director's most important jobs is to convince executives that top management cooperation is essential.

"Without this relationship with top management, I would be unable to do a proper job. Everyone must be convinced I reflect top management thinking and would be supported by them, if needed. My big problem, and this is one I share with anyone in this kind of position, is to be strong-willed and modest at the same time. I have to work with men in high positions; many are oldtimers who feel they are closer to the top than I am. I am not surprised if they are jealous and try to put me in my place. I must not give the impression I know more than they do. Quite the opposite: I have to take a deferential attitude and recognize their superior experience. Indeed, the long-term profit planner must walk a tightrope and he may easily get into trouble. Fortunately, although my troubles have been numerous, they have never reached the point where they jeopardize my usefulness in my job. Many others in jobs similar to mine have not been so fortunate.

"As soon as I had organized the long-term profit planning group, I requested the president and the executive vice-president to address a meeting of all supervisors, including those from our plants, to explain the purposes of my assignment and to point out the need for their support for my work. The speeches were made and questions from the floor were answered. To take advantage of the movement resulting from these meetings, I made arrangements for talks with all those attending so I could explain to them in detail what I intended to do and the cooperation I would need from them. No one rejected my suggestions, but I was left with the feeling a majority took a rather cool attitude. This was what I had anticipated. While those with engineering backgrounds showed understanding, the coolest reception came from financial executives, who were apparently afraid of possible encroachment into their specific fields.

"I decided to continue these efforts to gain confidence all around. I think I slowly made progress. I also prepared memoranda summarizing what I had said, with emphasis on the contribution expected from the various executives. More meetings followed to answer questions and I conversed personally with 'hard' cases—those who had reacted unfavorably. I finally concluded that a large majority would cooperate, though with a minimum of personal interest and involvement. This was borne out by later experience.

"I then held discussions with department heads on the details of their expected involvement in the long-term profit planning process. About three months before the end of the first year, I distributed a schedule of the due-dates for the various reports. As each report came in, I discussed it with the executive who prepared it, indicating necessary improvements in the future. I was aware that the first-year reports would be tentative only and of little value to management. After all reports had come in, I prepared a revised edition of the instructions, taking into account the experiences of the first year 'trial run.' "

Although it was difficult for many of the cooperating executives to think in the precise terms necessary, Mr. Jones emphasized to them that the development of numerical information was crucial for a useful long-term profit plan.

"The question most frequently asked during my discussions with our executives was how they were to compute the future-oriented data. Data for the one-year budget had been prepared for some years, and thus the functional executives were familiar with the problems involved. But to generate similar data for more distant periods appeared to them to be more difficult, if not impossible. Of course, the problems varied for the different functions. Our analysis of the company's budget procedures had indicated that the data used for the budget would be of little value to our work. I decided not to depend on these data but rather to make a new start by getting the long-term information independently. I asked our executives to develop their long-term information separately from the budget data, mainly on the basis of careful estimates. (I have already explained the review technique we used and pointed out that effective procedures had to be worked out as we went along, largely by trial and error.) Everyone involved participated in this effort. Each executive not only had to think in terms of his own activities but at the same time had to keep in mind the interests and needs of the whole company. The final result, the long-term profit plan, would, then, represent the thinking of all the participants.

"First, a broad analysis of each particular area had to be undertaken. The executive in charge of each function, as the principal specialist in his area of responsibility, had to consider the expected evolution of his area over the next few years. In the beginning we made no effort to develop specific figures. We were trying to determine, for example, whether current conditions could be expected to remain the same or whether they would change in ways that would require us to make additional capital expenditures. Should we expect new developments that would affect the particular function favorably or unfavorably? What would these be and when would they become significant? How would the function be affected by changes in other major functions, such as adding new products or services? What were the weaknesses of the function and the chances for removing them, either through internal measures or events that might come from outside the company?

"Based on suggestions from my group and from other participants, we prepared an overall list of factors to be investigated. As additional items came to mind, they were added to the list. In addition, each executive prepared his own list of factors that had a particular impact on his function. We anticipated that these lists and experience would make our analyses of increasing value. I am sure this is the crucial part of the planning effort. Individual figures are often difficult to determine with accuracy. But the results of these general analyses remain valid for a considerable time. But even these should be reviewed regularly and brought up to date as required. In order to compute specific figures, however, you must know the company's objectives and the resources available to achieve them. Moreover, you must know the sources of the data. The former budgets were deficient because of the inadequacy of this information."

Some of the problems involved in developing company objectives and acquiring the numerical data necessary for long-term profit planning were discussed earlier. Mr. Jones had similar problems in his company.

Top Management Provides the Ground Rules for Long-Term Profit Planning

Most companies assign responsibility informally for the different inputs into the profit plan. For example, more than half of the companies contacted indicate that they have no formal breakdown, by levels, of who will contribute what information to the long-term profit plan; this kind of responsibility is implicit in the company's organization structure. In an overall sense, however, general management provides the guidelines for anticipated growth, exercises leadership in determining company goals, coordinates the activities of the many contributors, makes final decisions, and approves the final long-term profit plan. The various staff groups contribute to the effort by assisting operating units in forecasting the items they need for profit plan development, by providing them with general staff assistance, by making preliminary reviews of their plans and suggesting revisions, by evaluating and recommending alternatives in a more formal way if requested, and, finally, by formally reviewing division plans. On the other hand, middle-level operating managers are charged with the formal responsibility for preparing the detailed plans for their areas of responsibility, including all revenue, expense, and cost estimates.

We have seen the important place of objectives in a company's long-term profit planning. Of equal importance are the assumptions a company's managers use in preparing their plans. Not all companies feel it is necessary to formally state the assumptions that will guide the planning effort, however. Among the companies contacted, about four out of ten do formally state their assumptions, the rest do not. When a company does formally state the assumptions its planners should use, these assumptions are usually set forth by the president, the chairman of the board, the planning director, the planning committee, or the budget department. Which group issues these important guidelines will depend, naturally, on how the company has organized for long-term profit planning. When assumptions are stated, they usually relate to such matters as general economic conditions, industry conditions, accounting principles, legislation, market conditions, sales forecasts, capital expenditures, technical conditions, financial conditions, and personnel matters.

The Importance of Profitability

In addition to serving as a tool for management decision making, the long-term profit plan is a constant reminder to all a company's executives of the importance of profitability. The particular functions (production, sales, research, and so forth) never are ends in themselves. Unprofitable sales should not be increased and products should not be made if there is not an adequate market for them. A well-developed long-term profit plan should help keep this fact before all the company executives.

Mr. Jones picked up again with his recounting of how he launched the company's long-term profit planning program:

"From the outset, Mr. Bright, with his background in the financial area, insisted that the profit plan be the focus of my activities and that all my work be directed toward providing the company with a plan. In my talks with the functional executives when I first started on the job, it was not easy to convince them not to concentrate exclusively on their own functions. Many of these men showed little grasp of the importance of financial factors. I discussed this matter at length with them to make them more aware of its importance. I believe I had some success, even among those who initially refused to accept my point of view as a matter of personal conviction. To some extent, at least, all our executives now appreciate the importance of the long-term profit plan as a part of the overall effort. This will be a never ending struggle, however, for the executives in charge of the functions will always tend to think only in terms of their specialties. But they all have to realize that their specific interests must be subordinated to the interests of the company as a whole. The long-term profit plan is probably the best device currently available for approaching, if not attaining, this much desired end."

In Franklin Jones's opinion, management must become familiar with the techniques of the functional planners if it is to use their efforts effectively.

"It is a fact that the viewpoint of top management and those of the functional executives are not always the same. The latter deal with a single function, while top management integrates all the functions. A technique that appears appropriate to a functional executive will not always be acceptable to top management, whose problems are different. So if top management reviews and perhaps revises a functional executive's planning techniques, this does not necessarily indicate a lack of confidence in the abilities of the functional executive. Of course, management can give this coordinating job to staff assistants if they are properly qualified."

At this point, Mr. Bright interjected an illustration of this problem and how management was trying to handle it.

"Let me just give you one illustration of what is involved here. You know I am familiar with current accounting practices and problems. I am equally aware that some of these practices are not in the best interests of business in general and our company in particular. Our controller, who handles our relations with our public accountants and the Securities and Exchange Commission, naturally is inclined to avoid trouble whenever possible. He will, therefore, accept their positions in advance, even if an alternative method would better fit our particular requirements. Take, for example, the argument about the 7-percent investment credit. The American Institute of Certified Public Accountants and, consequently, our auditors favor spreading the credit over the whole life of the assets in question. The controller tends to agree with them, though our management prefers taking the credit at the time of purchase, which tends to increase both profits and cash flow. Unless top management is familiar with these alternatives, the controller's point of view will prevail.

"I certainly appreciate management's reluctance to get involved in such questions. The temptation to let the experts decide on technical problems, including planning problems, is strong and easy to understand. But the results of doing this will not always be in the best interests of the company. Specialization is increasing, and management must learn to live with it. Frankly, I don't have a solution for this dilemma. I am in favor of top management having a general knowledge of the unique problems of each function. The planner will then be more inclined to present top management with the alternatives and let it make the final decisions. Top management can side with the experts, and usually will, or it can rely on its own knowledge of the situation."

Communication Regarding Long-Term Profit Planning

Effective communication is critical in designing and implementing long-term profit plans.

Most long-term profit planning efforts are started by the release of a statement by top management, or by the planning director in the name of top management, outlining the company's basic objectives and the long-term planning basic assumptions and intentions. These are intended to guide the departments that have to contribute their plans to the overall efforts. The problem is how to make sure everybody affected by the planning program has an *adequate* understanding of top management's objectives. But even more difficult is to ensure that everybody has the *same* understanding of these objectives. Each contributor to the plan has his own ideas as to what the company's objectives and preferences should be. These cannot help but influence the contributor's interpretation of top management's intentions and therefore the manner in which he prepares his own contribution to the corporate long-term profit plan.

Companies approach their communication problems in different ways. Some do nothing and hope for the best; this approach can easily result in major troubles and misunderstandings, although it may work in smaller companies where there is considerable personal communication among the company's managers. Another technique is to make the planning staff responsible for all communication; this arrangement can work satisfactorily. As explained by the planning director of a large corporation: "I have spent most of my time developing material for our several divisions to ensure uniform interpretation of management's objectives." As he said this, he pointed to a bookshelf with a number of large binders. "These binders include the material I have distributed to the divisions. In addition, I have visited the divisions for personal discussions with their managers and staffs to make sure that they knew fully what was expected from them." When asked what he thought of results of these efforts, he replied, "I certainly hope they have accomplished the desired results, but, of course, you can never be sure."

Another method used by some corporations is to schedule meetings once a year, or more frequently, away from headquarters. Top management and the corporate staff invite the division managers and division staffs. At the beginning of such a meeting the president or chairman of the board usually discusses the overall objectives of the company, while other members of top management deal with their particular specialities. These presentations are usually supported by materials or formal papers prepared in advance by the corporate staff. The talks are subsequently published for the guidance of the executives who participate in the planning program. The next step, often on the following day, is an open discussion in which everyone is expected to participate. This discussion affords the divisional representatives the opportunity to ask questions and, in turn, affords the corporate people the opportunity to explain in more detail their plans and how they expect them to be carried out. Sometimes, the final plan is determined at these meetings.

A worldwide manufacturer of consumer products—which did poorly during the 1950s but has greatly improved since a new management took over some years ago—uses still another approach. The vice-president of finance, formerly the company's vice-president of development, has charge of corporate planning. He explained:

"It is my settled opinion that one of the major factors that brought our company back to profitability was our long-term profit plan and the way we were able to get it accepted by all the people who contribute to it, including all the managers in our worldwide production and sales organizations. To make sure there is real understanding of management's objectives, I spend a considerable part of the year talking to these managers, wherever they may be. Our present goals are an 8-percent increase in sales and a 10-percent increase in profits annually. In recent years these goals have been exceeded. As part of our long-term profit plan, we constantly drive for savings, with the result that unit costs have been kept stable in the face of increasing wage rates. While sales have doubled, the number of workers has declined by some 10 percent. Top management has supported our long-term profit planning effort with enthusiasm."

8

Planning and Controlling Capital Investments and Management Manpower

I⊤ is customary to begin discussions of planning—especially short-term planning—with a discussion of the sales function, since this function has a decisive impact on the other planning functions. However, the company's long-term goals are more affected by and related more closely to investment decisions.

The Impact of Investment Planning on Long-Term Profit Planning

Investment decisions are typically long term. Expenditures are spread over a number of years, and the results of the investment—revenues and profits—may be realized only over an extended period. Therefore, a careful evaluation of an investment opportunity depends on having a long-term profit plan that will show the effects on profits in each of the planning periods. Determining the figures required for an evaluation of such an opportunity will often be difficult; therefore, a discussion of the techniques involved is especially valuable for those charged with the responsibility for developing or evaluating long-term profit plans.

Investment planning has been extensively researched, much more so than have the planning techniques for other functions. Decisions on investments are especially sensitive for several reasons. First, the amounts at stake are often quite large, and decisions once arrived at cannot easily be reversed. Moreover, investments may affect a company's situation for a long time ahead, even when the circumstances that led to the decisions have substantially changed. These are the reasons for the special care managements devote to these decisions, their strong efforts toward developing improved techniques for evaluating proposals, and their policy of reserving final approval to top management, even in highly decentralized organizations. Virtually all the companies included in our survey follow these practices.

The need for evaluating investment decisions over the long term has been recognized for some time. Before World War II these decisions were usually made intuitively and on the basis of short-term considerations. Investments were started during periods of booming business and discontinued as soon as a downturn occurred. Such a policy was accepted as good business practice, but in fact it was quite expensive and often resulted in inadequate facilities at the time of the next upswing. It finally became apparent that short-term considerations were not adequate in evaluating investment opportunities.

Management's attitude toward capital investment has in recent times undergone a dramatic change, in part as a result of the better understanding and control of business-cycle fluctuations. Most companies now tend to look at investment projects from a long-term point of view: investments are continued—although a company may slow down completion of some projects—even during the periods of business decline, as long as the decline appears to be of a limited duration. Also, new techniques based on quantitative data instead of on mere judgment make possible a more thorough and more adequate evaluation of investment projects.

Modern Evaluation Techniques Can Help in Analyzing Long-Term Investment Projects

The return on investment (ROI), the ratio of profit to the investment used to produce the profit, is a measure that has been used by a few companies for about half a century; it has now been widely adopted as an effective measure of the worth of investment projects. Special attention is being given to the time factor, which, though familiar to engineers and engineering economists, had until recently been disregarded by most accountants and managers. Measurement techniques such as discounted cash flow (DCF) and present value give special attention to timing considerations. The majority of the companies surveyed have not yet taken advantage of these techniques. There are, in fact, practical difficulties in applying these new measuring techniques.

Estimating future events is particularly difficult when the time span is long, as is often the case with investment projects. Introducing a time factor creates additional problems: in addition to estimating revenues, expenses, and profits, the time of their occurrence and a suitable discounting factor (interest rate) must be determined. For this reason even some large and progressive companies take a dim view of these techniques. But our survey indicates that a majority of large companies and some smaller ones either are using these techniques or are considering their introduction.

Determining the discounting rate to use in these calculations is sometimes laborious. The discounting factor for any given investment is the rate that will make revenues equal expenditures, when both are brought to time-period zero and considering also the useful life of the project. While there are many theoretically sound ways for determining these factors, in practice they are commonly found by trial and error. The advantages and shortcomings of these techniques have been hotly debated in recent years. The important point for management is that each method and each discount rate will produce different results, with the consequent varying impacts on the long-term profit plan. Therefore, management has to evaluate carefully the method being used by its experts before accepting their results. Unless this precaution is taken, the conclusions drawn may be highly controversial and even misleading.

In order to evaluate and then rank investment proposals in accordance with each one's profitability and rate of return, management must set a minimum required rate of return. Various factors enter into this determination. The cost of capital is one. Determination of the *cost of capital* is difficult since there are so many different sources of funds and often a combination of several sources is involved in a particular financing transaction. A special problem arises if internally generated funds are used, such as retained earnings or depreciation charges. What will be the cost of these funds? One widely used costing method is based on possible earnings from alternative investment opportunities, but this approach creates its own problems.

Risk is another important factor. There is a common assumption that risk and return go together: the greater the risk, the higher the required return. However, to measure risk in quantitative terms is difficult since the laws of probability are not readily applicable. So both the risk and the appropriate return must be determined by managerial judgment. A simple and widely used method of risk evaluation uses the payoff period—the time interval between the expenditures (cash outflow) and the return of the invested funds (cash inflow). Management uses its judgment to set the maximum acceptable payoff period, which is usually quite short—rarely more than three years. This method is concerned only with the return *of* the original investment and disregards the additional and more important return *on* the investment—what is received in addition to the return of the original investment. In its insistence on an arbitrarily short payoff period, management often excludes worthwhile investment projects that do not meet the arbitrarily determined time limits. It follows that this approach must be used with caution to avoid misunderstandings and difficulties. Many companies use this crude method for the preliminary screening of investment proposals and use other more sophisticated methods for the final selections.

Despite the use of elaborate approaches, managerial judgment remains a powerful and often decisive force. The motives that affect management's judgment may vary widely. Comments of executives in response to a survey made by a well-known business publication illustrate this fact. Thus a top official of a large conglomerate company explained: "Historically the capital outlays we defer always turn out to be our most expensive ones. There is little to indicate the benefit of waiting."

An executive who discussed the present low utilization of plant facilities said: "Most of the idle capacity is just not efficient. . . . Much of the capital spending . . . is caused by a desire to reduce costs by improving inefficient manufacturing facilities." Another executive remarked, "Businessmen take a two- to five-year look at family formations and markets just ahead, and they can't help getting pretty optimistic when they look beyond the current crop of short-range problems." Pressure of wage increases and technological considerations are cited as other factors.[1]

The LMN Corporation, a major manufacturer of heavy equipment, spends more than $100 million a year in capital investments. As part of a comprehensive long-term profit plan adopted several years ago, management decided to reorganize the company's procedures for investment planning, especially the procedures for selecting specific projects from

[1] *Business Week,* March 22, 1969, pp. 34–35.

among those submitted by the divisions. John Brewer, manager of corporate capital investment, described the company's practices:

> Our present procedures were adopted five years ago. Several years were needed to straighten out problems that developed and to give everyone involved, especially those in the divisions, an adequate understanding of the contributions expected from them.
>
> To keep costs down, the corporate capital investment group was kept as small as possible, but it was authorized to draw on corporate staff specialists for help in reviewing divisional proposals. This somewhat unusual approach has worked out satisfactorily, although the men we needed were not always available at the right time. But we have managed to deal with these problems in an amicable manner and to everyone's satisfaction.
>
> Our fiscal year starts on July 1; therefore, the long-term profit plan has to be submitted to management early in June. Each year in January top management indicates the amounts available for investment during the next fiscal year. We notify the divisions of their shares, which, however, can be adjusted in case of special circumstances. For example, a division manager who feels strongly that he has a project which should be financed, even though to do so would bring his total investment in excess of his share, can bring the matter before the corporate investment committee for final determination. In this way, we keep the system flexible and are able to meet unusual situations.
>
> Top management also sets forth the minimum return on investment expected from investment proposals; this figure usually remains unchanged for a considerable period. All projects are ranked in terms of indicated return. The total funds required to implement all the proposals are often in excess of the allocations. Some proposals, of course, may be rejected and others temporarily deferred. This brings the funds required for immediate projects within the limit of the allocation.
>
> Management may also give specific proposals a high preference ranking. For example, once it has decided to build a new plant or install new equipment, proposals for expenditures necessary to implement the earlier decisions will rank ahead of others.
>
> All proposals include a schedule of annual disbursements and revenues, if any. These are the amounts which will appear in the corporate investment plan and thus in the long-term profit plan. The investment plan also indicates the total amounts authorized for years beyond the current five-year plan to give management a complete picture of existing commitments.

At the division level, a small group may prepare the investment proposals or the job may be assigned to a single person, perhaps even on a part-time basis. These people keep in contact with the corporate group during the period of proposal preparation to test the acceptability of their proposals from the viewpoint of management policies. The corporate group, however, acts only in an advisory capacity. Divisions may disregard its suggestions and take their chances with the investment committee. This happens infrequently. Proposals may be submitted to the corporate group at any time, but there is a deadline if a proposal is to be submitted to one of the quarterly meetings of the investment committee. Copies of proposals are distributed to interested staff groups for review, and comments and these proposals are incorporated in the report the corporate investment group submits to the investment committee.

The investment committee consists of the executive vice-president, several corporate vice-presidents, and all division managers or their representatives. Thus each division has an opportunity to explain its proposals, especially if staff has commented unfavorably. Actual expenditures have to be approved by the corporate treasurer before the divisions make any disbursements, but planned disbursements and receipts are in the divisions' cash plans. The investment committee can make any changes in proposals it considers advisable, including deferring a project. A two-thirds majority is required for its decisions. The corporate investment manager serves as the secretary of the committee, but he cannot vote.

Divisions may appeal unfavorable decisions of the investment committee to the president who would initiate a review before arriving at a final determination. But this is quite unusual. In fact, there has been only one appeal since the introduction of the program, and it was rejected by the president on the recommendation of the staff group which made the special investigation.

A special group in the controller's department keeps track of all investment appropriations and prepares quarterly reports on the status of all projects which have not yet been completed. This group also advises the divisions of probable overruns so they can submit requests for additional appropriations. These are handled like new proposals. A special session of the investment committee may be called in cases of an emergency, but divisions are discouraged from bringing about such a situation. They are expected to submit their requests early enough so they can be processed routinely. There have been a few emergency cases, which were justified by circumstances that could not have been foreseen, such as strikes, floods, and so forth.

We have been using discounting techniques from time to time at both the corporate and divisional levels. But some of our top executives are skeptical regarding the value of these techniques. They believe there are too many uncertainties in the data to justify the additional computations. Our top managers base their decisions on all the available relevant information, their wide experience, and their familiarity with considerations inside and outside the company.

The Importance of Innovations in Long-Term Planning

Evaluating changes and new developments is at the heart of successful long-term planning. Nowhere is this more clearly apparent than in the field of technology. Innovation is the big challenge. Today, vast sums are spent for technological research, for innovation. This research may be directed toward the improvement of existing practices and equipment or toward completely new ones. This trend toward innovation does not affect all industries to the same extent. However, those that remain relatively static are in danger of falling behind and having their products replaced by new ones that are cheaper or better adapted to existing or future requirements. For example, the steel industry for a long time underestimated the impact of new materials such as aluminum and plastics, and it was slow to adopt new techniques such as the oxygen furnace. Thus this industry, which used to be highly profitable, became one of low profitability and return on investment.

Many managers concentrate their attention on short-term sales and profits and thereby fail to give enough time to new developments that may have a decisive effect on the future of their companies. These events may occur within their organizations, affecting, for example, their production techniques, or may occur outside among their customers. Long-term profit plans that reflect this short-run philosophy are of scant value as guides for decision making and can lead to grave disappointments. Alert managements tend to reject long-term profit plans that fail to evaluate fully forecast new innovations and their effects on sales and profits.

Our survey indicates that technological forecasting is an essential part of long-term profit planning in large *electric utilities*. The electric utilities industry is a typical growth industry: it has doubled its output in every past decade and is expected to continue growing at this rate in the future. These utilities have typically taken advantage of new technical developments, making possible significant cost reduction per unit of output. Investment decisions in this industry must take a long-term view, for the time lag between initiating a project and its completion is unusually long, in some cases more than a decade. Thus adequate technological forecasts are most important.

The planning director of one large utility explains how his company uses such forecasts in its planning.

"Determining our load factor for the next decade and beyond is our first step in approaching our planning program. This step requires the cooperation of various groups, especially engineers and marketing specialists. Measuring the future requirements of our customers is not as simple a task as it may appear to be for a company with a monopoly in its area. Technological expectations are of major importance. For example, some of our largest customers have their own facilities that supply part of their requirements. They will insist on the lowest possible cost per unit for the part that they receive from us. When we make a long-term contract with them, it has to take into consideration technological innovations that may still be on the drawing boards. But we must evaluate the impact of these innovations on our future costs and prices. If we don't realize the cost reductions made possible by these innovations, these customers may shift a larger portion of their needs to their own ultra-modern facilities. Also, the most efficient coordination of supply and demand at different times affects the cost of operations and is a matter of technological factors."

Another executive interrupted: "For a number of years, the demand expected for our area was not encouraging. High wage rates and a shortage of labor tended to induce a few large companies to move some production to other parts of the country. Our forward planning was in line with the opinion of most industry leaders that the increase in demand for power would be rather slow. These forecasts turned out to have been unduly pessimistic, but even after this situation became apparent, we were unable to modify our expansion program to meet the larger-than-expected demand. Delivery schedules for equipment on order could not be speeded up. Yet we had to meet the current demand, and the only way we could do so was to use obsolete facilities. These were high-cost units with large maintenance requirements: we had to absorb these costs for several years at the expense of our stockholders, since the regulatory agencies were unwilling to grant any rate increases. Our engineers had warned us that a delay in replacing these outmoded facilities could be dangerous, but we had relied on the opinions of our marketing specialists and of managers of industrial companies in our area. Here we had a situation where there was a conflict between technical and sales forecasts. Similar difficulties often develop when tight capital markets and high interest rates lead a company's financial experts to recommend slowing down expansion projects while the company's technological forecasters insist on new, lower-cost facilities."

At this point, the planning director resumed his presentation.

"The next steps are selecting the type of facilities to be built for the expansion program, and where. For these steps, the technological forecasters are most influential. However, other considerations often require modification of their recommendations. One such consideration is potential air pollution, now so much discussed. An excellent location for a coal- or oil-burning plant may be unavailable as a result of local opposition to the pollutants it is expected to emit. Installation of atomic power plants would eliminate this form of pollution, but there might still be difficulties because of explosions. And another problem might be conservationists' opposition to high-power transmission lines spoiling the landscape. The technological forecasters consider all such factors in their reports, and their recommendations are affected by them.

"Concurrently with considerations of possible locations for new plants, the technological characteristics of the new facilities have to be settled. The technological forecasters evaluate probable technical developments over the next few decades and the equipment to be used, always keeping in mind the goal of lowest possible unit cost. Each of the principal sources of energy—coal, oil, atomic energy, water—has its disadvantages and advantages, and the ways in which each is used will be improved technically in future years. Costs of construction (capital costs) and costs of operation (current costs) of different types of facilities are important in this context. For example, higher construction outlays may be offset by lower operating costs in the future. On the other hand, a shortage of capital funds may lead management to conserve present cash even though the result will be higher operating expenditures later.

"Another important factor is time. If demand is increasing especially fast and time is of the essence, the decision may be to put a new facility on stream at the earliest moment, even though that kind of facility would not have been selected on a strictly technological or financial basis."

Capital Investment: Plans and Reports of an Automobile Manufacturer

The importance of capital investments is also reflected in the large number of analyses and reports used for their evaluation and control. These serve three principal purposes. They (1) describe and justify proposals, (2) report progress on projects, and (3) compare the original proposal with actual performance to evaluate the accuracy of earlier estimates.

This company's manual has 15 sections and about 150 pages; it contains numerous sample forms used in administering capital investments projects, some of which are shown in Exhibits 18 to 21. Exhibits 22 and 23 show similar forms from other companies for comparison purposes. Excerpts from the manual follow.

Appropriation requests. Decisions that commit the corporation to acquire or dispose of capital assets are thoroughly evaluated and authorized at levels appropriate to the amounts of funds involved. The appropriation request (Exhibits 18 and 19) is used to present a proposal and obtain approvals. Approval of a program does not authorize commitment or expenditure of funds. Authority for such action must be obtained through a project request against the program. Appropriation requests up to $1 million can be authorized by the president or the administrative committee. Requests are submitted to the corporate investment analysis department and then reviewed by the appropriate corporate staffs. Other request forms used by the company are deviation requests, supplemental requests, lease requests, and disposal requests.

The controller of the activity submitting the request is responsible for preparing each request and for insuring complete documentation, including engineering data. Financial data, including cost analysis, financial evaluations, and accounting classifications, are furnished by the controller. Special instructions are provided for emergency and critical long-lead requests when immediate action is necessary to protect the interests of the company. Under extreme circumstances, authorization may be obtained by telephone, telegram, or other expeditious means while the written emergency request is being prepared.

An evaluation of all financial and nonfinancial implications is made on each facility, lease, or disposal request to ensure that the most beneficial alternative is selected. The evaluation is basically an estimate of the proposal's effect on operations and profitability and an estimate of the cash return that will result. (See Exhibits 19 and 20.) The depth of the analysis is contingent upon the nature of the proposal. The purpose of the evaluation is to determine the desirability of a proposal. Proposals are called financial if they can be justified primarily on the basis of measurable financial return. The most important yardstick is the percent return on the amount invested. Nonfinancial proposals are proposals that cannot be justified on the basis of measurable financial return, but that might still be desirable for other reasons. Nonfinancial proposals are more difficult to evaluate because there is no common yardstick, such as return on investment.

An effort is usually made to consider all alternative courses of action before selecting a particular course. They are evaluated prior to the preparation of an appropriation request. The financial evaluation considers the rate of return of each alternative. An attachment to the request describes the alternatives considered and includes a schedule showing the calculations for computing the rate of return or payout.

Appropriation requests are reviewed to determine the merit and attainability of proposed actions and to assist the approval authority in making its decisions. Each request is subject to a series of reviews by staff and technical specialists to insure that the proposed action is timely and consistent with approved plans, will accomplish the intent and purpose of the request, and is in keeping with the latest technology and availability of corporate assets. The investment analysis function coordinates technical and other reviews and makes recommendations to management. Controller and manufacturing staffs work together to ensure an adequate evaluation of overall aspects of appropriation requests and to provide sufficient information for the approval authorities.

Program/project control. Once approval of an appropriation request has been obtained, proper control is established and exercised to ensure that actual commitments and expenditures of corporate funds are kept within approved estimates, are made for a specific and approved purpose, and are properly approved. Program/project line item and commitment documents are the basic tools used for controlling the expenditure of approved funds. The controller exercises financial control; the manufacturing engineer exercises manufacturing control; purchasing exercises purchasing control; and each other function takes appropriate action.

All projects are closed as soon as practical. When a program or project is closed, the responsible operating executive sends a brief memorandum to the responsible group executive, with copies to the administrative committee member responsible for the operating activity and the manager of corporate investment analysis. The memorandum covers broadly the degree to which planned objectives were or were not attained and the major reasons for any significant deviations from the original plan.

Capital plan performance reports inform management of the indicated actual expenditure levels and compare these with planned expenditure levels. Exceptions and reasons for exceptions to planned expenditure levels are reflected to inform management of the current progress and to maintain a balanced effort toward the attainment of planned objectives. Reports are made monthly to the corporate investment analysis department. Group and division controllers are responsible for submitting consolidated reports and for maintaining close liaison with engineering personnel and those functionally responsible for projects to insure that cost estimates are realistic. Forecast data for approved and anticipated projects are kept as realistic as possible in recognition of the importance placed upon the capital expenditure forecasts and their relationship to projections of the company's total corporate cash requirements.

Postproject evaluation. Following the completion of a facility or investment action, a comprehensive review is made to compare and evaluate the actual results with the results projected at the time the action was approved (see Exhibit 21). The evaluation is prepared within 60 days following the first 3 months of actual usage of the facilities for projects over $5,000. It is to be submitted to the corporate investment analysis department for projects over $50,000. The controller who submitted the original project request is responsible for preparing the performance evaluation, which is based on the same principles of financial analysis used in preparing the original request.

Model-year capital expenditures plan. The corporate investment analysis department is responsible for preparing the corporate investment plan, which summarizes the reports submitted by some 25 locations of the corporation.

Management Manpower Planning

The impact of management on the profitability of business enterprises needs no discussion. The ever increasing complexity of managerial responsibilities makes it essential to plan for a supply of managerial talent on a formal basis if the company's future is to be ensured. The greater the knowledge and experience required for a particular position, the more planning is necessary to assure the availability of the right person to take over when the time arrives. Some companies have had programs for long-term planning in this area for many years. Young men of apparent executive timber are selected years in advance for an executive inventory. They are provided with extensive training within the company and, often, at educational institutions as well. Several individuals are selected for consideration for each executive position, should a replacement be necessary; in addition, expansion projects can be staffed from this reservoir of managerial talent.

Companies that overlook long-term manpower planning—and our survey indicates that many do—may face future difficulties; for example, new projects and expansion of facilities may be delayed for lack of trained managers. Not infrequently, the principal objective of a merger is less the assets of the company and more the possibility of adding a successful management team to that of the absorbing company. On the other hand, being acquired can disturb a company's carefully made plans for management replacement; the group taking over may be inclined to fill key positions with its own people and highly qualified executives of the acquired company may face discharge or substantial downgrading. If the acquiring company lacks depth in management, however, its acquisition of a company with a competent management may take care of this deficiency.

Admittedly, this type of planning can be expensive, and this is one main reason managements hesitate to use it. But the advantages are so obvious, and the dangers of a lack of capable management are so serious, that many engage in long-term manpower planning despite the cost.

9

Sales, Distribution Expense, and Product Planning

THE special importance of the sales plan results from the fact that sales are the principal source of funds for all other planned activities. There are other sources, of course, such as dividends, interest, royalties, and sale of assets, but they are usually less important. Our discussion, therefore, will focus on situations in which sales are the main source of earnings and cash flow.

One special feature of sales, and thus of sales planning, is management's difficulty in controlling what and how much can be sold. Designing a long-term sales plan is difficult, yet the sales plan is a principal component of the long-term profit plan. Another important factor is management's limited ability, in its attempts to maintain a desired sales volume, to control the relationship between sales and the related distribution expenses. Exhibit 24 lists a few of the factors one company considers in planning its marketing effort.

The Importance of Forecasting in Sales Planning

Management has traditionally given attention to forecasting and planning for sales. Whenever management focuses its efforts on such matters as volume of output or quality of production instead of on sales, the company will suffer and it may fail. Any product or service has value for a company only to the extent that it can be sold at a reasonable profit.

A variety of techniques has been introduced in efforts to improve sales forecasting and planning. We will analyze these techniques from the standpoint of their usefulness for long-term profit planning.

First let us review the distinction between forecasting and planning. Too often the two terms are used interchangeably. Forecasting is a prediction of something that is *expected* to happen. Planning, on the other hand, is concerned with the intended result—what we *would like* to happen. What we expect to happen does not depend to a major extent on our own actions: a forecast is made on the basis of situational factors we evaluate to get information about the probable future. But a plan *is* based on our own actions: we determine what we intend to do and what we wish to accomplish. Forecasting is necessary for planning, but, except for very large companies, plans have little effect on future events outside the company. From the standpoint of management, plans should be attainable but not easily so; usually, more than average effort should be required to realize them.

A forecast and a plan may be identical or they may differ markedly, as when the aims of a plan are far beyond what can be expected. Of course, there is the unlikely possibility that the goals of a plan are so modest that they are below the forecast. For example, management may be satisfied to maintain its present sales volume while its industry's sales are expected to increase. More often the plan goes beyond the forecast: the goal is to do better than expected performance, provided appropriate conditions exist. Planners usually look beyond forecasts and thereby create a gap between what they expect and what they want. Their plans are designed to close the gap. In order to achieve plan goals, management must take the specific actions outlined in the plan.

A forecast can be made without preparing a plan. But can a plan be made without forecasts? Probably not, for planning requires some expectations as to what is going to happen. Forecasting does not have to involve a formal process; in simpler cases it can take place in the planner's mind.

In recent years, many technical improvements have been made in sales-forecasting techniques. Mathematical statistical methods, such as multiple regression and input/output analysis, have been introduced with significant success. Large amounts of money have been spent on the development of improved forecasting techniques. Managements are fully aware of the value of adequate sales forecasts, and they have been willing, therefore, to finance the necessary research. Private market research organizations have developed new approaches using statistical and behavioristic methods to determining consumer attitudes and preferences. The usefulness of any one of these techniques in a specific situation must be evaluated carefully. Use of a technique is usually based on specific simplifying assumptions necessary to enable the vast quantities of data to be fit into the mathematical models and computer systems being used for the analysis. Here, as in many other instances, the significance of the basic data must be carefully evaluated, for it cannot be improved by computer manipulations. Despite sophisticated techniques, the judgment of experts with an intimate knowledge of markets and of the individuals who are responsible for making the decisions will usually be decisive. These executives will use all the information available, but they will evaluate it, taking into account factors computer models cannot catch or interpret properly.

The special difficulties in developing valid sales forecasts and plans make it especially important to recognize the unlikelihood of the sales forecaster and planner coming up with *specific* figures. The best that can be expected is the development of a *range* of probable future sales. Working with a range of probable future sales rather than a specific value may be an inconvenience to the planner and the manager, but it is more realistic. The need to work with a range of probable values is, of course, especially true for the longer period in which the problems of relating major, unavoidable fluctuations to specific time periods are especially difficult.

A long-term profit plan uses a wide variety of forecasts and estimates. To be sure, those prepared for the sales and marketing function are of particular importance. Almost all the companies contacted in the research prepare forecasts of product volume and prices. Such forecasts are prepared for individual products, product lines, product groups, and profit centers. Different companies carry these forecasts to different levels of refinement. For example, in one company, where the volume of a particular product is adequate and the data are available at a reasonable cost, a forecast for the product will be obtained. In another company, however, where individual product volume is relatively small or the cost of obtaining the information is high in proportion to its judged value, forecasts are prepared for product lines rather than for individual products. Naturally, the more information available on individual products at a reasonable cost, the sounder the plans based on these forecasts.

In addition to forecasting physical volume, companies forecast the extent of their market penetration, potential volume in new markets, and possible acquisitions. All sales forecasts are prepared for the length of the planning period, but usually are given in greater detail for the short-term future. For the longer period, companies forecast not only the sales of present products but also the sales of products they anticipate they will be adding to the line during the period.

Some factors important in developing the sales plan are estimated rather than forecast. In a sense these estimates are also forecasts, but they are based on the expert judgment of those who make the estimates rather than on more objective evidence or a wider sample of opinions about what might happen. So marketing management will estimate such matters as market trends, market share and potential, growth rates, profit margins, and—particularly for new products—sales volume.

The MNO Corporation operates several hundred retail stores in 20 states. Annual sales are around $300 million; after-tax profits fluctuate substantially but average 3 percent of sales. The stores vary widely in size, sales volume, and profitability. About one-third are located in large cities; one-third, in cities with populations of around 100,000; and one-third, in smaller towns in both industrialized and agricultural areas. These factors have a significant impact on the company's sales-forecasting and sales-planning efforts and make it difficult to get data suitable for management guidance.

Individual sales managers traditionally did their own sales forecasting; their figures were reviewed by the 20 regional offices and finally consolidated at corporate headquarters. These procedures were simple and inexpensive, though not particularly satisfactory to management. Like other companies in the industry, six-month budgets were used and thus sales forecasts had to be prepared twice a year.

A new president was asked by the board of directors to improve the company's profit picture, which was below the industry's average. Among other improvements, a long-term profit plan was introduced to supplement the present semiannual budgets. Fred Lang, the new president, explains his intent.

"Heretofore, there has been little, if any, long-term planning. Management's background was mainly in the merchandising area, and there was hardly an appreciation of financial planning. I was aware of the pitfalls and opposition I would face in trying to turn the company around.

"In this industry, sales volume means everything so far as obtaining profits. Therefore, sales forecasting and general long-term planning to improve sales had to be given preference in developing the profit plan. Substantial changes had to be made in the location and display of merchandise in many stores. But to determine the kind of merchandise that could be profitably sold in a particular store depended on proper market research and sales forecasting techniques. A thorough analysis of stores' conditions was essential if we were to measure sales for an extended period ahead. Up to now, such market analyses were more or less taken for granted and used for short-term sales forecasts. What we needed was market analysis in depth. To accomplish it, however, would take considerable time and money. Nobody in the company appeared qualified to undertake the job, yet time was of the essence. Lengthy discussions among top management and specialists in the company led to conclusions which we hoped would provide us with guidance for practical decisions. We selected 50 stores whose sales volume appeared to be low in relation to their particular locations. The selection was based on our best judgment. However, we found that even this limited investigation would require several months if conducted in accordance with the accepted techniques of market research. We thought this was still too long.

"We decided, therefore, on another shortcut. We would make a rough estimate of the sales potential for each of the 50 stores for the next 5 years. Each member of top management with merchandising experience and our merchandising experts would make their independent estimates and these then would be averaged as a basis for our sales planning. We were satisfied to find that the spread among these estimates was within a range of 10 percent in the large majority of cases. I will let Brian Rafferty, our senior vice-president for merchandising, explain to you how we carried out the assignment of developing long-term sales forecasts."

Brian Rafferty launched immediately into his explanation.

"Obviously, sales volume depends first of all on the market where the sales will be made. Two principal sources of information are essential to the market researcher. One is statistical data which are available from various governmental and private sources. The other results from actual questioning of potential customers. This is especially important if customers come from the general public. Such data are accumulated through mail or telephone surveys and actual face-to-face questioning. Electronic computers can digest enormous quantities of data and can classify and organize them as required by the researchers.

"All this material is just the beginning. The market researcher has to coordinate it in such a manner as to provide leads on potential sales. Since all the data refer to the past, their significance for the future must be carefully examined: this is especially so when the more distant future is at stake. It is the task of the analyst to evaluate the available information in terms of its implications for the future. Certain data can be extrapolated into the future with assurance. For example, the number of persons in the workforce ten or fifteen years ahead is already known, for all are now alive. We have fair estimates as to the growth of the economy, increases in productivity, and other data which permit reasonable calculations of the market potential for given classes of products and services in future years. Market research is not guesswork: it is different from traditional estimates that are the result of individual judgments based only on the experience of the estimators.

"Yet the uncertainties remain and they are formidable. Changes in techniques, consumer preferences, and so forth must be considered and these cannot be predicted to any significant extent. Use of sophisticated mathematical models can reduce the margin of error but won't eliminate it. Managers should not be misled by claims that accurate predictions of future sales, far beyond what can be accomplished with the tools that are presently available, are feasible."

Fred Lang commented at this point:

"All the techniques like market research can do is support the judgment and experience of individuals who are familiar with specific market situations. These people will often notice factors which the mechanistic approach won't detect. For instance, I have opportunities to talk to men in my own position who are concerned with the same problem of estimating their future sales. In this way, I can often get information which would not be available in any other manner. Similarly, sales and purchasing executives establish their own personal relations and sources of information. And this is equally true for a salesman who has a profound knowledge of many problems of his customers.

"One point I would like to emphasize is that you must always be prepared to recognize changes. There is a danger that a sales plan, once adopted, may be looked at as something which cannot and should not be modified. But the plan does not represent facts, only intentions and estimates. Changes and their impact on the profit plan must be recognized and evaluated.

"Our plan has worked out reasonably well. Our estimates have proved incorrect from time to time, and we did not hesitate to adjust them whenever we felt this had to be done. At present, we review our long-term sales plans once a year, but we continue to prepare our six-months' short-term budgets. Our vice-president–sales will explain briefly how he uses the sales plan for his decision making."

Joseph Bland, the company's sales vice-president, discussed sales' point of view:

"My approach differs somewhat from that of the profit planners. Our stores sell several thousand different items. For purposes of long-term profit planning, the inventory is divided into some 20 groups, and not much attention is given to changes within these groups. However, changes within the groups are of vital importance to us in sales management. We break down the 20 groups into several hundred and watch carefully the changes in product mix. We must know our profit margins for each group as well as the effect on the margins of the product-mix fluctuations. The use of electronic computers has greatly simplified our task of following up on changes in our sales picture."

Mr. Lang mentioned at this point the market research experts the company has acquired:

"We have been able to develop a group of market research experts. They cooperate with the store managers who now prepare not only their short-term budgets but five-year sales forecasts. We want them to think about opportunities for sales and profit improvements and not simply base their figures on a continuation of present conditions. We now schedule annual conferences for each region at which representatives from headquarters and the region explain our thinking to the store managers and answer their questions in detail. This has led to much better coordination of our forward planning.

"The market research group at the home office reviews the forecasts prepared by the stores and regions and may suggest changes which they will discuss with the people who prepared the plans. They are encouraged to think in terms of expansion and are given information and assistance on how to attain the larger goals."

Our survey indicates that most companies are attempting to broaden the scope of their sales planning by including lower management levels in their planning efforts. Some are not too enthusiastic, however, about the benefits of this approach compared with the time required to carry it out.

Planning for Distribution Expenses

It has been said that you can sell almost anything, provided you are ready to spend enough money promoting it. This may be an exaggeration, but it certainly contains a kernel of truth: sales volume and the cost of realizing it are closely related; one cannot be properly evaluated without the other. Therefore, both should be planned together and fully coordinated.

Distribution expenses cover most of the expense classifications related to the sales function, including advertising and sales promotion expenses. Most of these expenses are not directly related to sales volume. This contrasts with manufacturing costs, most of which fluctuate with volume of production to a major extent. Distribution expenses, therefore, have to be determined by management decisions, often without assurance that they will serve to attain the intended result. This type of expense is mainly designed to influence the behavior of consumers in some specific direction. (Consider the efforts of airlines to lure passengers by emphasizing the glamour of their stewardesses and the asserted excellence of their food.)

The primary aim of management when it authorizes large promotional expenses, without assurance of the desired results, is to improve profits. In many situations, especially in the case of consumer products with a limited profitable life, the long-term profit plan will be affected profoundly by these management decisions. If they turn out to be correct, profits may go up substantially; but with incorrect decisions, profits may plummet.

The situation is particularly critical for industries where promotional expenses represent a large part of total expenditures. The pharmaceutical industry is a prominent example in which promotional expenses have a decisive effect on profitability. One single successful television program can increase sales and thus profits substantially; while another, which turns out to be unsuccessful, will represent a wasted expenditure of millions of dollars and a heavy drag on profits. Thus the importance of planning ahead for such expenses becomes readily apparent. But even with planning, a sudden change in consumer preferences can affect profits considerably, despite promotional efforts. So all distribution expense decisions must be subject to review as circumstances change.

To reduce the unavoidable uncertainties, strong efforts are being made by many companies to establish significant ratios between sales volume, profits, and the expenses required to attain them. Use of these ratios is especially important for long-term planning, since they enable the planner to predict these expenses with reasonable efficiency. One approach, which has been partially successful, attempts to identify as far as possible the type of customers a specific promotion is supposed to reach. This approach has led some companies to switch advertising from nationally distributed publications to those catering to a particular geographical or special-interest group. Many magazines now publish regional editions to avoid carrying advertisements into sections of the country where they would be inappropriate—for example, advertisements for heavy winter clothing in the southwestern parts of the country. Also, mail promotions are often preferred as a medium for highly specialized promotions. For example, stores mail their catalogs only to their present or likely customers. Computers are now making possible highly selective promotions to small groups of customers.

Executives and specialists responsible for allocating promotional funds have a wide variety of opportunities for selective efforts to attain maximum beneficial results. Increased research in media selection can be expected, especially with the support of large computer memory devices.

Product Planning for Present and New Products

The close interrelation of the various parts of the long-term profit plan is clearly apparent in the context of a company's products. A company must be able to sell its products at a profit. Those that cannot find a market should not be produced by a profit-minded enterprise, regardless of how attractive the product might seem to the company's executives. The product's price less total costs and expenses per unit should leave a profit. It follows, therefore, that in the large majority of situations, costs must be adjusted to market prices, for it cannot be assumed that selling prices will always be high enough to produce a profit regardless of costs and expenses. This latter, infrequent condition arises in so-called cost-plus contracts.

Different problems develop in product planning depending on whether the product is produced currently or it is not yet in production. Generally, it is easier to plan ahead for products already being sold. Data for past sales are available and can be used for extrapolating into the future; also, the marketability of the product has already been tested. There may, of course, be fluctuations in demand—for example, downward movements following an upswing. On the other hand, no experiential data are available in the case of unmarketed products. Market research studies may suggest the acceptability of a new product in specific markets, but they do not necessarily provide a secure starting point for the planning effort. In evaluating the significance of these new products for the long-term profit plan, management must be alert to the uncertainty surrounding the profitability of those products that will reach the market for the first time in the future. This fact becomes especially important as the interval increases between the decision to go ahead with production and the time when the new product reaches the market, since consumer attitudes may have changed since the market research was completed. A substantial time lag may be unavoidable for technical reasons, as in the automobile production cycle. Ford's Edsel in the 1950s is a striking example of these dangers. Few of the companies contacted in our survey appear to give much attention to these important planning problems.

The Product Life Cycle

Every product has what can be called a "life of its own." It starts with a period of growth, which continues for a considerable time, often for many years. But sooner or later it is followed by a plateau and eventually, by a decline. After a period of decline, management may drop the product altogether and replace it with another with greater chances for profitable production and sales. The announcement some time ago by General Motors Corporation that it was going to drop its ten-year-old Corvair model is a case in point. Following heavy sales in the early years of production, sales gradually declined and finally reached the point where continuation of production was no longer worthwhile. It is natural to plan on the comfortable assumption that products with a ready market at present will continue to have one for an indefinite period ahead and that, therefore, plans can be made accordingly. However, the possibility of a change in present conditions should never be overlooked or lightly dismissed, particularly when there has been a lengthy period of stability.

Effective product planning requires that nothing be taken for granted. Every product line, and often individual products in the line, must be carefully analyzed to evaluate its future without prejudice. Every product is subject to "aging." The behavior of a product's aging curve must be watched for indications of a change in the direction of the curve, which may indicate the need for positive managerial action. It is not easy to evaluate changes in these curves and to distinguish temporary fluctuations from more permanent changes.

There are many examples of companies and whole industries that got into trouble through the overconfident expectation that prevailing satisfactory conditions would continue. In these cases management was surprised and unprepared for changed conditions, which often appeared quite suddenly. No plans existed as to what to do to meet the new, unsatisfactory conditions. Management therefore had to make decisions under pressure, without appropriate information, and often made a bad situation worse. Many companies can offer striking evidence of the benefits of long-term planning that provides for unexpected changes and outlines appropriate measures to deal with these changes in a manner of lasting benefit to the company.

Product planning is comparatively simple if a single product is manufactured. However, a majority of companies have a number of product lines and some companies have several hundred. These product lines must be coordinated with one another, with careful attention to fluctuations in the sales of different products resulting from changing market demands. Provided there is sufficient volume, a frequent practice is to set up each product line as a separate unit—for example, as a department, plant, or division—under a manager with considerable authority, who operates the unit as a part of a decentralized organization. The manager will be expected to prepare his own planning program, within the limitations of the companywide program; his plan will usually be reviewed at the corporate level before it is submitted to top management for final approval.

Product plans are determined by the customer demand represented in the sales plan. Product plans are usually separate from sales plans; but, of course, both must be fully coordinated to be effective. Additional complexities arise if a company manufactures a particular product in a quantity that fills only part of customer demands, the balance being met by purchases from outside. It is not unusual for a company to sell a product under its brand name even though it manufactures only part of its total sales volume of that product. In such situations, purchasing has to be coordinated, too, and the sales plan has to reflect both sources of supply. The purchasing department in such situations is responsible for assuring appropriate deliveries to meet its share of sales. Purchasing is also responsible for planning for the supply of raw materials, parts, and subassemblies necessary for the production of the planned units. Here again, close liaison among all the participating groups is essential for success.

Special problems arise in planning for the longer run as required for the long-term profit plan. Product managers are often reluctant to develop detailed plans for more than a comparatively short period, even a year, in view of the difficulties inherent in any effort to foresee all the many possible events that may have an effect on the plans. An educational effort may be necessary to convince them that no one expects them to accomplish the impossible. Their responsibility is limited to making the best effort based on their special experience and making adjustments whenever new information, which may have an impact on their previously developed plan, becomes available.

In a country as large as the United States, differences in demand exist for a given product, caused by climate, habits, and other factors. Therefore, product planning is concerned not only with volume, style, and quality of products but also with geographical considerations. Although this aspect of product planning is the responsibility of the sales organization, it can have a significant effect on the problems of product coordination, which the product manager has to control. Frequent and often unexpected changes in product mix will be reflected in changes in product plans, which represent unavoidable problems for the product manager.

Of course, there is always the question of what competition is going to do. The knowledge that another company is about to market a new product will certainly have an effect on sales and product planning. Moreover, if the company wants to maintain or expand its share of the market, it must plan to modify or replace products in the declining portion of their "aging curves." The anticipated reduction of their sales usually has to be made up in some way, often by expanding the sales of other products, some of which will always be in the ascending part of their "aging curves." Inevitably, new products will have to be considered too; but planners will usually concentrate first on present products.

Most companies now recognize the need for a steady supply of new products if they are to maintain their growth and profitability. They find it necessary, therefore, to develop plans that will ensure this supply of new products at the proper time. Proper timing is of utmost importance to avoid unwanted fluctuations of production, sales, and profits. The long-term profit plan depends heavily on this flow of new products.

For a long time, many companies left this all-important issue more or less to chance, to the expectation or hope there would be a sufficient inventory of new products for manufacture or purchase whenever needed to bolster sales. Today, however, it would be extremely dangerous for a company to depend on such vague hopes, for many companies now make use of planned obsolescence, and almost all companies engage in perpetual product and model changes resulting from extensive research and development efforts. A long-term profit plan on which management can depend must incorporate a supply of new products if the company is to meet the basic objectives of growth and profitability. Unfortunately, many companies have yet to learn this lesson. A number of the responding companies indicate their awareness of these problems.

Technological Forecasting in Product and Profit Planning

Present technological and economic conditions require formal procedures for analyzing future technological developments and their potential impact on the company's products and markets. Such analyses are necessary if a company is to have a realistic and successful long-term profit plan.

Technological forecasting as a formal technique is a recent development. Business has always given consideration to future technological events, but usually informally and only sporadically. Research management would follow new developments as a matter of professional interest. But there was no assurance that its findings would reach top management and, if so, there was no assurance that they would receive the attention they deserved. To make sure that prospective technological changes are duly incorporated into the planning process, a number of companies are setting up a specific organization to gather intelligence on technological areas of interest to the company.

Technological Forecasting in Realistic Sales Planning

Sales forecasting requires specification of the products to be sold. There is a tendency for planners to assume substantial stability of the current product mix. To be sure, introduction of new products and changes in the present product mix may be anticipated. Yet the attention given to these changes depends primarily on the sales planner's judgments. Although judgment will also be important and even decisive for technological forecasting, judgment about needed modifications of present products and promising new products can be significantly improved if qualified scientists and engineers are called in to contribute their professional opinions. All functions concerned must work together to secure forecasts of emerging technologies if the forecasts are to be of wide usefulness.

A few of the large aerospace companies have evolved an interesting approach to technological forecasting. Top scientists, engineers, and executives are asked to make independently their best guesses as to anticipated major technological changes in the years ahead, and the probability of these changes occurring. The ideas that appear most probable are carefully analyzed to determine alternative processes by which they might be achieved and the expected time of realization. Finally, the group reports to top management suggestions as to investments, market research, and so forth. The Delphi method is an approach that formalizes this technique. From lists of possible developments, those of greatest potential interest to the company are selected. Three basic considerations are used for the selection process—desirability, feasibility, and timing. This method "achieves a true consensus without sacrifice of important opinion and background information and avoids the difficulties and impracticalities of group discussion."[1]

An interesting illustration of the importance of technological forecasting in connection with long-term profit planning was provided by the financial vice-president of a large integrated corporation in the forest products and paper industry:

"For many years, fresh bread had been sold mostly in paper wrappings. Our company had been a major supplier of the paper used for these wrappings, and it represented a significant part of our total sales. Some years ago, our research people told us that efforts were being made

---

[1] Harper Q. North and Donald L. Pyke, " 'Probes' of the Technological Future," *Harvard Business Review*, May–June 1969. The same issue has another article on the same subject: Donald R. Schoen, "Managing Technological Innovation," which includes a detailed bibliography.

to replace the paper wrappers with a plastic material. The advantage of the new product would be that it could be used again and thus favored by the housewife customers. Our researchers, technological forecasters, suggested a study of the new product from technological, marketing, and financial standpoints. Management agreed and the study was completed in about two years. As a result, we were ready for the change-over. As soon as the new product reached the market and found the anticipated favorable reception, we were in position to supply the demands of our bread manufacturer customers. Most of our competition was unable to do so immediately, and this gave a boost to our sales of this product. As demand increased, we had to build a plant for the new wrappers and so found ourselves in the plastic-manufacturing business. Here you have an excellent example what alert technological forecasting can do to help protect the profitability of a company."

More and more managements are studying the benefits that can be derived from technological forecasting and are making appropriate arrangements for it in their planning activities. Exhibit 25 presents one company's efforts to help its managers keep alert to technological developments.

10

Production, Material, Labor, and Manufacturing-Overhead Planning

Now we shall concern ourselves with the planning aspects of the manufacturing process. These include the planning of the production activities and the factors required to accomplish them.

Production Planning

Production planning was one of the earliest applications of the planning concept in industry. It was part of the scientific management movement at the turn of the century, many years before the development of comprehensive business planning. The principles of production planning have been worked out in considerable detail in recent years so that optimum utilization of available facilities can be achieved. When done effectively, it is a major contributor to cost reduction and an important consideration in long-term profit planning.

One important objective of long-term production planning is to maintain production volume at as stable a level as possible. Most companies appreciate the significance of this concept, but they also appreciate the problems of putting long-term production planning into actual operation. Although the correlation between stable production and profitability is familiar to businessmen, profit-conscious managements make sure the relationship is fully accepted by their executives; unfortunately, such acceptance is often lacking.

A number of factors contribute to the difficulties in maintaining stable levels of production. We have discussed management's limited influence on the flow of sales from one period to another. The times when orders are received and when delivery is to be made are usually determined, within the limit of production capacity, by the customer. Some industries have been successful in getting their customers to let them, the supplying companies, decide on delivery dates so they can be coordinated with their production schedules. The steel industry is a well-known example. But even in this industry, the trend is to meet customer requirements as far as practical, even at the sacrifice of optimum production schedules. This frequent inability to anticipate and regulate the flow of incoming orders has a significant impact on production planning. Production planners must, as far as feasible, reconcile the customers' wishes with the requirement of minimizing the costs resulting from fluctuating production volumes.

One major benefit of long-term production planning is the opportunity it provides to evaluate, in advance, the alternatives for dealing with complex situations and to select the most satisfactory alternative, which may not be the most profitable in the short term. Among the alternatives often considered are expanding existing production facilities, acquiring improved equipment, farming out production, and replacing production by purchases from other manufacturers. Each solution has its advantages and shortcomings.

An examination of the possibility of expanding existing facilities—probably the most frequent solution—raises the problem of idle capacity with its production costs implications. Here long-term production planning will be especially important, for the decisive issue will be the extent to which the facilities will be used at or close to full capacity. For purposes of illustration, assume a company is using a five-year planning period. If the company can plan for 40 months of full production, its decision may well be to expand. If, however, it anticipates 20 months or less of full production, it may decide not to expand. Often the period of peak production is short—perhaps only a few months; in such a situation the company would probably not expand. However, if the company anticipates full production over, say, two-thirds of the planning period, it may decide to accept the remaining period of idle capacity since the benefits would offset the extra costs. One of the benefits of expansion would be the availability of sufficient in-house capacity to meet all customer requirements as to delivery dates, a very important selling point. Moreover, the company would have provided for expanded production—given the inaccuracies of sales forecasts—for the balance of the planning period and beyond.

Financial considerations also are often important in long-term production planning decisions. Even if a company has decided that expansion of facilities or replacement of inefficient equipment would be the optimum solution, it still may be unable to act because it lacks the financial resources. Many companies are reluctant to expand their fixed investment beyond a certain, often traditional, ratio to their total assets; and they may be equally unwilling to borrow the necessary funds. In such situations, a less satisfactory solution might have to be adopted. Many smaller companies, lacking adequate financial resources, must often accept wide fluctuations in capacity utilization resulting from swings in sales, with the consequent loss in profit.

PQR Manufacturing Company is a medium-size producer of parts and subassemblies for small appliances; it has sales of about $50 million. Management had considerable trouble coordinating production, sales, and inventory levels. Sales were concentrated among a number of large companies that assembled the final consumer products, and their orders fluctuated widely. Frequent model changes were a problem, as were minor adjustments required by the customers. These adjustments affected PQR Company's requirements for materials and parts. Customers' orders frequently called for changes in products and schedules on very short notice. In order to maintain their goodwill, PQR Company had to adjust itself to these demands, regardless of difficulties and heavy excess costs. To improve this unsatisfactory situation, management decided to install a long-term production planning program. This program reduced these troubles significantly, but it was not possible to eliminate them completely. However, the new plan was considered a distinct success.

Joseph Block, executive vice-president of PQR Company, described the installation procedures of the new planning program.

"We selected several junior executives and had them study the company's production planning problems and discuss them with experts. They informed us that in recent years a number of mathematical models had been developed to deal with this type of problem. In order to install such a model, however, a large amount of accounting and statistical data would have to be collected. Many of these data could be derived from existing records, but other data would have to be accumulated from several years' original documents. We realized that these data referred to the past, while our needs were for information about the future.

"Experience had indicated that models, incorporating probabilities of future events based on past occurrences, could make a significant contribution in planning if combined with traditional sales-forecasting techniques. Our job would be to provide the historical data and the sales forecasts, while the work of constructing the mathematical model would be done by the operations research specialists in our company. The formulas they developed would then be used by our production planning staff to get the desired results. It took us about six months to satisfy the demands of the operations researchers for information. But our efforts were not in vain. Correlation techniques used by the specialists uncovered definite relationships in our data which enabled them to anticipate—within a margin of error—changes in our customers' requirements.

"To appreciate the benefits which we derived from this work, you have to compare the situations before the program was started and after it was put into operation. Before, we were completely in the dark as to what would happen both within the short run, during the next few months, and over the more distant future. We just waited like sitting ducks for orders to arrive. There was no planning, we merely reacted to developments. Now we can proceed in accordance with our plans, which are derived from our customers' past behavior. Of course, these data are far from perfect, so we have to adjust them on a short-term basis. But the deviations tend to cancel each other out to a significant and surprising extent. We are confident that our production plan, even with a margin of error, is preferable to our former situation of no plan at all.

"Our model alerts us to turning points in the pattern and level of orders, similar to what is done in the analysis of overall business fluctuations. These points—with a specified probability of being correct—predict changes in the prevailing trends. When we know the probability that sales of a particular product or product line may decline, we may decide to review our production schedules and inventory levels. One important accomplishment is the development of flexible inventory levels, determined by the probabilities of particular levels of production and sales. As the probability of a decline in sales and production increases, we reduce our purchases and, thereby, reduce the inconvenience of having useless inventory to be disposed of, usually at a substantial loss.

"Don't misunderstand me. Our troubles are not over. No formula will ever completely free us from difficulties, for the number of alternative plans and schedules is virtually unlimited. However, certain events occur more frequently than others: this is the basis for our present planning system. Also, certain correlations are strong and, therefore, a change in one factor makes it more probable, though not certain, that there will be a related change in other factors. A careful evaluation of all these factors is still required, but now, at least, we have something to work with when we make our plans. This increases the chances that our decisions will be correct.

"We spent a lot of money investigating and installing the new system: for example, the expense for training the junior executives who worked on it and the overtime for the people who had to dig out the data, in addition to performing their regular assignments. We used part-time help to some extent, especially college students. We believe the money was well spent; we did not know this would be the case when we started, of course. We underestimated the total cost of the effort, as is usually the case. This was particularly true for the cost of digging out the old data. But once you decide to go ahead, you have to spend what is necessary, not set any arbitrary limits. These projects are similar to construction projects: you have to anticipate overruns."

Planning for an Adequate Supply of Materials

The importance of formal long-term planning for materials differs from industry to industry. If the required materials are plentiful and there are many sources of supply, no particular effort will be required. However, in numerous cases provision for an adequate supply may be a significant, even crucial, part of the long-term planning program. This is especially true for extractive industries and those dependent on agricultural products, which is the case for several of the companies included in the survey. Executives of a large manufacturer of paper and other products pointed out their need to coordinate the supply of their principal raw material—logs—with their manufacturing capacity and the major problems they have in trying to attain this goal. In the case of lumber, long-term planning of the supply of logs is virtually mandatory: trees grow slowly. And the length of time the company's money may be involved in assuring this supply may create serious financial problems for the company.

The situation is quite different for industries that depend on widely fluctuating supplies of agricultural products. Contracts with growers have to be made for several years in advance, and the contracting companies must accept the whole crop each year, regardless of its size and quality. Even the time when the raw product reaches the factories (canning plants) can vary widely from year to year. Management faces difficult decisions in trying to keep its operation on an even keel, and executives of these companies emphasize the effects of these decisions on profitability.

Problems of a somewhat different kind arise with products with international markets, such as coffee and cocoa. For such products, a United States processor may have little, if any, influence on the quantity of the product available—perhaps his principal raw material—and its price, and he must adjust to the varying quality of raw material he is forced to use. He may have prescribed specific standards in advance but be unable to get materials of high enough quality to meet product standards satisfactorily. This problem makes planning very difficult, since the company has practically no control of its raw-material supply. The same is also true for prices, which often vary substantially and erratically over the long term. These conditions have a marked effect on the long-term profit plan.

Oil companies exemplify a different type of situation regarding the long-term supply of a principal raw material. Their alternatives are to invest very large sums to secure their own supplies, often in foreign countries with unsettled conditions, or to purchase their requirements from producers under circumstances that also fluctuate substantially. And again the nature of the raw material—in this case, its chemical composition—has a significant impact on production techniques, costs, and profits. These complexities, pointed out by executives interviewed, have led these companies to use advanced mathematical techniques and computers to work out optimum short- and long-term solutions.

The Long-Term Labor Plan

Management typically looks at labor primarily as a cost. Labor is a particularly large, sensitive, and constantly growing part of total operating costs and thus has an important impact on the long-term profit plan.

In the "good old days," recruiting labor was fairly simple and thus did not require long-term planning. However, the situation has changed greatly as a result of new developments. First, the national policy for full employment has tended to reduce the available labor supply. Even more important have been the ever increasing mechanization and automation of operations, especially in manufacturing. Companies now need men with specific qualifications who, more often than not, are not readily available when needed in connection with an expansion of activities.

Frequently the shortage or actual unavailability of just one type of craftsman can have a decisive impact on management decisions. As one of the executives interviewed explained: "For a long time, it was our policy to concentrate our operations in this geographical area and thus get the benefits of centralization. But we cannot stick to this policy any longer. This area has a substantial labor shortage. Now we locate new plants primarily in terms of the adequacy of the existing labor supply, disregarding other factors that were previously more important to us." The same statement was repeated by other executives in the same geographical area; they indicated that time and time again plant expansions had to be deferred when it was found impossible to recruit the required number of qualified workers.

Another important reason for long-term planning of the labor supply is the need—to which many businesses have not been accustomed in the past—to provide for training their own workers as the only practical way to have them ready by the time required. This is a costly undertaking, and it usually has a substantial impact on profits. An executive of one of the large automotive manufacturers told us:

"We spent a lot of time selecting the location for a new assembly plant. One of the most important reasons for our final choice was that a nearby city was the home of a number of major metals-working plants. This gave us the opportunity to hire an adequate number of skilled workers, assuming we could attract them away from their present employment. But we also had to train a large number of semiskilled workers from scratch. As a result, the plant for many months operated at minimum capacity, virtually as a training facility for its future workforce. It took almost a year for the plant to reach the anticipated production volume. Of course, this was a very expensive procedure, but it was the only possible one in the circumstances. Every new plant today represents a heavy drag on our profit planning."

Manning tables are an essential prerequisite for satisfactory labor planning. They indicate both the numbers of employees and their required skills, by individual departments, for a particular volume of production. The tables are usually based on detailed job classifications so they will be effective as cost-control devices. Anticipated changes, especially progress toward automation, must be taken into account in preparing tables for the years ahead. Demand for unskilled and semiskilled workers seems likely to decline, while that for specialists seems likely to increase consistently and substantially. In order to make possible a smooth transition, the long-term labor plan must provide for training present workers for the more exacting tasks in the future. Unless workers are assured that automation will not bring about layoffs, their insecurity will create resistance to the changes through slowdowns and other obstructive behavior. Long-term planning is essential in this highly sensitive field for the long-term profit plan can be greatly affected by labor availability.

Negotiations with labor unions can also be facilitated if they are based on a long-term labor plan that enables both sides to develop their own policies and procedures, free from the impetus of sudden emergencies, with their unhappy effects. The overall objectives of management as they appear in the company's long-term plans are often revealed to all workers so they will be aware of the benefits that will result from improved productivity and profitability. Anticipated personnel reductions can usually be planned in such a manner so as to minimize hardships for the workers. This is the best way to secure cooperation when changes have to be made.

The fast transition from mechanical and manual office operations to widespread introduction of computer systems has provided a great deal of experience—some earned at a high cost—supporting the advantages of long-term planning for both management and labor. In this instance, most companies had sufficient time to prepare for the changeover with care, but some companies did not take advantage of the time they had. They kept their plans secret; as a result the grapevine carried all kinds of exaggerated rumors. Where employees were given a chance to learn new skills required for computer operations, fears of dismissals were avoided and needed reductions were accomplished through temporarily stopping the hiring of new employees.

Careful long-term planning for labor is the most satisfactory and the least expensive procedure for avoiding labor problems and for coping with unavoidable changes in current operating practices. The importance of long-term manpower planning for the long-term profit plan cannot be exaggerated.

As part of installing a program of production planning, PQR Company developed a proposal for a long-term manning plan to be coordinated with the production plan. It was hoped that such a plan would make possible steady employment for a large majority of the company's workers. It was felt that being able to give such an assurance would increase the probability that the company would retain high-quality help and thereby keep costs under effective control. Joseph Block, executive vice-president of the company, gave an explanation of the plan:

"For many years, we had no problem hiring the number of semiskilled people we needed. We staffed in terms of our historical ratio between production volume and direct labor costs. But as the national economy has approached full employment, we have been facing increasing difficulties in hiring. Yet management hesitated to change from hiring based on that ratio.

"It became increasingly obvious that a modification of the traditional method of hiring—and cost control—was unavoidable. Our labor relations experts told us that long-term planning of labor requirements would be necessary to improve the situation. Planning our production to minimize volume changes would be necessary so we could keep a steady labor force and thereby attract the better type of workers. Most of the data needed for long-term labor planning were available on payroll records but had never been analyzed for planning purposes. We did not have a formal system of job classifications. Because of the cost involved, management had been unwilling to install one. Therefore, our labor relations, payroll, and plant management people had to work out rough estimates as to the classification and distribution of our labor force.

"One tough, important question was how to measure the costs of discharging and again of hiring and training workers necessary to maintain the fluctuating level of workforce required by our traditional staffing ratio. Such a computation had never been made in the past; management looked at the saving that seemed associated with the procedure, but not at the additional costs involved. It was difficult to convince management of the significance of this approach. Some of our executives still are not assured of its value. What we can say, however, is that our labor costs have not increased in the face of rising wage rates. Layoffs and subsequent rehirings have declined substantially, and this fact has become gradually known to the local labor force. Indeed, there has been an increase in employment applications. We believe our long-term approach has justified itself and is making a valuable contribution to our overall long-term profit plan."

Planning for Overhead Costs

Traditionally, overhead costs have been controlled not by individual classifications but by overall rates based on short-term estimates. This practice is explained by the large number of specific classifications that compose the overhead figures, many of them too small to justify individual attention. But the ratio of overhead costs to total cost is steadily increasing, partly as a result of automation. Therefore, some companies evaluate individually and with care at least the larger overhead classifications, especially those related to automation, such as depreciation, maintenance, and local taxes.

The traditional approach to computing overhead rates is not acceptable for use in long-term planning. The inadequacies of traditional techniques have been familiar to cost estimators—a short-term activity; but they are even more critical for long-term planning. In the words of an executive who was interviewed:

"When I joined this company and reviewed its planning procedures, I found that in planning manufacturing costs it used its current overhead rates and merely increased them for expected price changes. The company felt this was a general practice. I failed to impress the controller and chief accountant when I raised the issue for consideration and possible change.

"I enlisted sales executives and industrial engineers to concern themselves with the matter in order to emphasize that this was not just an accounting problem. I pointed out that there was a danger that future costs were understated and expected profits overstated in the long-term profit plans submitted to management. Following extensive discussions, agreement was reached to develop separate data for the major overhead classifications based on the assumptions incorporated in the overall long-term plan. I have no doubt that many companies still use the traditional method; they will have to re-evaluate its suitability for use in long-term profit planning."

11

General and Administrative Expenses, Cash, and Financial Planning

MANAGEMENT'S influence on company expenses varies for the different functions. Manufacturing costs are closely related to volume and are the result of production procedures; they do not generally require specific management decisions. The situation is substantially different for non-manufacturing costs, which largely are not related to volume. Distribution and general and administrative expenses result in most instances from specific management actions. Distribution expenses are closely related to marketing policies; general and administrative expenses cover all the classifications that cannot be included in any of the other groups. They represent a wide variety of items that have hardly anything in common except that the amounts expended are the result of specific management decisions and are not related to measures or ratios in use by the other expense groups.

Since management is responsible for these expenses in the first place, it is easy to understand why they are the ones affected first and most whenever management decides to reduce expenses as a means of bolstering lagging profits. Reducing general overhead is a favorite device of professional cost cutters. In numerous instances, an incoming management has cut administrative or research expenses by 50 percent or more within a short time. Not long ago, a well-known manufacturing company announced that it had reduced its corporate staff from 1,510 to 125 within a matter of months in order to achieve profitability.

Long-Term Profit Plan and General and Administrative Expenses

Long-term profit planners always look for costs and expenses management can manipulate to facilitate attaining the profit plan without affecting the vital activities of the company. Corporate contributions are an expense of this type. Even if such contributions have been made regularly for a considerable period and the amounts are accepted as fixed and not subject to reduction, there is always the possibility of spreading them out over a longer time. Every effort should be made to keep such expenses as flexible as possible and not to let them become a permanent charge in order that they can be adjusted to requirements of the long-term profit plan. Management must take the position that the funding of these expenses depends on the attainment of the profit plan.

Many general and administrative expenses result from the company's organization, which has been determined by managerial decisions that can be modified when necessary. Experience has shown the potential dangers in a company having large staff groups, especially at corporate headquarters. When such groups exist at both the corporate and the division levels, expensive duplication of efforts may result. Also, new staffs are often added simply on a prestige basis, to keep in step with other companies in the same industry or location, whether or not a real need exists. For example, installations of expensive computer systems in many companies are not justified by the existing volume of activities suitable for computer processing.

Many companies plan general and administrative expenses on a long-term basis rather than adjusting them to individual good or bad years. An illustration of inadequate long-term planning is provided by reports of companies that have made long-term lease arrangements for space in a building, often before the building was completed, and have found themselves short of space only a few years later when they were ready to move into the new premises. Here we have a situation opposite to the computer case. Of course, planning space requirements is difficult because appropriate measures for decision making are usually lacking, but it appears that decisions frequently are made without a thorough evaluation of all relevant factors.

Cash Planning

Businessmen know the importance of cash to their operations; nevertheless, the significance of cash planning on a short-term basis and especially on a long-term basis has been recognized only fairly recently. Today, short- and long-term cash planning are accepted as essential sources of information. The incentive for cash planning came from lenders who wanted to know whether borrowers would be able to repay loans from future cash receipts. Borrowers were often surprised when this question was raised, since they shared a widespread belief that profitable operations would automatically provide the necessary funds. It was not easy to convince them that profitability does not necessarily go hand in hand with liquidity. Too many ostensibly profitable enterprises defaulted on their obligations because of a lack of ready cash. Nowadays, however, in most companies the *cash flow*—the company's ability to meet obligations when due—is evaluated and planned as carefully as its profitability.

The need for cash-flow planning is especially important in view of the tendency of many businessmen to concentrate attention on sales and profits and lose sight of the need to manage their companies' cash flow. Repayment schedules of loans and other obligations must be supported by careful plans that assure the availability of cash at the proper time.

Operating and cash conditions strongly interrelate, but they do not always move in the same direction; this makes the relationship difficult to evaluate. Profitability is not necessarily related to liquidity; nor is liquidity necessarily related to profitability. A business in liquidation will usually have a satisfactory cash flow since it will not be incurring new obligations.

There are various ways to improve a company's cash flow. Inventories or accounts receivable can be reduced. Payment of accounts payable can be delayed to preserve current liquid funds. And cash can be increased by short- and long-term borrowing and by selling stock. Cash planning selects the methods for generating and managing cash most suitable to the company's requirements at a particular time. On the other hand, neglect of cash planning may lead to management being confronted with sudden emergencies, such as an inability to meet its immediate obligations. Possible alternatives in such emergencies may be limited and not be in the best interest of the company. Sale of assets is one; raising funds under unsatisfactory and burdensome terms is another. Companies that overlook cash planning do so at their peril.

Except in the special case of financial institutions, cash flows result from actions in other areas, and therefore cannot be planned independently from these other areas. Cash planning, therefore, depends on these other plans and, since these other plans often depend on available cash flows, they may have to be adjusted to anticipated cash flows. Long-term cash planning is especially important in connection with large, expensive projects; most managements feel such projects should not be approved unless and until the necessary cash is assured. Most companies generate most of their cash internally; but, as necessary, companies can increase their available cash through outside financial transactions.

Like all planning, cash-flow plans are mainly the result of estimates. (Certain cash transactions are the effect of contractual arrangements and, therefore, can be accepted as facts.) In view of the special significance of the vulnerability of a company to a shortage of ready cash, cash-flow estimates are usually prepared with special care and with a strong sense of realism. In the case of sales forecasts, a certain optimism, and even exuberance, may not be out of place. But in preparing cash plans, such an attitude could be disastrous. These plans are most often prepared on a conservative basis and are designed to stand up to unfavorable developments. Many cash-flow plans have built-in reserves to be drawn on in emergencies. These reserves may be in the form of lines of credit with commercial banks or private funds of the principal owners or other interested persons. The owners, for example, may either contribute their own funds when needed or assist in raising them through their personal endorsement. The need to draw on these reserves may never arise, but if the appropriate arrangements exist, a company may be able to avoid dangerous troubles.

One unique aspect of cash planning is its sensitivity to outside influences over which management has no control; these can develop quite suddenly. The resulting dangers are especially critical for smaller companies. In the case of restrictions imposed by monetary authorities, for example, financial institutions will usually attempt to accommodate major customers while smaller companies are left without funds. With their customary sources of cash suddenly dried up, smaller companies may incur severe difficulties. Managements of these companies usually try to anticipate these contingencies, even though they may appear remote, and to plan in a manner to ensure their survival without undue harm to their future prosperity. Here again, conservatism in cash planning becomes particularly important.

The close relationship between the cash plan and the financial plan is readily apparent. The cash plan must be integrated with the financial plan, but it is by no means identical with the financial plan. The problems of cash-flow planning are specific and must be evaluated on their own merits.

STV Corporation, operator of a chain of supermarkets, has been expanding substantially over the years. Management has been under pressure to follow the trend in the industry in order not to fall behind in its market share. This is not so much a matter of prestige as it is an important factor in negotiations with suppliers on the accommodations that could be expected from them. As is customary in the industry, sales are almost exclusively on a cash basis—with the exception of some institutional organizations—which facilitates the company's cash operations. Management does everything possible to economize cash; not only the stores but also the major part of stores fixtures are leased rather than owned.

The corporation is closely held by the founders' families, who are unwilling to change this situation and possibly lose exclusive control. A conflict developed within management about how to reconcile this ownership situation with the desire for expansion. In the past, expansion had been financed from retained earnings and some contributions from the owners.

The younger managers wanted to continue the expansion, while the older group wanted to avoid any dilution of ownership and control. Since it was impossible to reach agreement, it was finally decided to get advice from the president of the bank through which the company transacted most of its financial business. The bank president would not make any recommendations without a cash-flow plan for several years ahead. If it could be shown that internally generated cash flow would continue to be adequate for financing the expansion, the present practices could continue. However, if cash resources would become insufficient some time in the near future, the company either would need a new policy or would have to modify or abandon the objective of maintaining the company's share of the market.

All the company's management agreed with these proposals in principle. The problem, however, was how to determine the cash-flow figures needed for the preparation of the long-term cash plan. The company had never done any such planning except short-term budgets for store managers. In order to compute future cash flows, estimates of sales and of other events that would have a major effect on cash were required. "We were faced with a real dilemma," said John Hughes, president of the corporation. "We needed cash-flow projections for the next five years;

to get them, extensive, time-consuming, and probably expensive efforts would be needed. On the other hand, we were not ready to introduce a comprehensive planning program. The possibilities for doing this had been discussed from time to time, but there had been a feeling that this was not essential for our operations and, in addition, would be quite expensive." He continued:

"After lengthy discussions with the bank, final agreement was reached that something rather unusual would have to be done to get the desired results fast and inexpensively. Our management group consisted of ten men, all thoroughly familiar with company affairs and industry problems. We agreed that each of us would estimate independently the cash balance at year end for the next five years on the basis of our generally accepted growth policy. Our estimates would be averaged and the result used for the determination of our long-term cash plan.

"Many objections can be raised to this procedure; certainly it was far from perfect. Probably its greatest weakness was that all of us would be biased in the same direction, that we would have similar prejudices which would affect the estimates. Yet we felt that there was no choice and our bank's president agreed. This was the only immediately available *practical* answer: we had to accept it. We found, happily, that differences in the estimates were comparatively small, mostly within 10 percent margin of the average. The cash-flow plan developed using this procedure showed that cash inflow would become inadequate to maintain our desired growth within three years. Therefore, within three years, a decision had to be made whether to reduce the rate of growth or to get long-term funds from outside, possibly even at the expense of some dilution of ownership and control.

"A committee of second-level executives has been appointed, all of them with many years of experience, to analyze the situation and study the alternatives which will be available when the time comes to make the final decision, probably after two years. Conditions may be quite different then, and the final decision undoubtedly will be strongly affected by that fact."

The Long-Term Financial Plan—
Final Step Toward the Long-Term Profit Plan

The long-term financial plan brings us to the threshold of the long-term profit plan. In our free enterprise system, financial considerations have a special significance. This does not mean that profits are the only objective of business activities, as too many managers seem to believe strongly; there are other important factors management must keep in mind. Yet profits, as they appear in the financial plan, are important: there can be no successful business enterprise nor a prosperous national economy without profitability. This has been demonstrated by the experience of those who have tried to eliminate profits as a principal consideration. This is why the long-term profit plan is *the* indispensable guide for managerial decision making.

Many managers with inadequate training in financial matters have a tendency to minimize the importance of this emphasis. They will insist that other factors are more significant and that profits are merely the result of successful performance in sales, product design, production techniques, and so forth. These, of course, are essential prerequisites of profitability, but none of them in itself will assure the future of the enterprise unless it is financially sound and shows sustained profitability.

Many companies have started their planning program with a long-term financial plan. During our field research, we interviewed a number of companies that were still more or less at this early stage or that reported that financial plans had been the beginning of their planning efforts. Often they had also planned in other functions, but had done so without any coordination with the financial plan, an essential prerequisite for establishing a true long-term profit plan.

In a formal sense, the financial plan is a pro forma version of traditional financial statements. But the financial plan is more than just a summary of the other functional plans in monetary terms—that is only one of its aspects.

In addition, however, the financial plan also is a plan of how to deal with the specific financial problems of the company. In particular, this includes the planning of cash flow to make sure that needed financial resources will be available to support the functional plans.

Resources That Support the Profit Plan

The financial plan deals with questions that arise from the reconciliation of the company's functional plans in financial—that is, money—terms. It reflects the importance of financial factors to the realization of the company's other plans. Neglect of financial factors can have unfortunate effects. Many businesses expose themselves to unnecessary, but foreseeable, trouble from the outset by starting operations with inadequate financial resources and with a heavy burden of long-term debt. The managements of new businesses usually find it wise to determine in advance the funds the business will need to attain its aims; the company's management will plan so that its resources will be adequate to its goals. The financial plan will vitally affect the long-term profit plan. Insufficient resources will cause the company to make plan attainment impossible.

As in cash-flow planning, a conservative approach to financial and profit planning is usually wisest. Unrealistic assumptions will render the plan useless, if not dangerous. To assume that every customer will always pay on time or that all expenses will be kept at a minimum will result in a plan of no practical value, one that will only mislead management. The financial plan usually reflects in broad terms managerial objectives for a number of years ahead. The plan will indicate the total funds required for each year, but it will not describe the methods of raising these funds; the methods used will depend on conditions at the time the decision has to be made. There are a variety of ways of acquiring needed funds, and the one selected will best fit prevailing conditions. For example, during an inflationary period, bonds may be unfavorable as a means of obtaining cash while stocks are favorable because people buy them to offset the effects of inflation. During a downswing, stocks may decline and, therefore, not be attractive; but bond prices may go up, since they provide a fixed return even though dividends on stocks decline.

The importance of coordinating all long-term planning, including the financial plan, has been mentioned before. The financial plan represents the final step of the planning program. Determination of future financial requirements depends on information about future activities. These future activities, in turn, are contingent on the availability of funds. Thus we see the close relationship of all planning efforts. Planning is iterative; there is no escape. But some practical approach must be found.

One approach is for management to announce in advance the total financial resources that will be available for each planning period; but these amounts would be considered tentative and not immune to possible changes. Some companies believe they must give an impression of inflexibility with regard to the total resources available to avoid an avalanche of demands for changes, which would frustrate the attempt to set a limit. Yet in taking this position, management, in fact, indicates its inability to make decisions on a rational basis. Most managements usually review proposals that claim unusual significance or profitability, even though they require resources beyond the announced limit and make a decision based on merit. They try to avoid giving the impression that changes are impossible under any conditions. Of course, the question will remain whether there is a way to raise the additional funds for desirable proposals that exceed the ceiling; most companies think it is worthwhile to try.

The planning manager, in cooperation with the company's financial executives, will usually make an allocation of the funds management has indicated will be available. This preliminary allocation may be changed in the course of developing the final plan. But the allocations will serve as guidelines for the preparation of the divisional plans. Dissatisfaction in the divisions with the amounts allocated must be anticipated, and arrangements for reviews must be made to ensure divisional managements that their requests are being treated fairly and the facts submitted in support of their proposals are being considered.

Psychological Factors in Long-Term Profit Planning

In companies with multiple profit centers, one approach is to let each part of the organization work out its own long-term profit plan, waiting until the consolidation of all profit-center plans before evaluating the resulting figure. Another approach is for management to announce its profit goal in advance—as is often done for financial resources—and then examine the completed profit-center plans to determine whether they have attained their expected share of the profit plan.

The first alternative gives more freedom to profit-center management to develop its own ideas: there is the possibility that their profit plan will exceed what management would have expected them to accomplish. On the other hand, additional work might be required if management is dissatisfied with the indicated profit and asks the profit center to revise its plans. Under the second alternative, profit-center management knows in advance what top management expects and will make every effort to meet the anticipated profit goal. However, complaints that the required profit is excessive and unattainable under prevailing conditions are common. In addition, lower management levels may manipulate figures to show the "correct" profit, knowing it will not be attained. Most managements impress on all concerned with planning that their figures must be as realistic as possible and usually insist on complete explanations of eventual differences between planned and actual results.

Psychological factors are important in this context. Some managers, favoring an autocratic approach, believe you have to push people to get results: they will usually prefer the second method. Those in favor of a more democratic policy usually tend to favor letting lower management levels show what they can accomplish if left to their own devices, as far as is practical; the final plan will be the result of discussions and negotiations and will represent a consensus among the several management levels. It is impossible to express a preference in favor of either method. Our interviews indicate that both are used successfully by some companies: each management determines its approach in the light of existing conditions. Some companies seem to adopt a middle position: management indicates a tentative profit goal which may be adjusted as a result of subsequent discussions and in consideration of the results of functional or profit-center planning.

XYZ Manufacturing Company, which produces components for the electronics industry, has been using one-year budgets for a number of years. However, coordination of the planning for the various functions left much to be desired, despite considerable efforts toward improvement. The company was closely held, and management had always been in the hands of the principal stockholders. It was decided to appoint an outsider as president in the hope that he would be able to increase the company's profitability. Joseph Miller, the new president, had been a vice-president of a large manufacturing corporation and had a reputation for drive and efficiency. Having made an extensive survey of the company's facilities, he remarked during an interview:

"The conditions I have found are not particularly unusual. They reflect a common ailment—namely, lack of adequate internal information and communication; one hand doesn't know what the other is doing.

"The company's budget has no real impact on operations. Few outside the budget department appear to realize that it should have an effect on their activities. Merely improving budget procedures would not be sufficient, however. In this industry, a constant flow of new products is needed if a company wishes to maintain or expand its position vis-à-vis its competitors. Only a long-term profit plan would really help. Substantial funds are required to support research and development programs: in this industry, several years are usually required to recover these outlays. We installed an integrated long-term financial plan to determine in advance the funds that would be required and the method we might use to make them available. This is not the type of a company which could appeal to the general capital market.

"My principal problem has been getting this approach accepted by the company's management. This was not the first time I had to undertake this kind of a job, and I was aware of the difficulties I had to anticipate. But we did accomplish the program to a substantial extent. You are probably interested in knowing how we did it.

"Fortunately, the financial situation of the company was very satisfactory. Our current ratio was approximately 3:1 and we had no substantial debts, except a mortgage at a low interest rate and with a comparatively small annual payment. But profits after taxes were only about

3 percent of sales. I had to get the business moving ahead. Fortunately, I had the complete cooperation of the owner–managers.

"I brought together a small group of specialists, most of whom had been working with me in my previous positions. They prepared a presentation, with films, slides, and a pamphlet, that I could use to explain the importance of the long-term financial plan to the company's executives. I put special emphasis on human considerations and the anticipated benefits of the new plan to company personnel. I always allowed adequate time for questions. In addition, I visited all company facilities for discussions with local people.

"One of the principal shortcomings of the old budget procedures was overcentralization. The controller's department assembled the data and distributed the completed budget to guide individual managers—who had no part in preparing it. The program was ineffective. I favor maximum decentralization. But to make an effective plan the functions involved in developing the long-term plans must be coordinated. I have always announced in advance my sales and profit objectives and the funds available for long-term investments, including development of new products.

"In time, the small group of specialists became the corporate planning department with the principal assignment of assisting the operating executives to develop their own short- and long-term plans. The planning department reconciles differences in plans and tries to achieve full coordination. Only if they are unsuccessful do I make the final decisions.

"The financial plan is a joint effort of the controller's and treasurer's departments, with the assistance of the planning department, which provides data from the functional plans. The treasurer's department prepares the cash-flow plan, including proposals on how to raise the funds required to support the company's long-term investment program.

"I also have frequent meetings of the principal executives to get them to coordinate their activities with each other. These meetings have brought about a much closer relationship among these men than had existed in the past. Previously, most of their contacts had been formal and in writing only. This has helped a great deal."

12

Presenting the Long-Term Profit Plan

THOSE who administer the long-term profit plan should never overlook the fact that its purpose is to provide a valuable tool for managerial activities, not to please the specialized interests of those who prepare it. The planners must avoid the danger of getting lost in technical details of no help to management; often such details lead only to confusion and an aversion toward the plan. The significance of the planning program is not measured in terms of the number and detail of the schedules included. It is usually a serious mistake to confront management with as much information as can be assembled and then leave it to select the usually comparatively few data of real value to its work. However, many people in charge of preparing long-term profit plans honestly believe that they have completed the task when they have accumulated the data and incorporated them in the reports; they feel they have neither the right nor the responsibility to make a selection among the data themselves.

Although including a large amount of data in long-term profit plans may impress management with the work the planners have done, important considerations argue for simplicity. First, the pyramid concept of organization and reporting attempts to reduce to the minimum the volume of management information reported at each level, confining de-

Presenting the Long-Term Profit Plan

tailed data to reports for the lower management levels. The exception principle to some extent parallels the pyramid concept: It calls for reporting to each manager only information indicating that he must make a decision or take some other action. Many companies feel it is unnecessary to report data that will not lead to action. More generally the basic idea is to have the recipient of a report determine the data he wishes to include in the report. The guiding principle is to provide a minimum quantity of highly relevant information. This information is usually identified best through a joint effort of the suppliers and the users. This approach is perhaps the best way to ensure a satisfactory solution to the problems of what to present, to whom, when, and how.

The usual format for reporting plans to management has been that of traditional financial statements, even though the plans present the results of the future-directed planning efforts, not historical data. Two principal advantages are claimed for this form of presentation. First, the format is familiar to managers, who therefore have no difficulty in interpreting the data. Second, and perhaps more important, comparisons between historical and planned data can be made readily and differences can be easily ascertained and analyzed. These benefits are usually worth keeping in mind when determining the format for planning reports to management.

The long-term profit plan, for companies following this approach, takes the format of a profit-and-loss statement presenting the planned profit for the period. The balance sheet accompanying the profit-and-loss statement indicates the assets, liabilities, and equity contributing to and resulting from the transactions involved in generating the particular profit figure. Long-term profit plans are usually prepared for annual periods: often the first year, and sometimes even later years, is broken down by quarters, especially if the differences between quarters are significant. Figures for past periods may be shown for comparison purposes. For example, the quarterly figures for the first year of the plan may be accompanied by data for the same quarters for the preceding year and, possibly, for the current year.

It may sometimes be more convenient to include annual averages of quarterly figures in addition to or in lieu of quarterly figures, especially if significant fluctuations make it difficult to ascertain longer-term trends. The first year of the long-term profit plan, in which near-term comparisons between actual and planned results are possible, provides management with information it can use for adjusting plans for subsequent periods so the company will have a better chance of attaining its profit goals.

The question arises whether the traditional pro forma statement is the most effective method of presenting plans. The pyramid concept, of course, calls for different presentations for the several levels of management, with fewer details included for each consecutively higher level of management. Moreover, if the needs of users are given careful consideration, we may have to assume that not all users will want the same information in the same form. Therefore, it will often be necessary to use more than one format in presenting plans.

The Long-Term Profit Plan for Top Management

The question of the proper format for reporting the long-term profit plan to top management leads us back to the fundamental concepts of planning. The objective of long-term profit planning is to furnish guidance to management for decision making by providing it with the essential relevant information. More detailed information, while always available if required by top management, will usually be included in the reports to lower operating levels for their guidance and control. The type of data top management will require will, of course, vary from case to case.

The timing and frequency of reports for the first year of the long-term profit plan, when it becomes operational, are also important. Reports generally are not submitted more frequently than is required for essential management information. Electronic information systems that produce real-time data tempt planners to forward all this information to top management to keep it "up to date on developments." Most companies strongly oppose this tendency. The need for specific data, not simply its availability, usually determines what is reported. Why forward monthly reports that hardly change from month to month—and so contribute no worthwhile information—when quarterly or semiannual reports might well suffice? Again, decisions as to type and frequency of reports should be made through joint consultations of suppliers and users. Some executives like to receive certain data more frequently than other executives do; their requests should be honored unless there are important reasons to the contrary. Past data may be included for purposes of comparison. Exhibits 26 to 33 present a small sample of profit planning reports, which show the different levels of details and the different time periods covered by such reports.

Analysis of Long-Term Profit Plan Data

Analyses of data supporting the long-term profit plan can be made in a variety of ways and extended in different directions. Quarter-to-quarter or year-to-year comparisons are most frequent. Equally important, however, is ratio analysis. Two of the most generally used ratios are earnings per share, which indicates the planned long-term profit per share of common stock outstanding, and the price/earnings ratio, which shows the relationship between profit and the current market value of the common stock. These ratios are popular in view of their simplicity. But as with many simple approaches, significant factors may be omitted or their impact lost. Each ratio highlights one particular factor only, often at the expense of others just as important. A more complete picture can be provided only by a comprehensive "syndrome" of ratios; to compute all these ratios may be time-consuming and expensive. Graphic presentations of ratios are valuable for indicating long-term trends. In any event, without proper analysis the significance of the long-term profit plan to management is substantially reduced.

Review and Approval of Plans

As we have seen, many levels of executives in all the functions of the business get involved in preparing plans. And at each successively higher level of management, the plans of the lower level are reviewed and approved. This procedure is usually carried out under the watchful eyes of the planning department or the planning committee. Among the companies contacted in the research, such groups as a corporate planning committee, a corporate staff, a corporate budget committee, a director of finance, a corporate long-term planning committee, and an executive committee lay down the guidelines for how the plans will be prepared and review the preliminary plans as they are submitted. Naturally, these groups or individuals give guidance to those preparing the plans.

After preliminary screening of the long-term profit plan has been completed and the managers responsible for its preparation are ready to formally submit it, to whom does it usually go for review? Companies, of course, differ greatly in their top organization. Among those participating in the research, however, final long-term profit plans are submitted to a corporate planning committee, senior management, the board of directors, the corporate president, or the corporate executive committee. And in almost all cases, it is this group that gives final approval to the plans submitted to it.

While all those involved in planning take great care to make each plan they submit as complete and accurate as possible, the fact that no one knows the future makes it inevitable that the future as it unfolds will be different from the future projected or assumed as the basis for the plan. In recognition of the slips 'twixt cup and lip and the dynamic nature of the environment both inside and outside the company, most companies revise their plans annually. Among the companies contacted for this study, better than eight out of ten indicated that they revise their plans annually. The others revise their plans as necessary; they have no fixed schedule.

13

Food Manufacturing and Wholesaling Companies: Selected Examples

THE four food processing and distributing companies described in this chapter illustrate the wide variety of current long-term profit planning procedures. One is a large company operating both in the United States and internationally; as a result of a recent merger, it has become primarily a distributor of drugstore products. Two others are independent subsidiaries of large international European companies. The fourth company is a major brewer.

Foremost-McKesson, Inc., San Francisco

The company is the result of the July 1967 merger of Foremost Dairies, Inc. and McKesson and Robbins, Inc. Sales in fiscal 1970 were $1,692 million and net profits were $29.2 million. The company currently breaks down sales and profits for its *principal* divisions: in 1970 Foremost's sales were $404 million and McKesson and Robbins' sales were

$747 million. The company is mainly a wholesale merchandiser, and has numerous distribution centers in the United States and in 25 foreign countries. The Foremost Foods Company is also a major processor of dairy products.

The company's strategy, as stated in its 1968 report, is "one of growth by means of accelerating progress in already established fields, emphasizing those with a better than average growth potential." The management believes the company will be "able to secure an increasing rate of return on investment by supplementing internal growth with a continuing program of acquisitions in areas of outstanding potential."

William J. Elbert, vice-president and corporate controller, explained that the company's four principal operating companies—drugs, food, liquor, and chemical—are subdivided into numerous divisions. Each of the companies has its own president and a separate staff and is considered an individual profit center. The company is highly decentralized; only cash is centrally managed.

Mr. Elbert indicated that Foremost Dairies has been using budgets for many years and long-term planning since 1962. McKesson and Robbins has now been included in this program. The same people are engaged in long-term and short-term planning. Budgeting is carried to the lowest management level—foremen and so forth. Long-term planning is restricted to divisional managements and staffs. The presidents of the four principal operating companies are executive vice-presidents of the corporation and members of top management, which also includes the corporate controller, the treasurer, and the general counsel.

All long-term planning is carried on by the companies, and their plans are reviewed by corporate management. Plans are revised twice a year as required. Short-term planning is administered by a budget director.

The companies also are responsible for capital planning, with projects over $100,000 having to be approved by the board of directors. Capital plans are developed in detail for the next year and in more general terms for two more years; they are tied in with the companies' general long-term plans. A monthly capital expenditures statement is prepared and summarized in February, prior to the start of the corporation's fiscal year on April 1. The financial effects of projects are evaluated by means of the discounted cash-flow technique. Since the company is mainly a distributor, the amount of capital investment is comparatively small. A range of acceptable returns on investment, with acceptable levels varying for the different companies and for different kinds of projects, is used in evaluating proposed projects.

The corporation's forecasts of sales and profits have been quite accurate. Mr. Elbert said that the corporation's objectives include an annual

10 percent growth from internal sources and another 10 percent from acquisitions. The growth through acquisition objective has not been attained because of a lack of suitable candidates, but management is looking vigorously for prospects.

The long-term profit planning program is still being developed, but all levels of management find the present program useful. The management bonus program is tied in with the achievement of plan objectives; this increases its importance to managers. Some of the corporation's managers assert that general management is now better aware of the future needs of the company, that financing is done in a known and consistent manner, and that prices can be set to meet long-term objectives.

The F. & M. Schaefer Brewing Co., New York

The company is the largest brewer in the East; it produced and sold in excess of 5.4 million barrels in 1969. Net sales after excise taxes were $169 million, and net profits were $5.6 million. The company was founded in 1842 and was privately held until 1968, when it became a corporation. It was admitted to trading on the New York Stock Exchange in early 1969. Schaefer operates three breweries and one malting plant in New York and Maryland; its market is the 14 eastern states and some export business.

The company's profit planning program was explained by David C. Webster, controller:

> The program has five principal parts. The annual master plan, the budget, is developed in detail for all functions and in application constitutes a responsibility accounting system covering close to 200 cost centers. A media/market plan is developed in connection with the master plan so we can evaluate product and customer profits by market. The monthly reporting system, including statements and analyses, is geared to present actual and planned data and indicates variances from the plan. Profit projections for the current year are built from an analysis of results to date. Finally the long-range, five-year plan is reviewed and adjusted annually following the approval of the budget. Special attention is given to the development of plans, costs, and profits by responsibility centers, subject to the review process and coordination between functions.

As far as organization arrangements are concerned, Mr. Webster indicated that:

The long-range planning program was started in 1959. Both short-range and long-range planning activities are combined and performed by the same people. The market research group prepares sales forecasts for five years ahead. Long-range planning is performed on the corporate level only. But the individual plants prepare their own budgets with the assistance of the corporate staff. Some 25 persons are involved in the planning program at all levels, some on a part-time basis only. Sales and profit objectives are determined in the spring by top management. Capital investment projects are evaluated by return-on-investment techniques, but not by the discounted cash-flow method. The annual budget reflects the first year of the long-range plan. The detailed data developed for the budget are extended into the future for use by the long-range plan. The budget itself is prepared in the fall.

Mr. Webster indicated that Schaefer's management considers the long-range plan essential for maintaining adequate profits in an industry as strongly competitive as the beer industry.

Nestlé Company, Inc., White Plains, New York

The company is the U.S. subsidiary of the worldwide Nestlé Company of Switzerland (Nestlé Alimentana S.A.), which also holds a 36-percent share of Libby McNeill & Libby, Inc., Chicago. The U.S. company does not publish figures on sales and profit, but it is understood that it makes a substantial contribution to the profit of the parent company.

The U.S. company is a leader in the food industry.

According to Patrick D. Reidy, manager of financial analysis and planning, the U.S. company operates virtually independently of its Swiss parent. The top executives of the subsidiary maintain liaison with the parent and visit the headquarters at Vevey in Switzerland from time to time.

Mr. Reidy stated that in the early 1960s the company introduced a ten-year plan, which was later abandoned. In 1968 the parent company reinstated long-range planning, and the preparation of a six-year profit plan is now required. The parent company's initial objective is at least to equal the average performance of the food-processing industry in terms of return on investment.

Evaluation of capital investment projects is based on return on investment and discounted cash-flow techniques. All planning is done by a special group in the controller's department. Forecasts are developed by the marketing organization in conjunction with the controller's area.

Since the company is still in the early stages of its long-term plan, there is no readily available way to evaluate its effectiveness and usefulness to management.

A Food Company

The company, part of a worldwide concern with headquarters in Europe, is mainly a distributor of canned foods, but also manufactures some food products.

Both the president of this company and the vice-president of operations, who supervise the company's planning activities, attribute the rapid progress of the company in recent years to the techniques they used to introduce and operate the long-term planning program. As described by the vice-president of operations:

"Every two or three years, top and second-level management meet for a couple of days away from corporate headquarters to discuss and determine the company's objectives for the next several years. These objectives are based on a detailed evaluation of the company's strengths and weaknesses. The president and the other top managers lead the discussion, to which everyone is expected to contribute. Out of these meetings comes a list of individual projects, each of which is assigned to a particular manager for investigation and report by a specific date. The president himself monitors the timely submission of these reports." (See Exhibit 34.)

"From these reports, the five-year long-range plan is developed. The company has a budget committee and a planning committee. The division managers submit their plans for review by these committees. Differences can usually be straightened out by correspondence. Only infrequently are division managers asked to headquarters for discussions."

The president and vice-president of operations insist: "The techniques we use have the beneficial effect of involving all members of management in the planning effort. By using them, we avoid the common complaint that middle management is so absorbed in its daily chores that no time is left for considering long-range planning problems. With our approach, every manager is given his specific assignment and is required to consider its long-term effects. All managers are strongly motivated to work cooperatively for the benefit of the company as a whole. This has resulted, we think, in more substantial improvements and cost savings than probably could have been accomplished in any other manner. Every manager is expected to make his own decisions within the framework of the plan, rather than wait for orders from the top. On the other hand, top management considers it its responsibility to help and advise these managers. The plan is a joint effort, not imposed from the top."

The vice-president of operations was asked whether, in his opinion, this approach was so successful because in his comparatively small company close cooperation among managers was practical. Would the same method work in a much larger company? He replied, "Of course, I cannot give a definite answer since I have no experience outside my own company. But I feel strongly that the concept is sound in principle and could be applied in a large company, with appropriate adjustments to fit it to specific conditions."

14

Retail Merchandising Companies: Selected Examples

A NUMBER of practices are common and significant for this industry. Long-term profit planning has been essential in retailing to guide the large expansion of outlets in the postwar period into the suburbs of the metropolitan areas. Careful planning was required if a company was to obtain suitable locations, particularly in newly built shopping centers. And each new location required thorough financial, merchandising, and personnel planning. But there has been little truly comprehensive planning. All the companies contacted have been using short-term budgets, and few have made special organizational provisions for long-term planning. And in those companies that do both kinds of planning, all planning is usually performed by the same people.

The planning period is usually comparatively short, and in most instances does not exceed three years. However, in view of the scarcity of desirable locations in many areas, location planning may cover much longer periods.

The retailing companies interviewed seem to have a somewhat conservative attitude in connection with the introduction of newer management techniques such as the use of electronic equipment for managerial purposes.

A Department Store Group

This company is a department group store in the Midwest. In recent years it has established a number of large and small branches in its area. Sales in 1968 were $372 million and net profits, $8.8 million.

The company has been an early user of short- and long-term planning, the latter in connection with its program in the postwar period to expand into the suburban areas. The same people are responsible for both short- and long-term planning; only one person works full-time on long-term planning. The planning program was reorganized in 1964.

The process of long-term planning was described in a talk by the company president. He pointed out:

"The research department maintains up-to-date information on areas that may be considered for stores in the near future. Available data are gathered on current and probable future population, income levels and spending on department-store-type merchandise and on number, size, and characteristics of competing stores.

"Initially, data are obtained from government reports, trade publications, and other published media. However, as a given area becomes a prime candidate for consideration, additional detailed information is obtained directly by the research staff. For example, a complete canvass of competing retailers in a given area is often conducted by visiting all of the stores, listing their locations and dominant characteristics, and pacing off their dimensions.

"Another method of obtaining information is through consumer surveys. These can be useful, for example, in estimating the store's current share of the market in specific areas, or in determining the acceptance of existing retail facilities. Such surveys can also determine consumers' knowledge of the store and how their attitudes and shopping habits would change if the company located a certain type or size of store nearby.

"Once an area has been identified as having potential for a unit, specific sites are investigated. Selection of a site is based on a number of factors, such as size and price of available tracts, adequacy of the surrounding road network, size and distribution of the surrounding population, adjacent land uses, zoning restrictions, terrain, and drainage considerations.

"Following site selection, store size and timing must be determined. Utilizing the data previously collected, the research department makes several volume estimates for various store sizes five, ten, or even fifteen years into the future. The company has programmed its computer so that several estimates for various store sizes are possible; formerly, only one or two estimates could usually be made. Frequently, outside consultants make independent evaluations and sales volume estimates before the board of directors finally decides.

"Once timing, site, and size and kind of store have been determined, store operating and merchandising executives select the store layout, design, and operations and departmental space allocations.

"General management is closely involved in expansion plans for the next few years and is involved in a more general way for the more distant future. Division heads receive working forecasts of the future, in total dollar and unit sales, so they can prepare adequately for future workloads in activities such as warehousing and delivery.

"It is important that the working forecasts used in planning capital investment be as accurate as possible. The company has hired economic consultants who have experimented with complex computer programs, cyclical analysis, exponential smoothing, and so forth. The company is trying to find a single source or technique it can rely on to the exclusion of others. Consultants' estimates have been fluctuating substantially. Forecasts looking ahead 20 years or so, made just a few years ago, contain assumptions about trends that already appear to be changing significantly.

"In preparing long- and short-term forecasts, staff economists gather pertinent information from many sources, including results from the use of mathematical techniques and the data and reasoning behind the company's consultants' predictions. They consider all the possible positive and negative influences, trends, and so forth, and finally arrive at a forecast by a process that is perhaps closer to collective bargaining than scientific computation. Forecasts produced by this process have been substantially more accurate than those that would have been possible by relying exclusively on any one of the consultants. The company's maximum error during the recent periods was 8 percent; two consultants had errors of 12 percent and 14 percent. The company's official sales plan, based on forecasts made three months before the beginning of each quarter plus the judgment of key executives, has had an average error of 2 percent for the same period, with a maximum error of 5 percent.

"As to the future course of this company's long-term planning, it will become extensive and formalized, leaving as little as possible to chance. The company's activities, and the alternatives open to it, are becoming more complex, yet the penalties for inflexibility or ill-conceived change remain severe. The company has so far established no rigid long-term planning cycle, but it has found that some guidelines are necessary to insure that no important aspects are neglected. Every major executive is provided with long-term estimates of probable dollar and unit sales every year or two. In addition to the actual forecast, these reports discuss the probable future economic environment and the expansion plans on which the estimates are based.

"The company's long-term plans are based on several basic types of information, which it attempts to re-examine every few years to identify changes and trends and refresh memories. One key category is information about consumers. As it becomes more difficult for management to keep personally in touch with customers, it becomes increasingly important to study consumers formally. In addition to day-to-day activity in consumer research, a thorough re-evaluation has to be made periodically of the company's market share in its major merchandising lines among various kinds of consumers, particularly among those groups that are growing in importance. The company tries to stay aware of the contribution of various ages and income levels to its total sales; it tries to keep up with changes in the habits, needs, preferences, and attitudes of various consumer groups.

"Evaluation of operating effectiveness—that is, the company's ability to accomplish current objectives efficiently and at a profit—is another continuous process that must be thoroughly reviewed to be sure that routine procedures are effective."

Jewel Companies, Inc., Melrose Park, Illinois

The company has expanded greatly in recent years. In fiscal 1970, sales were $1,464 million and net profits were $21.4 million. The company operates several hundred supermarkets, partly through subsidiaries in the United States and through affiliated companies outside the United States. Many supermarkets are connected with drugstores opened by the company. The company has also branched out into self-service department stores, convenience food stores, restaurants, and the manufacturing of food products.

Howard O. Wagner, executive vice-president, finance, explained:

> The organization has changed substantially in recent years. During the 1950s the company operated with a five-year expansion plan. This planning was restricted to the corporate level. Since then the company has become widely decentralized. The operating companies have their own management staffs and largely operate independently.
>
> All the operating companies have short-term annual budgets, which are very detailed and extended to the store level. The operating companies submit their plans to corporate management for review. Long-range

planning is done mainly at the operating company level. Each company submits detailed statements of funds required, including inventories and other current requirements, and profit projections. Many of the stores are leased from corporate-controlled real estate companies.

A three-to-four-day conference of top executives of the corporation and the subsidiaries is held annually, away from headquarters. At that time the long-range plan is reviewed and another year is added. The long-range plan now covers three years. Management feels that a longer period would be unrealistic in view of the number and rapidity of unforeseeable changes in this industry.

A capital planning committee makes the final allocation of available funds and the operating companies then plan the use of their respective shares. A minimum return of 10 percent on investment is required, and considerably higher for riskier projects. The analysis is based on the discounted cash-flow technique.

There is no separate planning organization or staff. Top management of the corporation and the operating companies, with their staffs, do the planning. Management believes that this method is economical and works satisfactorily. The company has been highly successful in regularly exceeding the growth rate of the industry.

Special attention is given to recruitment and training of personnel and the development of the supervisory and executive personnel needed to support the planned expansion programs. There have been no problems in staffing new facilities from the available inventory of trained personnel.

Montgomery Ward & Co., Inc., Chicago

Montgomery Ward (a division of Marcor Inc.) has had a checkered history since World War II. Before the war its sales about equaled those of Sears, Roebuck and Co., whereas in 1968 they were less than one fourth of Sears'. In 1968 sales reached $1,990 million and net profits were $34.4 million, almost twice those of the preceding year. In the fall of 1968 the company joined Container Corporation of America to form a holding company, Marcor, Inc., of which Ward's is by far the larger partner. The recent development of the company started in 1961 when Robert E. Brooker, a former Sears executive, took over and brought in a large number of other former Sears executives. Traditionally, the company had catered to the rural areas of the country; most of its stores were small. This has gradually been changed. An increasing number of modern stores have been built, and these now provide the bulk of sales and profits. The company's catalog business is proportionally higher than Sears'—more than 26 percent of total sales as compared with about 20 percent—in part as the result of the Catalog Sales Agencies, which are franchised organizations established since 1965.

The company began to organize a long-term planning program only in 1968. J. K. Stow, manager of corporate analysis and special studies, has been given charge of the new program. Prior to 1968 planning was informal. During the credit crunch of 1966 the company had to restrict credit sales for lack of funds; this move had a very unfavorable effect on earnings. Most planning, especially for the expansion of outlets, was done in the company's four regions. However, the company, like others in the industry, always used short-term budgets prepared by the individual branches. These budgets were reviewed by successively higher levels of management in the field, in the region, and at the corporate office, and finally were approved at the corporate office. Mr. Stow explained,

> The budgets were prepared, reviewed and approved within the context of a set of sales and earnings objectives, which, in the light of our experience, usually proved overly optimistic.
>
> The real estate staffs of the regions worked under a system of priorities which served as a guide in building new stores. These staffs were supported by others on the regional and corporate level. Considerable long-range planning was also done in the merchandising area, where there has been a substantial upgrading of inventories.

Mr. Stow described the preparatory work for the long-term planning program.

> We arranged numerous courses on long-range planning that were attended by several hundred of our executives. We are also preparing procedural guides for the regions. We believe the result has been satisfactory. One important question has been whether store managers should be as involved in long-range planning as they are in short-range budgeting. The regional vice-presidents differ in their opinions, but we propose to give the store managers a limited part in long-range planning as well.
>
> No final decisions have been made as to the organization of a corporate long-range planning staff or whether I should continue my present job as manager of corporate analysis. We intend to complete the first five-year plan in the near future. We expect to update this plan annually. The first year of the long-range plan will be the basis for the short-range budget. However, there are many issues still to be decided.

Sears, Roebuck and Co., Chicago

This world leader in the merchandising field, with fiscal 1970 sales of $8,863 million and profits of $441 million, has an interesting approach to planning. In addition to the catalog mail-order business in which it originally started, it operates more than 800 department stores and hundreds of catalog stores in the United States, Canada, Latin America, and Spain. The enormous expansion of the company's operations becomes apparent if we compare its sales of about $1,000 million in 1945 with its fiscal 1970 sales of $8,863 million. All this has been accomplished without any formal centralized planning group.

The company does not have a corporate planning department, nor is there a planning department in any of its major geographic divisions. Planning work is spread among a number of departments. Over the short term, the geographic territories develop seasonal plans and budgets based partially on corporate economic analyses, local conditions, and other known factors. These seasonal plans are carried down to the individual stores, which complete budgets with territorial office guidance. Long-term planning derives from the company's expansion goals determined by top management. This planning requires the company to project funds needed and funds available for expansion and to project capital expenditures and the allocation of funds to specific programs.

The company is sales-oriented throughout; sales projections are the start of all long-term financial and profit planning. The comptroller's department prepares long-term projections for five to ten years from time to time as required, not necessarily on a predetermined schedule, beginning with prescribed sales assumptions and rates of growth. A spokesman for the department explained:

> These projections are in the form of pro forma statements. This approach is preferred by top management since it enables them to make ready comparison with past periods. The finance committee of the board of directors, made up of top officers and outside directors, meets several times a year and reviews updated projections prepared by the comptroller's department.
>
> The comptroller's department, before preparing new projections, consults with the other principal functions and receives information of anticipated changes which may affect future activities and profits. These functions, such as merchandising and credit, prepare their own forecasts, with the comptroller's department translating the data into financial terms and projecting results assuming different fund-raising

techniques. The actual raising of funds is the responsibility of the treasurer.

No personnel are assigned full-time long-term planning work. Those who consult with other functions and prepare financial projections have other duties in addition to long-term financial planning. This arrangement is flexible and is suitable to the often changing requirements of large retail organizations.

The general approach to the long-range planning for capital expenditures is as follows:

1. The initial step for new selling units is a demographical study projecting urban and suburban population directional thrusts; this analysis is made by both the territories and the corporate market research division. The same is true for the small catalog sales offices; but for these the analysis of future markets is primarily the responsibility of catalog order plants and does not receive the same attention from the corporate market research division.

2. Based on these analyses, locations for future stores and expansion of existing ones are determined.

3. Based on the expansion program adopted, the merchandising function formulates its own plans to insure sources of supply for the merchandise to be offered by the new stores; the personnel function makes plans to recruit and train the necessary staff; the operating function plans necessary changes for transportation and distribution; and other staff functions make similar plans for their future activity.

4. Based on approved plans, the territories move to acquire or lease the land for future stores. This may be done through the company itself or by a real estate subsidiary. Land acquisitions may precede actual construction by many years.

5. Availability of financial resources, of trained personnel, and of physical capacity to handle new store openings influences the speed of expansion.

Elaboration on some of these steps may be helpful.

Analysis of markets. The director of the merchandise research department described his department and its work:

> The department consists of seven groups which study consumer attitudes and location problems and develop economic and statistical data. The department is the principal source of long-range projections of future sales, which provide the basis for long-range planning throughout the organization. The staff consists of some sixty persons, five of whom are working full time on the economic aspects of long-range planning. Outside consultants are also retained for advisory services.

The department itself serves as an adviser on marketing problems to other functions of the company, for example, on pricing new products. Some of the new techniques—operations research and correlation analysis—have been introduced in the last few years to support the long-range projections.

Special long-range planning efforts are undertaken in connection with introducing new products, since new products often require decisions on promotion, production facilities, and so forth to be made far in advance. It is essential that these activities be coordinated so the company can move as rapidly as possible to bring new products to the marketplace.

In an interview, Arthur M. Wood, president of Sears, indicated that market research had enabled the retailing operation to increase its sales, upgrade the quality level of its product mix, and increase its profits—higher priced "top of the line" products bring a larger percentage of profit. The company's market research program, started in 1966, has been expanded in recent years.

Real estate planning. As mentioned earlier, real estate operations are critical in overall long-term planning for expansion. Real estate planning is generally carried out in the territories that prepare five-year location programs. However, the need for closer coordination of real estate operations led to the appointment of a vice-president for real estate and property. He explained:

The job of the department is to review and coordinate the work done in the territories. A separate subsidiary, Homart Development Co., was organized to develop shopping centers, usually in cooperation with other interested groups. Sears builds its own store in each center while Homart rents out the remaining space and takes care of the administration of the center.

The growing scarcity of suitable space for establishing these shopping centers requires long-range planning and decision making, often a long time before actual construction of a store begins. Joint sessions with the real estate specialists in the territories, who have first responsibility for making proposals, are scheduled frequently. New listings of possible locations are updated monthly.

The real estate function's plans are an important consideration in the preparation of the company's long-term financial projections by the comptroller's department.

Merchandising and sources of supply. The method of buying merchandising is an exception to the company's basic pattern of highly decentralized organization. There are some 50 buying departments, located either at the corporate headquarters in Chicago or in the headquarters office in New York. These departments were described by the general merchandising controller:

> They negotiate the contracts with the suppliers. The stores and catalog order plants then order directly from the suppliers in accordance with the terms of these contracts.
>
> In view of the size of the orders negotiated by each buying department—their actual annual buying volumes are between $35 million and $200 million—special planning is required. It is frequently difficult to find vendors who are able to supply economically the quantities needed by the company and to meet its specifications. Sears generally prefers to deal with manufacturers that are able to stand alone, but it will assist in the financing of production or expansion of facilities where necessary. It will not take an equity position in a supplier unless there is no other way to obtain the desired supply economically. All these actions require long-range planning and close coordination with the other functions of the company.
>
> Each buying department has an annual budget and a free hand to operate within the budget limitations. These budgets may be increased when required, possibly affecting the long-range financial plan.

Sears' largest wholly owned subsidiary, Allstate Insurance Company, contributes close to 20 percent of corporate profits. Allstate has its own planning program; its officer in charge of corporate planning reports to the vice-chairman of the company. Allstate's planning activities are strongly centralized, and all initiatives originate from the corporate planning group. A new long-range plan is developed approximately every five years and the current plan is updated annually. The current long-range plan, termed "New Dimensions For Allstate," spells out in narrative form and with charts and tables the company's principal objectives, and especially its expectations for growth beyond that of the industry as a whole.

15

Manufacturing Companies: Selected Examples

This group includes a wide variety of companies. Most operate mainly in the manufacturing areas, but, following the trend toward diversification, they have either branched out into other fields or have themselves become subsidiaries of larger, conglomerate types of organization. Several of these companies have been growing phenomenally in the last decade, and therefore their experiences in the long-term profit planning area are of particular interest. Although they may have considerable planning experience in some particular functions, most have become involved in formal and comprehensive long-term planning only in recent years. They are still experimenting to find the most appropriate approach to long-term profit planning for their companies.

An Electronics Manufacturer

One of the most important parts of this midwest electronics manufacturer's planning process is its programs for major new products. This part is the responsibility of the groups who propose, approve, and monitor new products. To assure rigorous analysis and opportunities for high-level review, minimum standards for the information required and appropriate formats for new product proposals have been established.

There are three major phases in the cycle for preparing and approving new product programs, but not all of the programs will pass through all the phases. These phases are

1. Preliminary investigation or basic technology study.

2. Major study or advanced development project.

3. Major product program.

The preliminary investigation explores whether an idea or concept is worth pursuing. At this stage there is little definitive or quantitative information available. But what is to be accomplished, why it is considered important, how long it should take to complete, and what it may cost can usually be determined.

Once the idea or concept is accepted, a major study is undertaken to reduce the idea or concept to practice and to demonstrate its feasibility. Approval at this phase requires specific statements of objectives and plans.

The final stage, a major product program, consists of four sections:

1. *Program analysis:* enables the manager to appraise the overall attractiveness of the program.

2. *Product development plan:* indicates how the program will be put into effect and what it involves. Since a large part of this plan must be completed before the program analysis, major portions of these two sections will usually be prepared at the same time. Of special importance to the product development plan are identification of specific problems, designation of individuals responsible for problem solution, and deciding when the problem will be solved. Exhibits 35 to 41 are the forms to be completed in submitting plans for management approval.

3. *Quarterly evaluation:* points out changes that have occurred and discusses reasons. Plans to meet previously unforeseen problems are outlined, as specifically as possible.

4. *Program review:* provides operating management with an independent evaluation and helps the program manager to obtain the resources needed for the successful completion of the program whenever problems with a program indicate a need for special attention. The review is authorized by the group president. Usually the vice-president for corporate development is appointed chairman of the review board and works with the group president in selecting members of the board. Outside consultants may be selected as members. Members are selected in recognition of special skills and represent a broad cross section of skills

related to the technology of the program. The ideal panel is completely objective and highly skilled; this ideal cannot always be attained. The panel is given access to all program records and information. It can discuss any aspect with any person associated with the program. The board usually spends from two to five days' work on its investigation, and defines the things to be corrected or investigated further by program personnel. Conclusions are discussed with the program manager, who either can accept the recommendations, can convince the board to withdraw them, or can leave them unresolved and consider them as differences of opinion. After the discussion the report is revised, if necessary, and presented to the group president at a meeting attended by the program manager and members of the line management. The group president is free to accept or reject any of the panel's recommendations.

Continental Can Company, Inc., New York

Continental Can holds a leading position in the packaging industry. Originally it made only metal containers, but it has now branched out into other packaging materials—paperboard, plastics, and composites—so it can offer its customers a more complete line of products. Increasing emphasis is being placed on providing packaging materials systems to solve customers' total packaging needs, rather than supplying only packages. The company is expanding into other related areas as well, including large holdings of forest land in the South. The company is organized into several main groups—metal operations, paper, plastics, and closures and consumer products—each consisting of several divisions. It has substantial operations in Canada and recently has made major acquisitions overseas. In fiscal 1969, revenues were $1,780 million and net profits were $90.4 million.

A comprehensive long-term planning program was initiated in 1965, led by the director of corporate planning, Warren W. Nissley, reporting directly to the president, E. L. Hazard. Recently, long-range planning has been integrated with previously existing short-term budgeting and control procedures. The entire financial planning process now is administered by a three-man "plans review office" reporting through the controller, David R. Arnold, to the chief administrative officer, Charles B. Stauffacher.

The company's overall planning philosophy was presented in an introductory section on planning in its annual report for 1967:

Planning is a key management function at division and group levels. . . . The company's basic philosophy for achieving its objectives is "increasing reliance upon individual creativity and initiative." Toward this end, planning methods seek to strengthen its decentralized organization structure, in which each division general manager is held fully accountable for the performance of his division.

Within the operating groups and divisions, planning activities are shaped by the annual requirement to submit a written long-range plan and by the constant requirement to provide guidance for technical and market development activities. Each group and each division organizes for these tasks in the manner best suited to its particular size, complexity, competitive position, and management team. Although the approach may vary, each participant is encouraged to think broadly about the relationship of his function to the entire business. In all cases, preparing the annual long-range plan is a key general management function.

Corporate management reviews planning on a company basis. At the corporate level planning procedures revolve primarily around two standing committees: long-range planning and research policy. The *long-range planning committee* reviews division long-range plans on the basis of overall company objectives. These objectives are defined by top management who give final approval to all long-range plans. These management reviews insure that the plans reflect realistic marketing strategies and sound financial planning, and that fulfillment of the plans will result in acceptable contributions to the company's growth.

The *research policy committee* establishes directions for corporate-initiated activities, evaluates the merits of large development projects proposed by the operating units, and periodically reviews the progress of major technical programs, whether initiated at corporate or operating levels.

As Mr. Hazard pointed out in a talk to company managers, "the key words are 'participation and communication.' Management wants wide participation at every level in defining objectives, developing strategies, and setting goals."

Mr. Hazard initiated long-term planning with a letter to all division vice-presidents and general managers dated March 22, 1965. (See Exhibit 42.) The director of corporate planning prepared a *Guide for Preparing a Divisional Long-Range Plan,* which was intended to suggest topics that the division managers might wish to discuss in their plan. It pointed out that "the key to efficient planning lies in coming to grips with the issues that are really important and in avoiding the proliferation of excessive and irrelevant details." (See Exhibits 43 and 44.)

While in general the format of the plan was left to the divisions, two schedules in standardized format were required: Projection of Sales, Income, and Return on Employed Capital for 1970; and Forecast of Annual Capital Requirements through 1970. (See Exhibits 27 and 45.) The purpose of the standardization was to permit projection of the total corporate picture to 1970 and to facilitate coordination of long-term planning with the three-year capital budget. In addition, each division was requested to summarize any corporate support other than capital funds required to pursue its long-term plan, such as corporate R&D services, staff services, and managerial assistance.

The projection presents the logical financial implications of strategies and action plans developed by the division. While the projection is not intended to be unsupportably optimistic, it is supposed to set forth the most challenging goals the division believes are attainable. If two or more substantially different strategies are under active consideration by the division, a separate projection is provided for each such strategy. The divisions are expected to consider the market forecasts distributed by the marketing analysis department; a division may substitute its own market forecasts, but if it does, it is expected to indicate its reasons.

Guidelines concerning trends of overall U.S. prices and labor costs are given to the divisions by the corporate staff. The guidelines include information such as "the consumer price index will rise by _____ percent per annum; industrial prices, on the average, will rise _____ percent; average hourly labor costs, including fringe benefits, will increase by _____ percent per annum." Projections of sales and income, however, are not based on the assumption that relevant prices and labor costs will conform to these overall guidelines. On the contrary, the price levels and labor rates for a given division are usually forecast primarily on the basis of demand, supply, and competitive factors specific to the division's situation.

The projection is usually accompanied by a description of the major assumptions underlying the financial projections. In a recent year the planner had to state his assumptions regarding the factors listed below with respect to product group A:

A. *Sales*
   1. Growth or decline of specific end-use markets.
   2. Participation in specific end-use markets for 1965 and participation forecast for 1970.
   3. Net volume anticipated from new products, after allowing for substitution effects.
   4. Impact of selective selling programs or other policy changes that will affect volume and participation.

5. Price levels and trends, if not covered under "Major Assumptions Throughout."

B. *Income*
List major assumptions regarding income levels projected for 1970, which should account for any anticipated changes in profit margins for 1970 as compared with 1965 as a result of
1. Raw material prices.
2. Labor rates.
3. Effects of automation and other manufacturing cost reduction programs.
4. Overhead expenses of plant and division.
5. Effects of sales programs and trade-mix shifts.
6. Selling and administrative costs.
7. Effects of new product developments.

C. *Employed Capital*
Identify cause of major changes in employed capital, with particular reference to large fixed-asset projects and to changes in inventories and receivables if disproportionate to sales. Identify any specific major retirements anticipated through 1970.

The second year the company went through its long-term planning cycle, the long-range plan had to be organized into six major sections:

1. *Progress:* Brief review of progress toward goals established the preceding year; comments on implementation of major projects and strategies; and status reports on incomplete studies relating to strategic issues.

2. *Environment:* Significant changes in forecasts of customer requirements and of the competitive situation; new opportunities or threats identified since the last year.

3. *Franchise:* Redefinition of business in which to compete, specifying reason for changes from preceding year's statement.

4. *Strategy:* Summarize briefly major elements of business strategy. Discuss alternative strategies for dealing with newly identified opportunities and threats. Select and justify alternatives that will best deal with the future as you see it now.

5. *Goals and Support:* Summarize projected financial results for years 1967 through 1971; specify the corporate support necessary to implement your plan. Corporate marketing services department will provide economic assumptions and "broad brush" market forecasts. Desires for market studies in depth should be discussed with marketing services department.

6. *Program:* Develop a timetable for implementing the key elements of your strategy. Specify actions required, dates to accomplish them, and individual responsibilities.

The third year the company went through its long-term planning cycle, divisions were asked to prepare charts depicting (1) at least five years' historical performance, (2) the 1966 long-range plan projection, and (3) the 1967 long-range plan projection. Each of these was to reflect sales and income, total employed capital, net changes in employed capital, and return on employed capital.

The instructions for this third planning cycle continued:

While the minimum period will remain five years, a brief letter should be added outlining important matters affecting prospects beyond five years. It should call attention to potential problems and opportunities, major facility projects, possible organizational changes, new management techniques, diversification activities, or other matters which ultimately may require corporate policy decisions and/or support. The long-range plan should be the basic tool for building and maintaining a healthy, satisfactorily profitable business. The quality of long-range planning, therefore, is of great interest. In virtually every plan, there appears room for continued improvement in most or all of these areas:

1. *Market Evaluation and Strategy.* Have you explored the future in sufficient depth from your customer's or potential customer's viewpoint, giving attention to every key factor he will consider in major procurement decisions?

2. *Manufacturing Programs.* Are you preparing to exploit all three basic avenues for increasing return on capital, without inviting additional competition or self-manufacture:
   Lower manufacturing costs?
   Reduced fixed assets per unit of production?
   Reduced inventory and receivables per dollar of sales?

3. *Technical Development.* Are the business plans for your major divisional projects adequately thought through? Have you suggested the corporate-sponsored projects which might have important implications for the division?

4. *Personnel Planning.* What is your program for recruiting, holding, and developing the truly outstanding individual?

These indications of the top management's continuing effort to improve the usefulness of the long-term plan illustrate the need to make long-term profit planning a permanent part of the company's management process. A company is only beginning when it first introduces long-term planning.

Miehle-Goss-Dexter, Inc., Chicago

Miehle-Goss-Dexter is a corporation that resulted from mergers made in the 1950s. At present there are six divisions: the Goss division, by far the largest, manufactures large web presses of both standard and custom design; the Miehle division makes sheet-fed presses; the Dexter and Lawson divisions produce various types of binding equipment; the Fincor division manufactures electronic speed, temperature, and position controls; and MGD Pneumatics, Inc., makes blowers and pumps. The company has subsidiaries in Canada and Great Britain and sales offices in many other countries. In fiscal 1968 sales were $154 million and net profits were $9.1 million.[1]

According to Robert Peterson, who is director of planning and research and has a background in engineering and business administration:

> The company is highly decentralized; each division has its own president and staff, though some of the divisions are rather small.
>
> Several years ago, the company started a long-range planning program; prior to that time, planning had been informal. Both the corporate headquarters and the divisions use people whose major responsibilities are in other functions of the company to develop the long-range plan.

The present procedure was described by Mr. Peterson:

> Long-range planning starts early in the year and is scheduled for completion during May and June. [See Exhibit 46.] The scope of the plan has been steadily expanded during the last four years, with emphasis placed on elements of the plan which analysis of prior plans indicated would become critical in the future.
>
> We also prepare a one-year plan (budget), which we call our profit plan, during August–September for the fiscal year beginning November 1. It should be nearly identical with the first year of the long-range

---

[1] In the spring of 1969 the company announced the signing of a merger agreement with North American Rockwell Corporation of El Segundo, California. It was stated at that time that the merger should mark a new era in the graphic arts industries, with North American's aerospace technology to be combined with MGD's extensive experience to produce more efficient printing systems.

plan with appropriate adjustments for new information that has become available since the completion of the long-range plan.

The same people, in general, are preparing both the long-term and short-term plans. Corporate and division managements take a major interest in the preparation of the long-range plan. Staff support personnel from several departments—especially planning, operations, and market research—participate in the work.

> The company's business is a blend of expansion and replacement. The larger newspapers, magazines, and commercial printing shops have many presses and replace them according to some schedule which can be highly influenced by current economic conditions; for replacements can be deferred if required by financial considerations. On the other hand, replacement can be accelerated by new technical developments, especially changes in processes or increases in productivity, which are especially important in the printing industry. The company considers itself as a growth enterprise and is so looked at by investors, which include many institutions. The objective is to get a larger share of the growing market.

> The divisional plans are reviewed at the corporate level. While the divisions look at their specific problems and interests, the corporate review analyzes the plans from a companywide point of view.

At the start of the planning period, Mr. Peterson issues what is called *Contents and Instructions for Preparation of Long-Range Plans*. The required reports consist of nine parts:

I. Summary of Operating Results
   Exhibit A. Shipments and forecast demand (new orders).
   Exhibit B. Level of shipments or forecast demand including a trend line and the compound percentage growth per year.
   Exhibit C. Charts on (1) prime gross profit and operating profit as percent of sales; (2) operating profit and net profit before taxes and capital charge; (3) return on net operating assets.

II. Product/Market Plans and Forecasts: New orders received based on actual past experience for each product line to cover the following information:
   A. Record and forecast of new orders for five past years and five years ahead.
   B. Markets to which the product is sold and basic information considered in developing the market estimates:
      1. Total size, in terms of installations and customers.
      2. "Aging" of in-place equipment.

3. Dominant factors contributing to new orders.
4. Customers' attitude and financial resources for expansion and replacement.
5. New marketing programs, if any, which you foresee as required or desirable.

C. Pricing and financing:
1. Current price information, expected price changes and time to place them into effect for new orders for 1968–1970; effects of price adjustments on competition.
2. Financing and credit terms presently required and changes to be required and included in the forecasts.

D. Product evaluation:
1. Competitive strengths and weaknesses, highly competitive features, most serious detriments to forecasting a greater share of the market.
2. Engineering and development programs included in the plan and affecting products' market performance during forecast period. Programs already decided on and pending.

E. Competitive evaluation:
1. Who is competition, approximate share of business, recent activities to make them stronger or weaker.
2. Possible effect on MGD's market share, adequacy of stated marketing and engineering programs in respect to competition.

F. Future marketing:
1. Best opportunities or requirements for marketing corollary products or services to these customers. Availability and desirability of opportunities for additional growth.
2. Basic trends of this market for this type of equipment during the late 1970s in respect to market trends and probability of significant technical obsolescence.

III. Planning, Development, and Engineering Programs
A. Planning projects: Current and anticipated programs, their objective and status grouped as
1. New products.
2. Major products model change.
3. Market information and analysis.
4. Technical awareness projects.
5. Acquisition/diversification study.

B. Development and engineering projects: Group current and anticipated development efforts by product lines and supply statement of objectives and status or anticipated starting points and rough cost projections. Designate within each product group projects oriented toward:
1. New product development.
2. Model change.
3. Product improvement.

4. Cost reduction.
5. Miscellaneous.

Also describe process or material technical developments with most significant impact on equipment design and/or market potential for specific equipment. Plans for development work along these lines. Possible requirements for external development work by other groups.

IV. Capacities; Sources of Capacity and Demand
  A. Factory capacity: Tabular and chart form of information in factory productive hours:
    1. Present and expected maximum plant capacities available by plants.
       a. Division facilities at practical maximum level of manning regardless of present employment level including 10 percent overtime average.
       b. Equivalent capacity, in hours, of subcontract facilities used whether internal or external to MGD. Rough estimate of productive hours required if produced in plants of the division.
    2. Forecast of productive-hours demand (marketing forecasts in terms of productive hours).
    3. Forecast of shipments: productive hours included in operating results as shipments.
    4. Excess or deficit of capacity:
       a. demand versus shipments
       b. expected maximum plant
    5. Record of production hours shipped 1963–1967.
  B. Engineering Capacity
    1. Forecast of engineering hours required to support shipments forecast.
    2. Forecast of engineering hours required for product-design maintenance and/or new models.
    3. Forecast of engineering hours required for major new equipment designs or new product development as outlined in III.
    4. Total hours requirements.
    5. Present availability (MGD, subcontract and total).
    6. Past input of engineering direct hours for the years 1963–1967 (MGD, subcontract and total).

V. Production Plans: Where multiple facilities are used, provide table per year (1968–1973) of productive hours for each product to be produced in each facility.

VI. Facilities and Facility Capital Budgets
  A. Project requirements for major new facilities; amounts of funds in the plan to acquire these facilities or future requirements for funds not yet committed in the plan.
  B. Specific plans for disposal of facilities, anticipated results, and whether reflected in forecasts of long-term plan.

C. Existing machinery availability by broad machine types, degree of use, age groups for reviewing need for replacement programs (required every four planning cycles).
D. Capital budget requirements; 1969 and first six months of 1970 on a quarterly basis: when funds would be appropriated and when actually expended.
E. Specific new equipment known or forecast to be required for new designs or new products, cost of required equipment, approximate time of installation.

VII. Other Major Programs
Major projects with an appreciable effect on operating results such as
A. Major systems projects.
B. Major manufacturing programs for cost reduction on particular equipment.
C. Any major departmental organization programs or training programs.

VIII. Plan's Major Decisions and Sensitivity
A. Recapitulation of major decisions incorporated in the plan, required final approvals, and date by which plan must meet objectives.
B. Forecasts sensitive to decisions; programs and assumptions included in planning preceding the projections.
C. Programs which by the nature of the risk may be either delayed, less successful than forecast, or fail and thus have highly visible impact on divisional operating profits. Give rough estimate of extent of impact.
D. Areas in which specific corporate or external assistance may be required or desirable in any of these programs.

IX. Forecast of Operating Results: It is expected that pertinent footnotes or comments will be provided as a supplement to these statements to cover any specific assumptions (not covered in other portions of the plan) which are used in developing these projections. Particular attention should be given to supplying comments regarding any significant changes forecast in the levels of employment of direct and/or indirect personnel.

Sales (shipments) will be based on the forecasted price levels for 1968–1970. Accordingly, all prime costs and expense items should be adjusted, as appropriate, to reflect the level expected in these respective years. In 1971–1973 sales price levels, prime costs, and expense rates will be forecast using the 1970 levels.

Although these very elaborate instructions are designed for the needs of a particular company, they may well be useful as a guide in other situations, with appropriate adjustments to fit special conditions. They represent an interesting effort to combine quantitative and qualitative information into a unified whole.

Texas Instruments Incorporated, Dallas

Texas Instruments is a well-known growth company with a reputation for excellent organization and long-term planning.[2] The company was founded in 1930; by 1960 it reached a sales volume of $233 million, and in 1969 sales were $832 million with net profits of $33.5 million. The goal is $3 billion in the late 1970s. The company's basic strategy is "one of deliberate innovation in the create, make, and market functions and of managing this innovation to provide continuing stimulus to the company's growth in usefulness to society." The key to creating change is research and development. The sum total of the company's research, development, and engineering is the *total technical effort,* to which large amounts are earmarked, since it is a principal factor in determining the company's future business.

TI's management of innovation and its programs to motivate all its employees—efforts that are of great importance to their long-term profit planning—are of particular interest to us here.

The company is organized into more than 70 "product-customer centers" (PCC's). This structure reflects the company's fundamental philosophy that all company efforts should be oriented to products and customers rather than to functions, as is the case in most other companies. Each PCC must have the basic capabilities of creating the product, making the product, and marketing the product to the largest possible extent. As explained by Patrick E. Haggerty, chairman of the board, each center regardless of size is like a complete small business with its profit plan and responsibility.

Each PCC can be looked at as a series of three concentric rings. The inner segment is the "create-make-market" ring. The second ring includes the staff activities, while the third, outer ring is an elaborate system of management planning and control procedures focusing on objectives, strategies, and tactics (OST). OST starts with establishment of corporate objectives, exploratory research activities, intracompany objectives and business objectives. For each objective, specific strategies—consisting of detailed tactical action programs (TAPS)—are developed to outline how the objective will be achieved. The performance of the whole system is tested by a variety of measurements.

There are a number of different strategies, according to Mr. Haggerty, such as hold-the-line strategies, modest-gain strategies, and breakthrough

---

[2] This write-up of Texas Instruments' approach to profit planning is based on interviews with executives of the company and Jack B. Weiner's article, "Texas Instruments: 'All Systems Go,'" *Dun's Review,* January 1967.

strategies. However, only breakthrough strategies will have a major impact on the growth and prosperity of the company if they are successful. As many as a hundred strategies may be followed at a particular time; about one fourth of them may be breakthrough strategies with a significant effect on profits.

The acid test of the system, of course, is performance—the extent to which employees, particularly middle management, are willing to accept it. According to Willis Adcock, strategic planning manager in the corporate staff, middle and top managers are deeply involved in the company's programs. Some of the strategies won't have their impact "until the 1970s, but there is nothing more satisfying than a good hard goal, especially if you have played a role in setting it."

One unique feature of the company is that in addition to its regular operating organization it has another highly fluid strategy organization made up of so-called strategy managers. These men have regular jobs where they spend most of their time, but in addition, they have responsibility for one or more specific strategies. As explained by Mr. Adcock, "Just as strategies cross division lines, you can also cross [these] . . . lines for somebody whose services you need. It's really a superimposed organization." A prime strategy, for example, is to reduce costs on a predictable basis to maintain profit margins. Each strategy is implemented with specific tactics. Such a tactic might be a planned program of innovations in production technology to keep the company's cost below competitor's costs.

Each cost center engages in annual bottom-up planning. Each cost-center manager determines his needs for personnel, capital expenditures, travel, overtime, supplies, and so forth. Operations are run on a four-month rolling forecast, which is reviewed and adjusted monthly. Many indexes are employed to optimize costs and performance in all areas, including standards on many indirect costs.[3]

The principal control device is a looseleaf book of *Monthly Performance Reports* kept by each PCC manager, with 55 computer-prepared separate financial statistics for each operating unit. Included are figures for gross profit margin, receivables, cash flow, net sales billed, and percentage return on assets; a profitability summary compares actual results with plans. Another monthly comparison measures operating results. Variances serve as error signals, suggesting analysis and corrective action.

Management has a unique approach to innovation. Too often, Haggerty points out, innovation is associated strictly with research and

---

[3] Ibid., p. 70.

development in the physical sciences. "But [it] . . . can also occur in manufacturing or marketing as well as in 'creating.' The most effective innovation is the one that can be found in all the three categories of create, make, and market."

Senior management has made a serious attempt to institutionalize the process of innovation by developing a system for managing innovation. Management is still struggling to comprehend the process of innovation, to improve the environment for innovation, and to install and operate the OST system for management innovation on an equally effective basis across the whole organization. This system attempts to remove the uncertainty about objectives and strategies and to establish policies with respect to invention and innovation required in general business and technological areas. When innovation has been managed properly and advantage has been taken of the OST system, the amount of significant invention and innovation has been impressive. However, the company's experience so far has indicated that in too many cases strategies have not been well conceived and the resources required have not been properly assessed or managed.

TI has launched a program to involve most employees in team efforts to manage and improve their own jobs in the company, and, through these efforts, to upgrade themselves, add to the overall level of innovativeness, and markedly improve company productivity. Hourly employees now receive salaries in recognition of their increased responsibility for managing their own work. This is part of the company's long-term effort toward having people at every level more involved in planning, doing, and controlling their own work and the work of their natural work group so they will be better able to solve their own problems and achieve personal and company goals.

In the opinion of Mr. Haggerty:

> The board of directors must evolve mechanisms which will allow it to examine and influence, and in the final sense take responsibility for, corporate self-renewal by ensuring that:
>
> 1. The corporate structure, policies, and practices are realistic, sufficiently elastic, and yet powerful enough to cope with the external national and international environment not just as it now exists, but as it will be through future years, and over the entire corporate span of interest.
>
> 2. The corporation's products and services are truly innovative and really are contributing in a major way to constructive change in the world around it.

3. An innovative, aggressive, properly educated and experienced staff of professional managers, scientists, engineers, and other specialists is available and being generated in sufficient depth and talent to meet the corporation's long-range goals.

Fulfillment of this responsibility for self-renewal appears to make it desirable to have directors with the title "Officer of the Board" in addition to the present full-time operating officers serving as directors. This would provide high-level, capable people who have the time to study, to think quietly about, and to comprehend the impact of the rapidly changing internal and external environment and the relationship of both to the company's self-renewal. The officers of the board would have no operating responsibilities. Their duties would relate entirely to their functions as directors and advisers to the board.

One such officer of the board has been added whose principal experience has been developed as a senior executive of TI. Two additional directors have been added whose principal experience has been developed outside the company.

Xerox Corporation, Stamford, Connecticut

The Xerox Corporation has been conspicuous for its tremendous growth over a very short time. In 1960, when Xerox introduced the first 914 copier, profits were $2.6 million on revenues of $40 million. By 1969 profits had increased to $161.4 million on operating revenues of $1.483 billion. Joseph C. Wilson, chairman of the board (chief executive officer from 1946 to 1968), guided the company through this period of dynamic growth.

As the company has grown and diversified, its organization structure has undergone a steady metamorphosis in order to meet changing needs. In the early 1960s the company was organized along functional lines—that is, manufacturing, research and development, marketing. But the growth of operations and the steady expansion into related fields led the company to reorganize, and it now consists of eight basically self-sufficient operating units and four staff groups. The operating units are the business products group; the Xerox education group; the communication products division; the special products and systems division; the Latin American division; Rank Xerox Limited; Xerox Computer Services, Inc.; and Xerox Data Systems, Inc. The four staff groups are research and development, which includes the Palo Alto Research Center; finance and planning, which is responsible for both the operating plan and the long-term plan; marketing, which is responsible for reviewing and advising the president on all marketing plans; and administration, which is responsible for reviewing and advising the president on legal, communications, facilities, procurement, and personnel issues.

The Xerox Education Group, Xerox Data Systems, and Electro-Optical Systems within the special products and systems division became part of Xerox as the result of one or more acquisitions. The most recent acquisition was Scientific Data Systems (since renamed Xerox Data Systems), a scientific and real-time computer manufacturer that operates as a subsidiary corporation rather than as a division; the merger took place in May 1969.

Xerox Corporation, founded as the Haloid Company in 1906, was headquartered in Rochester, New York, until September 1969. At that time, the president's office and more than 150 staff people were moved to Stamford, Connecticut. Headquarters for the Latin American division were also relocated in Stamford at that time. The Xerox Education Group was previously located in Stamford. The Business Products Group—which accounts for more than three-fourths of the company's revenues—and the Communication Products Division are located in Rochester. Xerox Data Systems is located in El Segundo, California. The Special Products and Systems Division is located in Pasadena, California. Rank Xerox headquarters is in London. Corporate headquarters was relocated to remove the company's top command to "neutral" ground—away from the extensive operations in Rochester—on the theory that this removal would make it easier for top management to concentrate on its unique responsibilities.

Before 1965 there had been some formal planning, primarily within functional organizations and without a great deal of coordination between organizations. Recognizing the importance of a coordinated planning effort, in 1965 the company set up a formal planning organization reporting to the president and chief executive officer. Planning groups were also set up within the larger divisions.

At present, the chief planning position of senior vice-president of finance and planning is vacant. It formerly was held by Joseph B. Flavin, now an executive vice-president. Reporting to the vice-president as director of planning is Dr. Robert M. James. Reporting to Dr. James are six planners, organized primarily along organizational lines; that is, each planner is responsible for being the corporate planning representative with one or more operating units.

The planning department coordinates all planning activities, evaluates operating unit plans, and tracks the performance of their programs. It also consolidates information for reports to top management and serves as a coordinating group for corporate staff involvement in reviewing operating unit strategies and plans.

The importance of coordinating long-term planning with short-term financial planning is emphasized within the planning role. In 1967, to facilitate this coordination, the company began to use two-year budgets, which are referred to as operating plans because the term budget implies restraint. Mr. Flavin has noted that "a large company can't plan on a one-year basis because this doesn't provide for the impact of a new product or activity in subsequent years. You cannot concentrate on today; concentrate on tomorrow and today will take care of itself." The long-term plan, which includes the two-year operating plan plus plans for five years beyond, serves as a planning bridge between current operations and development programs and the long-range goals and strategies of the company. The long-term plan is an expression of future business opportunities, problems, and strategies linked to, but not extrapolated from, the operating plan. A longer frame of reference requires less detailed planning, but more strategic analysis with broader assumptions and more options to counter the greater uncertainty.

The organization and responsibility for planning are handled somewhat differently within each division, so no overall generalizations can be made. Within the business products group, the marketing organization is responsible for business and product strategy, while the responsibility for generating the assumptions that go into a plan is divided among the various functional organizations. The appropriate groups estimate market demand, marketing costs, manufacturing costs, development costs, and so forth. The coordination of these assumptions and the generation of the forecast per se is the responsibility of the control department. Extensive use is made of computers in this process since the product line is broad, interactive, and spread among a large number of customers.

In order to provide a target against which plans can be developed, top management annually reviews and, if necessary, revises long-term corporate and operating unit objectives. In a statement prepared for the information of company personnel, several guiding principles were described in the following terms:

1. To be oriented always towards our customers' needs and to translate those needs into product concepts within our field and capabilities.

2. To maintain well-trained and aggressive sales organizations backed by imaginative advertising and sales promotion.

3. To maintain a creative, strong program of organization for basic and applied research, product development, and engineering.

4. To maintain progressive and competent quality- and cost-conscious manufacturing organizations capable of making complex mechanical,

electrical, and optical equipment and highly specialized supplies.

5. To plan and carry out our activities under effective management control so that predetermined profit goals are achieved.

6. To recognize the dignity of each individual in the organization and maintain a concern for both his welfare and his desire to excel.

7. To recognize that a successful business must serve well its customers, its shareholders, its people, and its suppliers and must fulfill its responsibilities to society.

In addition to these philosophical goals, specific financial objectives are given to each operating unit in terms of revenue, profit, and ROS (return on sales). The difference between the operating unit plan and the objectives specified by the corporation is known as the "planning gap." It is believed in Xerox that a planning gap is essential, since, if there is no gap, the target is not rigorous enough. Each planning gap becomes a target for improvement of the strategies and plans of the operating units.

Because of the dynamic growth of the company and broadening of its markets, difficulties have been encountered in fully developing and implementing a planning cycle. However, the current planning cycle is this: Top management sends out a set of objectives and goals in April; the operating units prepare their plans and submit them for corporate review; the planning department coordinates the review of the operating unit plans by the functional corporate staff groups; comments and recommendations developed by the staff groups are forwarded to the operating units and to corporate management; in June top management holds a review with each operating unit; during the summer the units respond to management's questions, aimed at closing the profit and review gaps that have been identified in each unit's plans; and then, in the fall, a two-year operating plan is prepared, consistent with the long-term plan that finally evolved. A long-term plan is based primarily on a series of program plans aimed at achieving chosen business strategies; that is, the corporation's planning and development activities are basically oriented toward the program-management concept. Each development program is broken down into a series of task plans, with associated manpower and expenses. These task plans form the basis for the functional development plans. Revenue forecasts on a program basis form the basis for manufacturing and marketing departmental plans that cut across programs. Hence, the flow is from business strategy to product plans to functional plans, since the basic organization structure within operating units is on a functional basis. There is, of course, feedback as well from functional plans to product plans to improve the operational implications of functional plans.

While these mechanisms have remained relatively unchanged, the overall thrust of the planning function has changed substantially with the growth of the corporation. From the origination of a formal planning function through 1969, the goal of diversification beyond the base being built by the 813, 914 and 2400 product families had a major influence on planning activities. While the internal and external opportunities considered were numerous and varied, the ventures and acquisitions undertaken were always directed toward specific goals related to the established corporate capability and toward interest in businesses related to the utilization of information. While the business products group concentrated on development of the xerographic technology and on planning for improved reproduction products, corporate management assembled a strong base of operations in the education and computer fields. In 1969 a new agreement was negotiated with the Rank Organization of London to give Xerox a firm control over its destiny worldwide and to enable Rank Xerox to market other than xerographic products of the corporation.

With these achievements, Xerox now has a foundation for developing a broad leadership in fields related to what the president and chief executive officer, C. Peter McColough, has termed the "architecture of information." The 1960s were characterized by the dramatically successful development of the xerographic copier/duplicator business, the identification of long-range corporate goals, and the establishment of basic worldwide operations for fulfilling these goals. The 1970s will be characterized by continued growth and refinement of the existing office product, education, and computer businesses, with a rational blending of these business capabilities to strengthen and extend the offering of products and services in chosen fields. For example, the graphic and communication technologies within the business products and communication products divisions have potential application in computer system peripherals; copier/duplicator products are already prevalent in educational institutions; computer and communication products have potential uses in education; office document reproduction and distribution systems of the future may utilize computer and communication technologies; systems application opportunities for these technologies are numerous; and the internationalization of manufacturing, engineering, and marketing operations is far from complete.

Therefore, the development of strategies and plans during the 1970s must involve the joint efforts of managers throughout the corporation. Decisions must be made with a common frame of reference concerning the objectives, assumptions, and risks of strategies. A chief role of planning will be to help bring various frames of reference into reconciliation and to facilitate communication among levels of management and across functions, extending from near-term realities to long-term objectives. Planning will assist management in defining these frames of reference and in evaluating them for realism and consistency with long-term goals.

In this role, planning serves as a catalyst. The planner must inspire interest in strategic issues, draw out management judgments, channel information, question assumptions, assure that strategies and plans are thoroughly developed and evaluated, seek resolution among points of view, coordinate efforts, track assumptions and progress, and see that plans are kept alive through updating. To perform such functions effectively, one must induce candor and trust by remaining objective and open-minded. The natural tendency to cling to concepts or plans that one participates in developing must be suppressed. In order to accommodate differences among issues and differences among managers, planning procedures and documentation formats must be flexible. At the corporate level these functions are carried out by a small staff team working informally with operating unit management to complete necessary staff work in advance of scheduled management decisions.

The status of planning at Xerox reflects both the difficulty of instituting a good planning process in a dynamic growth company and, simultaneously, the importance of having a good planning process in order to guide that growth adequately.

16

A Process Company: Standard Oil Company (Indiana)

Process companies differ from most manufacturing companies primarily in terms of facilities planning and production planning and control. Process companies are capital intensive in most instances, and their cost structures are different from those of less capital-intensive companies. This influences their approaches to buying raw materials and to setting prices for their finished products. In addition, the size and time horizons of their capital investments require a special effort in capital budgeting.

To be sure, international petroleum companies have major planning problems associated with insuring their supply of raw material at an acceptable price. They also must anticipate political developments within the countries from which they obtain their supplies and to which they at present—or might in the future—sell. Perhaps their planning horizon is a bit longer and their raw material and marketing planning are more worldly in terms of the factors they must consider, but the essence of their long-term profit planning task is similar to that of the other companies already considered. Of special interest to us, however, is the systematic way in which Standard Oil Company (Indiana) has planned its planning process.

With its consolidated subsidiaries, Standard Oil of Indiana forms one of the largest integrated organizations in the petroleum industry. It is engaged in the exploration, production, and transportation of crude oil and natural gas and in the manufacturing, transportation, and marketing of all major petroleum products, including petrochemicals.

In the United States, Standard Oil of Indiana ranks sixth in crude oil production, third in refinery runs, and fourth in gasoline sales. Through subsidiary and associated companies it also carries on business and operations in some 30 foreign countries. In 1969 total revenues were $4.322 billion and net earnings were $321 million. Total capital and exploration expenditures were $846 million. At the end of 1969 its total assets were $5.151 billion.

Since 1961 Standard has functioned as a parent company concerned with overall policy guidance, coordination of operations, performance evaluation, and financial planning for the corporation. Its operations are carried out through four major subsidiaries, all wholly owned, as follows:

- *Pan American Petroleum Corporation*—exploration and production of crude oil and natural gas in North America.
- *The American Oil Company*—refining, transportation, and marketing of petroleum products, marketing of liquefied petroleum gas, and manufacture and sale of fertilizers in the United States.
- *Amoco International Oil Company*—foreign petroleum operations.
- *Amoco Chemicals Corporation*—manufacture and sale of chemical products worldwide.

The Corporate Planning Philosophy

This corporate structure dictates some of the subject matter with which planning at Standard Oil of Indiana must be concerned. To some extent at least, all Standard's operations are interrelated in various ways. The questions considered at Standard in the planning process include: What overall balance of operations is desirable in order to survive and operate profitably in an uncertain future? What strategic hedges are appropriate against possible changes in ground rules such as prorationing, import quotas, and depletion allowance? In controlling the reinvestment of funds, should Standard concentrate on the domestic main line, where it has its greatest experience and competence? If so, which end of it? Or should more emphasis be given to the branches such as petrochemicals and liquefied petroleum gas? How much foreign operations does Standard want and how much can it afford? Should Standard be partially diversifying out of the petroleum business?

Although Standard Oil of Indiana has been engaged in the long-range planning of major facilities since the early 1950s, integrated planning on a broad and formal basis was not instituted until 1961. Consistent with the operating philosophy of the corporation, Standard's detail planning is done by the subsidiaries on a fully decentralized basis. The corporate planning department in the parent company is involved in the development of corporate objectives and is directly concerned with broad allocation of resources among subsidiaries, general guidance regarding subsidiary planning procedures and report requirements, and review and consolidation and evaluation of the subsidiary plans. The parent staff, with assistance from subsidiary staffs, also formulates a consensus position on key aspects of the environment for the plan period.

Each subsidiary prepares its own plans within guidelines furnished by the parent and develops projections of capital spending, profits, and cash flow, as well as projections of sales and production volumes and other operating parameters. The central staff reviews subsidiary plans, consolidates them, and evaluates the overall program for feasibility and desirability in the context of consolidated resources and objectives. Frequently, the subsidiaries and the central staff work together in making any adjustments that may be necessary to produce a satisfactory and feasible plan. The plans cover a ten-year period and are updated annually.

These ten-year plans provide a framework within which current decisions are tested and resolved. In accord with this concept of the planning process, Indiana Standard does not consider its ten-year plan to be a blueprint of its future activities. Instead, it is the starting point for the preparation of such a blueprint. For a corporation, the control budget comes closest to the concept of a blueprint. At Standard, the first two years of the ten-year plan serve as a basis for the preparation of the two-year control budget. Thus the near-term operations of the corporation are continually assessed against a ten-year perspective.

The Planning Organization

The planning and economics department of Standard Oil Company (Indiana) is staffed with about a dozen professionals. It reports to the vice-president, planning and coordination, who in turn reports to the executive vice-president of the parent company. Overall policy guidance for the planning function is provided by Standard's planning committee, whose present eleven members include seven representatives from the parent company, all of whom are directors and/or officers of the corporation, and one representative from each of the four major subsidiaries. One of the subsidiaries is represented on this committee by its president and the other three are represented by their executive vice-presidents. The committee is chaired by the executive vice-president of the parent company.

This involvement of top management in the planning process facilitates ready communication at the top level and a free interplay of ideas as the plan is being developed. The ten-year plan, with its breakdown of profits, expenditures, and cash flow by subsidiaries, has also become the vehicle by which the parent's broad control over future subsidiary operations is exercised.

The central planning staff comprises three divisions which reflect the three general areas of activity in which it is engaged. The economics division concerns itself with broad aspects of environmental forecasting, which leads to the selection of planning premises in regard to the setting in which the corporation will function during the plan period. These premises are developed jointly with staff economists and other appropriate personnel from the subsidiaries involved. The planning development and procedures division is concerned with research on the planning process and how it can be improved. This group is operations-research-oriented and maintains liaison with the central computer sciences department. The planning division is responsible for coordination of the planning activity with the subsidiaries and for interpreting and evaluating the subsidiary plans from the parent company's viewpoint. The latter two divisions are only loosely divided, and the backgrounds and talents of their members are largely comparable and interchangeable; in practice, though, it has been fruitful to assign an individual to each subsidiary for in-depth follow-through. The departmental organization is deliberately kept somewhat flexible, with overlap in functions to take advantage of the strengths of the people involved. In particular, the planning development and procedures function and the subsidiary coordination function overlap significantly.

This effort of the central planning staff in the parent company is supplemented by the detailed planning activity in the major subsidiaries, which also have formalized planning procedures. The general office of every major subsidiary has planning groups charged with responsibilities for coordination of all ten-year plan activities within the subsidiary, consolidation of divisional plans prepared by the operating divisions, and liaison with the parent company planning staff. The planning group within each subsidiary receives policy guidance from the subsidiary top management and usually operates through a ten-year-plan working committee of ten to fifteen people who represent, on a part-time basis, each one of the operating departments. In turn, these representatives are responsible for insuring that the divisional plans prepared either in the field or in the general office reflect the best thinking of the operating management, consistent with the policy guidance from the subsidiary top management.

Evidently, the long-range planning at Standard Oil of Indiana is not an ivory-tower exercise carried out by a few specialists. Rather, it is a grass-roots effort involving the participation of scores of individuals in every major subsidiary. This procedure not only provides an excellent perspective for operating managers in their day-to-day responsibilities but also secures their identification with the objectives of the plan and a commitment to attain them. The plan is not imposed on the managers from the top but is built from the ground up. Representatives of the parent planning staff sit on the subsidiary ten-year-plan committees as appropriate to insure good communication throughout the corporation during various phases of the planning process.

The Planning and Control Cycle

The continuous planning activity at Indiana Standard is implemented annually according to this approximate schedule—

Planning Guidelines	December
Subsidiary Planning Statements	February
Subsidiary Ten-Year Plans	April
Consolidated Ten-Year Plan	June
Control-Budget Guidelines	July
Evaluation and Strategy Report	October
Two-Year Control Budgets	November

Planning guidelines are issued by the parent company in December and are largely limited to the broad allocation of capital expenditures to each subsidiary over the period of the plan. Usually there are no specific restrictions as to the operating programs subsidiaries may include within the allocated capital budget. For the time being, it has not been practical or advantageous to establish profitability standards for the ten-year plans of the individual subsidiaries, although of course the subsidiaries are quite selective in regard to the programs they include. The calendar year during which the consolidated plan is issued follows the first year of the prior control budget and is not part of the planning period; however, the subsidiaries have discretion in regard to the second year of the control budget, which becomes the first year of the ten-year plan. Typically a subsidiary begins its ten-year-plan activity in October, subject to revisions in scope and basis when parent planning guidance is received.

Concurrent with the planning guidelines, the parent company issues planning premises representing a common specified environment so that the ten-year plans of the individual subsidiaries can proceed from a consistent base. These are developed in joint forecast committees composed of knowledgeable individuals from each of the subsidiary companies under the chairmanship of a parent company staff economist; they represent a consolidated company consensus position on certain key aspects of the environmental outlook. The environmental forecasts cover the long-range demand/supply picture for all energy in general and petroleum in particular, with price projections for the latter; background projections are prepared of the general economy, the state of present and future technology, and the impact of domestic and international political developments. Each of the several elements tends to impinge on the others. At Standard the forecast typically starts with the general economy first, then considers the demand/supply for energy, and, finally, the demand/supply and prices for petroleum products. Technological forecasting is relatively difficult to come to grips with, and for the most part the burden of technological forecasting rests on the perception of informed people in each subsidiary.

The assessment of political developments is an even fuzzier area. The political economy in a country can change suddenly. More frequently there are subtle forces at work that can easily go unnoticed and yet have a profound influence on the operating results. When a major environmental uncertainty faces the industry as a whole, as during the recent debate in Washington on the crude oil import controls, Standard finds it expedient to develop a contingency plan with an alternate set of environmental assumptions.

Planning statements usually received from the subsidiaries in February provide a concise description of the objectives, strategy, key assumptions, and major features that form the basis of the subsidiary plan. They also highlight any major variations from previous plans. Besides indicating the course chosen by the subsidiary to implement the planning guidelines, the planning statement furnishes sufficient quantitative information to insure intersubsidiary coordination in regard to material flows.

Subsidiary ten-year plans are received by the parent company in April and are distributed to the planning committee immediately. However, a discussion of these plans is held in abeyance while the consolidation is in progress. The narrative portion of each subsidiary report includes a brief statement of objectives and strategy, a statement of environmental as well as developmental (that is, program) assumptions, a statement of operating and financial results, and a section on evaluation. The evaluation section provides subsidiary management's own appraisal of its plan and includes a consideration of the realism of the plan, balance among functions, cost and productivity trends, and so on. It also identifies the timing of major decisions—that is, decision lead times; decisions that are assumed in the plan, but that are dependent on the turn of environmental events; and sequential events that are dependent on the outcome of earlier actions. It includes a summary of work currently in progress and work indicated as desirable to resolve issues raised in the plan.

Numerical data are transmitted by the subsidiary to the parent in a specified form suitable for computer input for consolidation purposes and are also tabulated in the ten-year-plan document itself. The data received in the plan period vary from subsidiary to subsidiary but the detail is usually somewhat greater than that generally contained in the historical statistical section of the annual report of major oil companies. These include the profit-and-loss, cash-flow, and balance-sheet schedules. The plans record in greater detail the discretionary spending projections of the subsidiary, by functions and by geographic areas. The term discretionary spending includes all items of an investment nature, regardless of the conventional accounting treatment. In particular, expensed reinvestment such as exploration and research expenditures are included in this category. Considerable detail is provided on personnel to permit long-range manpower planning. The data usually include a current inventory as well as a projection of requirements of personnel by academic training and job classification. The subsidiaries use their own computer programs during the various phases of plan preparation.

The consolidated ten-year plan, issued by the parent planning department in early June, is expository in nature with a minimum of evaluation. The purpose of this document is to provide a frame of reference against which individual subsidiary plans can be appraised by top management without an undue time gap between the completion of the subsidiary plans and discussion of them by the planning committee. The consolidated plan document includes the consolidated company results as well as summaries of individual subsidiary plans. The presentation includes ten years of history for all of the key parameters.

The review of the results of the subsidiary and consolidated ten-year plans by the planning committee and management, together with any updating information, leads to the formulation of guidelines for the two-year control budget in July. The control budgets are prepared by the comptroller's departments of the subsidiaries and are coordinated by the parent comptroller's department. However, because of their familiarity with the

A Process Company: Standard Oil Company (Indiana)

bases implied in the control budget guidelines, the central and subsidiary planning staffs are frequently consulted while the budgets are being formulated by the subsidiaries. Concurrent with the control budget guidelines, the parent company planning department also issues updated specific environmental assumptions for the budget period; these are to be used uniformly by all the subsidiaries. Like the ten-year-plan premises, this consensus position is a responsibility of the joint forecast committee under the chairmanship of a parent company staff economist. These budgets are received by the parent company in November.

In the meantime, the central planning staff is engaged in the preparation of the evaluation and strategy report. This report, usually issued in October, is designed to furnish staff support to top management on matters of policy concerning growth, balance, direction, etc. The format and content of this report are flexible to accommodate the needs of the currently relevant issues, which seem to change from year to year; it usually includes, however, a comparison of the results with the company's past history and with the performance of other oil companies. This report sets the stage for development of planning guidelines for the next plan, and the cycle repeats again.

The dynamic nature of the environment and massive scope of the company's operations makes annual updating of the plans a meaningful and rewarding exercise. The annual revision not only adds a year to the planning horizon but provides scope for integrating the long-range implications of the company's actual operations for one more year. It also permits updating of the environmental outlook and company's response to any new challenges that become evident after the preparation of the previous plan. Evaluation work carried out in the interim period also leads to improved strategies, which are then translated into the revised plan. Although the ten-year-plan document per se is updated annually, broad scoping studies throughout the year by the central planning staff lead to continuous updating of the major financial parameters.

Discussion

Two characteristics of the company's planning not always found in the planning function are active participation in policy making and deep involvement in the immediate future. Active participation in policy making does not mean that the planning staff makes policy. Rather, the mechanics of putting together a master plan for the total operation forces management to make vital policy decisions. In many respects, the planning personnel serve as staff to the board of directors in its policy-making role. It is also through the planning process that the new policies are being put into effect.

Since in many areas a significant change in direction occurs as a result of this process, planning is inevitably concerned with the short-term future. While long-term considerations may have dictated the new policies, the most pressing problems created are immediate ones covering the next two or three years. Planning's familiarity with the background to the change, the principles involved, and the development of the relevant statistics has made it a logical participant in short-term activities.

Indeed, the objective of Indiana Standard's long-range planning process is not so much to schedule action in the distant future as to influence current decision. For use as a scheduling device, planning would logically be designed to attain a preset and specific goal through the precise integration of its many details. There may be considerable stress on efficiency in such a plan all up and down the line, and it may lend itself admirably to the setting up of an effective monitoring system. However, such a plan provides little room for true creativity and innovation in any broad sense. The resulting plan would be fixed rather than dynamic. At Standard the endeavor is to get away from the scheduling concept of planning (although some of this is inevitable in such a massive corporation) and to emphasize the innovative and evaluative aspects of planning.

Standard Oil of Indiana views its long-range planning program as an articulation of the company's strategy for the future and the evaluation of that strategy in terms of probable consequences. The plans thus give a focus and a sense of direction to the operations of today, so that the company will best be able to cope with the cloudy and uncertain problems that lie ahead. The purpose is to test out a given program or strategy to see what the consequences will be and determine what change, if any, should be made in the near-term course of the corporation. In a sense, this type of planning is an aiming device, like the telescopic sight of a gun, to see what end result may be logically expected if the enterprise proceeds on its present course or along some new direction under study.

The fact that the new plan deviates considerably from the old plan is, in itself, no condemnation of the planning process. In fact annual updating is rather pleasantly anticipated, for the planning process would have to be sterile not to germinate better new approaches. This attitude also explains the close integration of planning and the control-budget process at Standard, inasmuch as a major contribution of planning at Standard is to influence the selection of control budget guidelines that determine the near-term course of the corporation.

Exhibits

1. Framework for Business Planning, Stanford Research Institute   167
2. Annual Corporate Planning Process, United Air Lines, Inc.   168
3. Preamble to Corporate Objectives and Guidelines for Operating Planning, Sylvania Electric Products Inc., a Subsidiary of General Telephone and Electronics Corporation   169
4. Statement of Corporate Objectives, Hewlett-Packard Company, October 1969   170
5. Corporate Objectives, Sylvania Electric Products Inc., a Subsidiary of General Telephone and Electronics Corporation   170
6. Statement of Goals, a Large Manufacturing Company   171
7. Strategic Planning: Objectives and Definitions, Sylvania Electric Products Inc., a Subsidiary of General Telephone and Electronics Corporation   172
8. Long-Range Planning, Excerpt from Corporate Financial Manual, Northrop Corporation   174
9. Five-Year Business Plan, Raytheon Company   175
10. Preparation of Long-Range Plans, American Airlines, Inc. (Excerpts)   207
11. Position Description for Senior Vice-President–Economic Planning, United Air Lines, Inc.   208

12. Statements of Basic Function for Economic Planning Positions, United Air Lines, Inc. 209
13. Position Description for Corporate Director of Development Planning 210
14. Position Descriptions for Director–Planning and Business Development and Director of Financial Planning, Samsonite Corporation 211
15. A Selection of 1968 Newspaper Display Advertisements for Planning Executives 218
16. Planning Committee Functions, Trans World Airlines Inc. 220
17. Duties of the Central Corporate Planning Staff at American Airlines, Inc. 221
18. Appropriation Requests, Corporate Procedure Manual, an Automobile Manufacturer 221
19. Financial Analysis Summary, Appropriation Requests, Corporate Procedure Manual, an Automobile Manufacturer 223
20. Request Justification, Corporate Procedure Manual, an Automobile Manufacturer 224
21. Postproject Evaluation (Projected and Actual Accomplishments), Corporate Procedure Manual, an Automobile Manufacturer 225
22. Project Appropriation Request, Appropriations Manual, Ford Motor Company 226
23. Project Worksheet, St. Regis Paper Company 227
24. Checklists for Market Positions and Market Developments, Continental Can Company, Inc. 228
25. Checklist for Technological Developments, Continental Can Company, Inc. 229
26. Form for Division Cash Plan, a Food Company 230
27. Form for Projection of Sales, Income, and Return on Employed Capital for Divisions' Long-Range Plans, Continental Can Company, Inc. 231
28. Form for Sales and Net Income by Year for Divisions' Long-Range Plans, Continental Can Company, Inc. 232
29. Instructions for Preparing Financial Summary of Long-Range Plan, Continental Can Company, Inc. 233
30. Form for Consolidated Long-Range Financial Plan, St. Regis Paper Company 234

31. Form for Cash Flow and Ratios for Long-Range Financial Plan, St. Regis Paper Company — 235
32. Long-Range Plan, Phase I, Operating Income Worksheet, St. Regis Paper Company — 236
33. Instructions for Completing Long-Range Financial Planning Forms, St. Regis Paper Company — 237
34. Illustrative Planning Strategies, a Food Company — 240
35. Form for Summary of Major Product Program Analysis, an Electronics Manufacturer — 242
36. Form for Reporting Commercial Potential for Major New Products — 243
37. Outline of Analysis of Product Objectives and Description for Major New Product, an Electronics Manufacturer — 244
38. Outline of Analysis of Market Opportunity for Major New Product, an Electronics Manufacturer — 244
39. Form for Calculating Effect on Annual Profit of a Major New Product, an Electronics Manufacturer — 245
40. Form for Reporting Allocation of Manpower and Detail of Development Costs for a Major New Product, an Electronics Manufacturer — 246
41. Form for Reporting Unit Costs and Profitability for a Major New Product, an Electronics Manufacturer — 247
42. President's Letter Announcing Start of a Formal Long-Range Planning Process, Continental Can Company, Inc. — 248
43. Introduction to "Guide for Preparing a Divisional Long-Range Plan," Continental Can Company, Inc. — 249
44. Table of Contents for "Guide for Preparing a Divisional Long-Range Plan," Continental Can Company, Inc. — 250
45. Form for Forecast of Annual Capital Requirements for Divisions' Long-Range Plans, Continental Can Company, Inc. — 251
46. Memorandum from Director of Planning and Research, Outlining Contents and Approach to the Preparation of Divisions' Long-Range Plans for 1969–1973, Miehle-Goss-Dexter, Inc. — 252

Exhibit 1. Framework for Business Planning, Stanford Research Institute

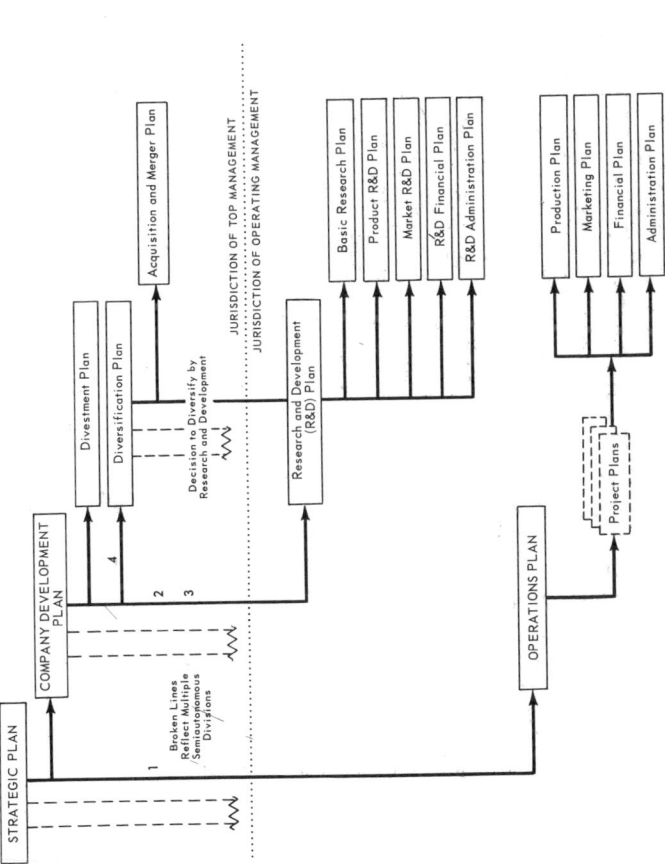

Exhibit 2. Annual Corporate Planning Process, United Air Lines, Inc.

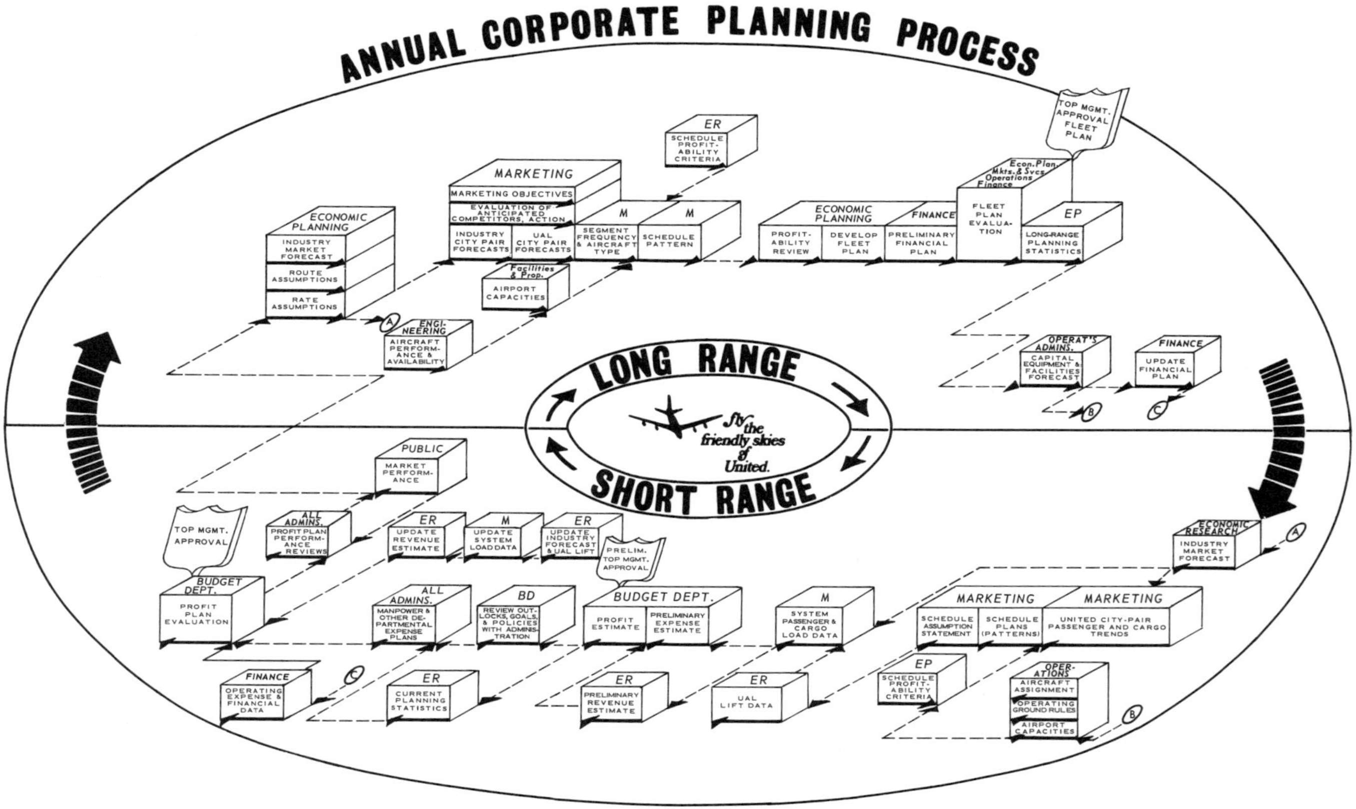

Exhibit 3. Preamble to Corporate Objectives and Guidelines for Operating Planning, Sylvania Electric Products Inc., a Subsidiary of General Telephone and Electronics Corporation

The process of long-range planning is an energetic, continual process through which management develops strategies for the accomplishment of its objectives. To insure that the planning process at Sylvania is ambitious, realistic, and a "way of life," the company must revise its goals and actively project its course of action in a constantly changing business environment. The planning procedure must continually examine different methods of operation: What new markets are available? What changes should be made in our product policy? What will be the future resource requirements? How high a rate of return must we achieve? How is profitability going to be improved in the future?

Long-range planning for our company is *not:*

- A statistical extrapolation of past performance.
- An end in itself.
- A hopeful projection of the future without a sound foundation of facts.
- The formation of a distinct activity completely separate from other phases of managing our business.
- The creation of a rigid master plan depriving line management of its initiative and flexibility.

Long-range planning, as we envision it for our company, is a pervasive and integral part of managing our business. It includes:

1. Formulation of broad corporate objectives and objectives for each division and function compatible with the broad corporate objectives.
2. Review of short- and long-range economic outlook.
3. Evaluation of strengths and weaknesses in terms of competitive position.
4. Establishment of goals which define specific measurable accomplishments to be made currently and in the next four years toward the established objectives.
5. Preparation of specific operational plans, after considering possible alternatives, to set forth in detail how the goals are to be attained, with a built-in provision for periodic reviews and modifications as conditions change.
6. Coordination of all our planning to increase cohesiveness of the company, to insure integration of efforts, and to avoid wasteful diversions.

Exhibit 4. Statement of Corporate Objectives, Hewlett-Packard Company, October 1969

Profit: To generate the highest level of profit consistent with our other objectives.

Customers: To provide products and services of the greatest possible value to our customers.

Fields of interest: To enter new fields when the ideas we have—together with our technical, manufacturing, and marketing skills—assure that we can make a needed and profitable contribution to the field.

Growth: To let our growth be limited only by our ability to develop and produce technical products that satisfy real customer needs.

Our people: To help HP people share in the company's success, which they make possible; to provide job security based on their performance; to recognize their individual achievements; and to insure the personal satisfaction that comes from a sense of accomplishment in their work.

Management: To foster initiative and creativity by allowing the individual great freedom of action in attaining well-defined objectives.

Citizenship: To honor our obligations to society by being an economic, intellectual, and social asset to each nation and each community in which we operate.

Exhibit 5. Corporate Objectives, Sylvania Electric Products Inc., a Subsidiary of General Telephone and Electronics Corporation

With Respect to Product:

1. To provide high-quality products and services in the lighting, electronics, communications, and related fields, at the lowest possible cost to our customers consistent with the objectives of General Telephone and Electronics and with the profit objectives below stated; and to develop new and improved products and services in these fields by anticipating future needs of our customers and constantly increasing our overall competence.
2. To maintain a position of leadership in all areas of the company's business.
3. To maintain and strengthen the corporate image of GT&E as well as Sylvania, including recognition of the brand name "SYLVANIA" and to achieve an ever growing customer recognition of Sylvania as a single entity through greater cohesiveness in all areas of the company's operations.

With Respect to Profits:

4. To maintain earnings sufficient to provide a reasonable return upon the capital employed in the business—i.e., an amount sufficient to meet the dividend requirements of GT&E and provide additional capital for Sylvania's future growth.

5. To exploit fully all markets, existing and new, where Sylvania's capabilities give reasonable assurance of a level of return on investment compatible with that expected by GT&E, giving due consideration to the risk involved.
6. To maintain a pattern of sales growth at a profit level surpassing the average of each industry in which Sylvania competes.
7. To realize the maximum income attainable through vertical integration within Sylvania, consistent with the foregoing objectives, and through use of the capabilities of the other companies of the General System.
8. To plan the overall business of Sylvania so as to reduce to a minimum the effect of seasonal or cyclical economic swings.

With Respect to Employees:

9. To provide our employees, without regard to race, color, creed, or national origin, with an expanding opportunity for challenging and rewarding work under favorable working conditions, with competent leadership and competitive compensation.

With Respect to the Public:

10. To maintain high ethical standards in all our dealings with customers, employees, suppliers, and the public; and to sustain and strengthen the recognition of our company as a "good neighbor" in the various plant and laboratory communities in which we operate.

Exhibit 6. Statement of Goals, a Large Manufacturing Company

The ultimate achievement of division objectives depends upon its ability to perform according to plan. Intermediate standards of performance are required to monitor progress toward this end.

Goals are defined as those statements which specify the quantitative results that are to be achieved during the planning period. Goals must be realistic if they are to be more helpful than harmful. Therefore, goals are *not* predetermined. Instead, they evolve during the later stages of the planning process as targets or standards of performance against which actual results can be measured. Goals which are developed in this manner will serve as stepping stones in the attainment of division objectives.

Goals must therefore be established within the framework of division objectives. The greatest motivational value will be realized if all managers participate in setting their own goals. However, in order to avoid suboptimization, these standards of performance should be selected only after careful evaluation of all possible alternatives. The final selection of program plans and strategies will establish division goals which will become the standards of performance.

Goals fall into two categories, both of which have attainment dates:

1. *Statistical goals* such as sales, profit before taxes, return on capital employed, return on sales, capital turnover, and share of market.
2. *Milestones* such as program milestones and project milestones.

For example, the goals of the company might be as follows:

Statistical Goals	1969	1970	1971	1972	1973
Sales (millions of dollars)	72	76	82	86	90
Return on capital employed (%)	8.8	8.3	9.4	10.4	10.9

	Milestones	Quarter
1969	Initiate cost improvement program at main plant	1
	Complete design and field testing of sorting machinery	2
	Complete construction of warehouse at _____	3
	Begin construction of new plant at _____	4
1970	Start shipping from new warehouse at _____	1
	Kick-off marketing program of new machine type _____	1
	Introduce new sorting machinery	2
	Establish new regional office at _____	3
	Complete construction of new plant at _____	4
1971	Establish new dealerships in western states	1 and 2
	Direct major advertising effort to wholesalers in the Midwest	2 and 3
	Begin redesign of machinery type _____	4
1972	Establish new dealerships in mountain states	1
	Begin construction of new warehouse at _____	2
	Field test new machinery type _____	2 and 3
	Continue advertising effort to wholesalers	3
	Complete construction of warehouse at _____	4
1973	Start shipping from new warehouse at _____	1
	Direct major advertising effort for new machinery type _____	2
	Introduce new machinery type _____	3
	Begin design of new machinery type _____	3 and 4

Exhibit 7. Strategic Planning: Objectives and Definitions, Sylvania Electric Products Inc., a Subsidiary of General Telephone and Electronics Corporation

I. Objectives of the Strategic Plan
   A. Primary Objectives
      1. *Flexibility:* the plan should contain discrete elements which are meaningful for the divisions to prepare and which lend themselves to various analytical techniques at the corporate level.
      2. *Motivation:* division personnel should be encouraged by the plan guidelines to be imaginative, to "stretch" their division; planning must be substituted for projection.
      3. *Control:* the plan, when translated into expected financial results,

should be structured so as to pinpoint responsibility and accountability for achieving these results.
    4. *Informative:* the plan should provide the kinds of information about the division's future so as to foster a more meaningful approval process at the corporate level.
    5. *Integration:* coordination of all facets of planning should be provided for in the plan.
  B. Secondary Objectives
    1. *Uniformity:* the plan must culminate in a definite financial budget for publication, and fit any GT&E and Sylvania requirements for such.
    2. *Adaptability:* the more it resembles our current planning procedure, the easier the plan will be to sell.
    3. *Simplicity:* the simpler the definitions, guidelines, and techniques of the plan, the easier it will be for the divisions to understand and meaningfully follow; the plan should avoid multiple or "flexible" definitions.
    4. *Communication:* allowance should be made for free interdivisional exchange of plan information; sought here is coordination of interdependent divisions.
II. Definitions
  A. Operating Plan
  A projection of operations which has as its base the current level of division strengths and weaknesses. . . .

  We are encouraging the divisions, in the operating plan, to examine carefully how they can maximize their future position using only the tools which are available to them *as of today.* No substantial "help" from other Sylvania sources should be included or expected. By limiting the resources available, the operating plan is expected to be relatively unimaginative and conservative and show only nominal growth at best.
  B. Development Plan
  Composed of specific activities, projects, or acquisitions having a favorable profit impact. Plans which will cause decreased profits now but profit improvement later will be included as a development plan—their acceptance will depend on the particular circumstances.

  These are discrete, strategic decisions involving significant shifts in emphasis or direction from current levels of operations. The development plan allows the divisions to come forward with ideas which they would never dream of incorporating into their profit plans as currently prepared.

  New York will approve or disapprove each development plan. Those approved will be incorporated into the operational plan, resulting in a strategic plan. The divisions are committed to this package and should prepare full-blown financial statements to reflect the dollars involved.
  C. Acquisition Plan
  Corporate and/or group acquisition strategies designed to fill the gap between internal growth (sum of all division strategic plans) and

corporate growth objectives (regardless of their source). End result: sum of operating plans plus sum of development plans approved plus acquisition plan equals SEPI official strategic plan. . . .

"Arbitrary" goal-setting can be done at any level, at any stage of the plan. Corporate staff can analyze, concur with or disagree on any element of division operating or development plan; or can set its own corporate goals. Top-level corporate management is "forced" to do some original, formal planning of its own.

D. Future of Strategic Planning

The hope is . . . that division personnel will gradually grow accustomed to the system. Eventually, we should be able to transfer much of the initiative for good, imaginative planning to them from corporate management, freeing the latter to concentrate on overall corporate direction and image through the acquisition plan.

The more comprehensive analysis which is possible through examination of discrete budget parts will enable us to feed better information to corporate management—hence more informed decision making.

Exhibit 8. Long-Range Planning, Excerpt from Corporate Financial Manual, Northrop Corporation

---

Policy: To provide for the achievement of corporate growth objectives and goals, each division, subsidiary, or profit center will submit on an annual basis a complete, integrated long-range plan. It will encompass the following operating plans: marketing, overhead technical activity, facilities, manpower, and business or financial.

The long-range plan, when approved by the respective operating manager, shall be submitted to the corporate office for review and approval in the manner set forth below.

Procedures

A. The initial stage in the development of the long-range plan is the establishing of the overall corporate objectives and the goals for reaching these objectives. Normally, the corporate objectives will be established by the president and disseminated to the operating managers at a corporate management conference or at an executive council meeting.

B. The second stage of the long-range planning cycle will be the issuance of overall planning guidelines and procedures by the corporate office. A principal element of the planning guidelines will be the identification of the environment in which the company will be operating during the forecast period. This identification on an overall basis would include: financial and economic environment, marketing environment, technical environment, and industrial relations environment.

C. The third stage of the long-range planning cycle will be a scheduled review of preliminary estimates of contract acquisitions, major program efforts, and resources requirements with the operating managers. . . . No specific formats are to be followed for the above review. It is expected that each operating manager will be prepared to discuss his operations.

D. The fourth stage of the long-range planning cycle will be submission and review of product-line or program forecasts. The goals to be accomplished in this stage of the planning cycle are as follows:

1. Review and selection of major programs or product lines to be pursued.
2. Establishment of probable levels of contract acquisitions and sales.
3. Establishment of probable levels of overhead technical activity.
4. Review and evaluation of preliminary projections of income, resource requirements, and return on investment.

To accomplish these goals, each division and subsidiary will submit its product-line or program details. . . . A forecast sheet is to be submitted for each major product line or program, together with a summary sheet indicating division or subsidiary totals.

Supporting detail for capital-asset requirements not associated with a particular [program] or product-line forecast is to be submitted on a separate attachment. . . .

To facilitate the corporate office review of the program or product-line forecasts, a concise statement of the rationale behind each forecast is also to be submitted. . . .

In addition to the long-range plan . . . each division, subsidiary, and profit center will submit, on an annual basis, a complete, detailed annual business plan. The annual business plan will encompass forecasts of sales, costs, income, financial position, cash requirements, overhead technical activity, facility, and manpower requirements. The annual business plan, when approved by the respective operating manager, shall be submitted to the corporate office for review and approval. . . .

Exhibit 9. Five-Year Business Plan, Raytheon Company

General Policies and Procedures

SUBJECT: FIVE-YEAR BUSINESS PLAN

1. *Purpose.* This statement establishes the broad guidelines for preparation and annual review of division and subsidiary company Five-Year Business Plans. Economic and other specific guidelines and assumptions will be issued annually by the planning office.

2. *Policy.* The Five-Year Business Plans of the operating divisions and subsidiaries of Raytheon are to be updated as important changes occur. To provide an opportunity for executive office review, a current version of the plan covering the forthcoming budget year and four subsequent years will be submitted to the executive office in mid-October of each year. A company strategy meeting will be scheduled for late October or early November, at

which time formal presentation to, and review by, company management will occur. The guidance provided at the company strategy meeting will confirm the basis for developing the next year's budget. A generalized milestone schedule of key events is included under Section 10.

3. Applicability. This policy is applicable to all divisions, separate operations, and all majority-owned subsidiary companies of Raytheon.

4. Responsibilities. Division general managers and subsidiary company presidents are responsible for compliance with this policy and for the development and implementation of such divisional or subsidiary company procedures as appropriate.

5. Introduction
   A. The business plans are summarized by the use of information exhibits and by an accompanying commentary. This commentary should be held to a minimum, would by preference be in outline form, and should cover the following principal points (organized, as appropriate, by business area):
      - The charter of the division or subsidiary company and its underlying management philosophy.
      - Current and future circumstances of the served market.
      - The division's or subsidiary company's percentage penetration of the served market vis-à-vis major competition.
      - Objectives of the business-area or product-line grouping, given the presumptions of the above two points.
      - Strategies to be followed to achieve the stated objectives.
      - Significant, longer-range problems to be faced in achieving the objectives, including consideration of manpower, plant and equipment, and other resources.
      - Management development.
      - Interrelationships with other divisions and subsidiary companies of Raytheon.
   B. The information exhibits and commentaries are assembled into a plans book, which forms the data base for examining and evaluating the direction and growth performance of the Raytheon Company. Except for assignment to group executives, and members of division and subsidiary organizations in which the plans were developed, such books (the number of copies is specified each year) are distributed only to the planning office from which a controlled reassignment is made.
   C. Presentations of the plans, after appropriate review and approval by the group executives, are made by invitation to the company's operating and staff management group in the fall of each year. Such presentations cover the points set forth in 5A above, and provide the basis for intracompany discussion directed toward the objectives of better coordination, cooperation, and management effectiveness. Information shown at these presentations is drawn from the data base

and commentaries set forth in the plans books. Separate instructions are provided by the planning office relative to the outline for plan presentations.
D. The first year of the five-year planning period (including changes that result from the fall meeting) is detailed under the direction of the controller's office for measurement purposes and, upon approval, is established by the executive office as the company's profit budget.

6. Procedure. It is suggested that the plans book be organized in accordance with the following generalized outline and the related commentary. Specific exhibit titles and applicability to Raytheon divisions and subsidiary companies are set forth in Section 7, below. Discussions as to the content of exhibits and other explanatory material are set forth in Section 9, along with facsimiles of the information exhibits.

A. *Executive summary.* This section is devoted to the general manager's or president's summary of important aspects of his division or subsidiary company. Two of the four subsections are specific information formats; the other two parts may be presented in whatever format is appropriate to the general manager's or president's style of presentation.

B. *The business-area or product-line summaries.* This section contains the fundamental objectives, strategies, assumptions, and discussions of expected results for each of the business-area or product-line groupings identified for the purpose and as specified by the group executives. Separate program or product-line detail should be prepared and held available under the guidance of the division planning office.

C. *Functional plans.* This section contains the analyses, plans, and strategies for developing and improving the functional organizations of the division or subsidiary company. This review would include an assessment in some depth of personnel skills on hand, expected departures and replacements, and entirely new requirements for expansion and upgrading, and would cover at least the major function of the controller, industrial relations, manufacturing, marketing, research, and engineering.

D. *Facilities requirements.* This section is composed of information exhibits discussing (1) floor space, (2) the relationship between floor space and manpower, and (3) laboratory and manufacturing machinery and equipment requirements (including scientific data processing equipment).

E. *Divisional statistical summaries.* This section contains particular summary exhibits which have proved to be of importance in support of plans, or which are useful as reference throughout the year.

F. *Raytheon Europe.* This group comprises both government-oriented and commercial businesses. Plans books will be made up by selecting forms from the exhibits to this procedure, as appropriate. Each subsidiary company within Raytheon Europe will have a separate plan.

7. Plans book organization.

Plans Book Table of Contents
Content Specification

	Form No.	Govt. Group(a)	MPTD Semi-conductor, Computer	Subsidiary Companies(b) and Research
Executive Summary				
General Manager's Summary		x	x	x
Comparison with Budget and Last Year's Plan		x	x	x
Summary of Key Measures	10-1583	x	x(c)	
Summary of Key Measures by Business Area	10-1584, 10-1602	x	x(c)	
Summary of Key Measures by Operation or Product Line	10-1585, 10-1603		x	x
Planning Highlights (Extended)	10-1586, 10-1587	x	x(d)	
Planning Highlights	10-1589, 10-1590			x
Business-Area or Product-Line Summaries				
Business-Area Objectives and Strategies		x		
Operation or Product-Line Objectives			x	x
Business-Area Summary— Government	10-1591	x		
Operation or Product-Line Summary	10-1592		x	x
Project Funding Sheet— Government	10-0204	x		
Program Summary— Government	10-1593	x		

(a) Includes Raytheon Service Company.
(b) Amana, Badger, Caloric, D. C. Heath, Seismograph Service, United Engineers.
(c) These divisions may wish to use the more extensive chart form because of the importance of orders and backlog to their businesses. If so, the form should be modified locally to indicate key measures by operation or product-line groupings.
(d) Commercial divisions should modify terminology on these forms, as applicable.

Plans Book Table of Contents
Content Specification

	Form No.	Govt. Group(a)	MPTD Semi-conductor, Computer	Subsidiary Companies(b) and Research
Functional Plans (Discussion in Prose Form)		x	x	x
Manpower Requirements (End of Period)	10-1594	x	x	x
Facilities Requirements Summary of Floor-Space Requirements by Major Locations	10-1595	x	x	x
Summary of Floor-Space/Manpower Relationship	10-1596	x	x	x
Summary of Machinery and Equipment Requirements	10-1597	x	x	x
Summary of Manufacturing Load by Program Served	10-1606	x		
Divisional Statistical Summaries				
Summary of IWRs OUT	10-1604	x	x	
Summary of IWRs IN	10-1605	x	x	
Long-Range Balance Sheet and Funding Plan	10-1598	x	x	x
GOR and Programmed Expenditures Summary—Government	10-1599	x		
Summary of Floor-Space Investment Plans	10-1600	x	x	x

8. Additional information on interdivisional transfers. Transfers IN and OUT reflect the execution of IWR orders placed or accepted. Forms 10-1577 and 10-1578 are available as worksheets to aid those who need elaboration in transforming orders into "sales." No submission is required.

9. Discussion on information exhibits. Noted on face of exhibit facsimiles.

10. Schedule of key events. The chart attached as Exhibit A gives general timing of incidents important to the planning program. Specific dates for any given year are transmitted under separate memorandum by the director–planning.

Business-Area Objectives and Strategies

This is the section where specific and pointed commentary is of critical importance. The future of the business area, circumstances of approach and attack on the market, details of new and improved resources, anticipated response of competitors, and the like should be examined. In the discussion of what is to be done to achieve objectives, the business-area manager should be as specific as possible in respect to his marketing plan and the utilization of external aids (advertising, brochures, and the like), to promote the business area's position.

Operation or Product-Line
Definition, Objectives, Strategy, and Competitive Analysis

Product-line definition. Identify the product line. Special market segmentations are of interest here but must be consistent with your definition of served market.

Objectives. Support your specific objectives for sales, profitability, and market share growth for the five-year plan period.

Market characteristics. This should briefly cover at least:

- Market growth during past five years and Raytheon's growth in this market over the same period.
- Projected five-year market growth and fundamental reason for growth.
- The most important changes in product in next five years.
- The most important changes in end-use buyer requirement in next five years.
- The identity of the ultimate customer. How do you reach him?

Strategy. Detail the principal points of the strategy you will use to meet your objectives and deal with the market characteristics for the five-year period.

COMPETITIVE ANALYSIS

Major Competitors	*1970 Sales*	*Market Share*
_____		
_____		
_____		
_____		

Distribution Channels — List and, if appropriate, comment on distribution channels used by competitors and Raytheon. Specifically, comment on whether competitors have other products in same channels. Does Raytheon?

Competitive Evaluation — Comment on how Raytheon product compares with top competitors' product in terms of quality, price, utility, customer acceptance.

Competitive Strategy — What factors are most important in maintaining or improving our competitive position? Describe Raytheon's competitive strategy.

EXHIBIT A

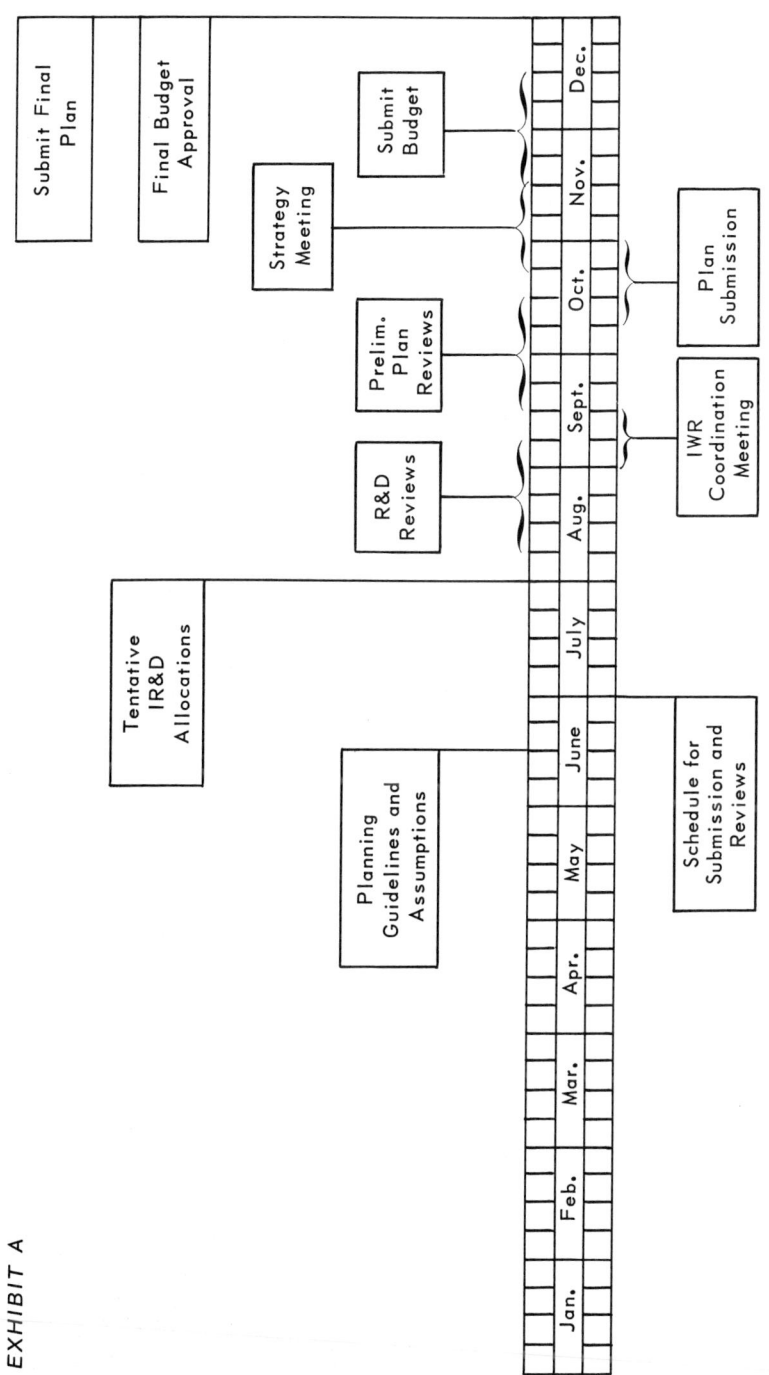

SUMMARY OF KEY MEASURES
(DOLLARS IN MILLIONS)

COMPANY PRIVATE

DIVISION _____ DATE SUBMITTED _____

ORDERS, SALES, AND BACKLOG

	LAST YR 19__	CUR. YR 19__	BDGT YR 19__	19__	19__	19__	19__
BEGINNING BACKLOG							
GOR (OUTSIDE) + IWR (IN) − IWR (OUT)							
TOTAL ORDERS (NET)							
NET SALES - IE							

REPRESENTS LEVEL OF ORDERS AVAILABLE AFTER DEDUCTING IWR OUT; IS BASIS FOR NS-IE

IWR IN
GOR (OUTSIDE)
BEGINNING BACKLOG-IE
NS-IE

182

SUMMARY OF KEY MEASURES BY BUSINESS AREA   COMPANY PRIVATE

DIVISION _____ DATE SUBMITTED _____

NET SALES
(INTERNAL EFFORT)
(DOLLARS IN MILLIONS)

Business areas should be identified with segments of vertical bars, using alternating black, gray, and white. The legend should be at the left of the chart. Example:

- Bus Area "A"
- Bus Area "B"
- Bus Area "C"
- Bus Area "D"
- Bus Area "E"
- Bus Area "F"

LAST YR 19___ | CUR. YR 19___ | BDGT YR 19___ | 19___ | 19___ | 19___ | 19___

BUSINESS AREA

183

SUMMARY OF KEY MEASURES BY BUSINESS AREA

COMPANY PRIVATE

DIVISION _____ DATE SUBMITTED _____

PROFIT AFTER TAX
(DOLLARS IN THOUSANDS)

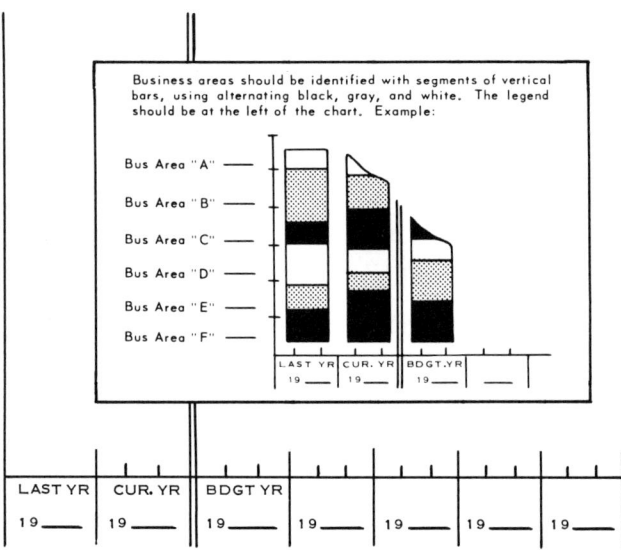

BUSINESS AREA

SUMMARY OF KEY MEASURES BY OPERATION OR PRODUCT LINE

COMPANY PRIVATE

DIVISION _____ DATE SUBMITTED _____

NET SALES
(DOLLARS IN MILLIONS & TENTHS)

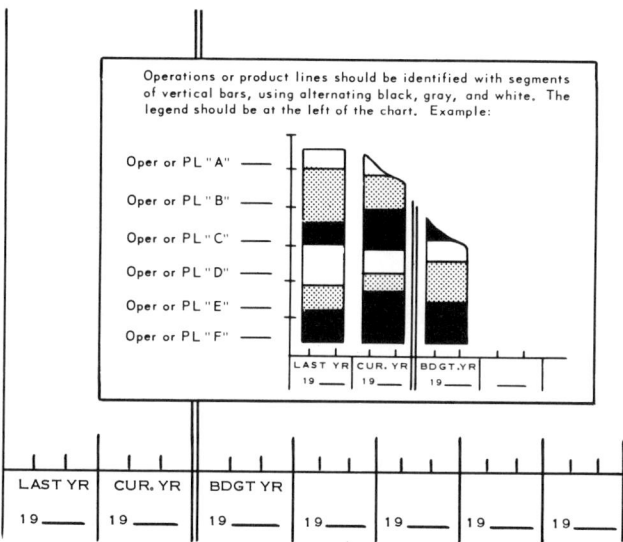

	LAST YR 19__	CUR. YR 19__	BDGT YR 19__	19__	19__	19__	19__
OPERATION OR PRODUCT LINE							

SUMMARY OF KEY MEASURES BY OPERATION OR PRODUCT LINE

COMPANY PRIVATE

DIVISION _____ DATE SUBMITTED _____

PROFIT AFTER TAX
(DOLLARS IN THOUSANDS)

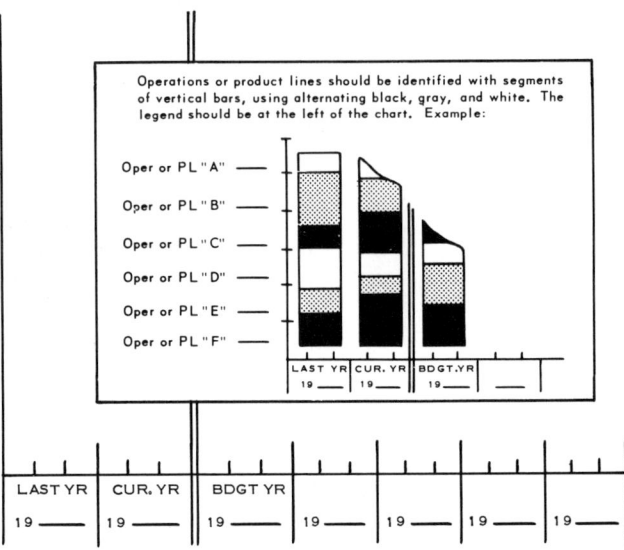

PLANNING HIGHLIGHTS
(EXTENDED)
(DOLLARS IN MILLIONS & TENTHS)

COMPANY PRIVATE

DIVISION _____ DATE SUBMITTED _____

	LAST YR 19___	CUR. YR (a) 19___	BDGT YR 19___	19___	19___	19___	19___
Gross Orders Received Outside Interdivisional (IWR In)							
•							
•							
•							
• Other							
TOTAL							
Memo: Interdivisional Orders Placed (IWR Out)							
•							
•							
•							
• Other							
TOTAL							
Net Sales – Internal Effort Engineering Production							
TOTAL							
Memo: Foreign Sales							
Memo: Net Sales – Outside							
Backlog (End of Period) Outside Interdivisional							
TOTAL							
Memo: Government Only							
Profit Before Tax NS-IE							
Net Income							
Programmed Expenditures Independent Research							
Ind Development – Govt Pool							
Ind Development – Other							
Bid Proposal – Govt Pool							
Marketing – Govt Pool							
Marketing, etc. – Other (Excl Corp)							
Administration (Excl Corporate)							

> Emphasis has been placed in this exhibit upon the circumstances of interdivisional orders. Accordingly, space is provided to identify major interdivisional customers and suppliers, as appropriate.

> If appropriate, sales by location may be used for an approximate separation of sales into engineering and production sales.

(a) Current year estimate includes accounted period thru _____.

PLANNING HIGHLIGHTS
(EXTENDED)
(DOLLARS IN MILLIONS & TENTHS)

COMPANY PRIVATE

Page 2 of 2

DIVISION _____ DATE SUBMITTED _____

	LAST YR 19___	CUR. YR (a) 19___	BDGT YR 19___	19___	19___	19___	19___
Capital Investment Matters (b)							
Approvals							
— To Be Capitalized							
— To Be Leased							
Expenditures (c)							
— Carryovers							
— Current							
— TOTAL							
Depreciation and Amortization							
Assets (End of Period)							
Current							
Noncurrent							
TOTAL							
Funding:							
INC (DEC) in Customer Advances							
(INC) DEC in Total Debt							
Miscellaneous							
Cost-to-manufacture Base							
Manpower (End of Period)							
Employees							
Contract Labor							
TOTAL							
Additions:							
Total Manpower							
For Replacement							
For Growth							
Engineering and Scientific							
For Replacement							
For Growth							
Royalty and Know-how Income (Pretax)							
Key Measures (End of Period)							
Current Assets Weeks Wks							
Return on Sales (NS-IE) %							
Asset Turnover (NS-T) X							
Return on Assets %							
NS-IE per Person (d)							

> Under Capital Investment Matters, the "Approvals" lines are separated between the values of property plant, and equipment to be capitalized as compared to that which is to be leased. In both cases, the amounts to be shown represent purchase cost, and the separation should be in line with current philosophy and should have the concurrence of the treasurer's office.

> In the Manpower section, provision has been made to display the expected annual manpower change for replacement as opposed to for greater workloads. The office of research and development and the office of engineering may ask for additional support in regard to engineering and scientific manpower additions.

(a) Current-year estimate includes accounted period thru _____.
(b) Include matters relating to building space and capital goods, irrespective of financing method, in accordance with definitions contained in finance manual section 25.2.
(c) Involving capitalizable property only.
(d) Include contract labor; use average based on year-end positions.

PLANNING HIGHLIGHTS
(DOLLARS IN MILLIONS & TENTHS)

COMPANY PRIVATE
Page 1 of 2

DIVISION _____ DATE SUBMITTED _____

	LAST YR 19__	CUR. YR (a) 19__	BDGT YR 19__	19__	19__	19__	19__

Gross Orders Received
  Outside
  From Other Company
    Entities
  TOTAL							

Memo: Orders Placed
  with Other Company
  Entities							

Net Sales — Total							
Memo: Foreign Sales							
Memo: Net Sales — Outside							
Backlog (End of Period)							
Profit Before Tax % NS-T							
Net Income							

Programmed Expenditures
  Independent Research
  Independent Development
  Marketing, etc. — Other
    (Excl Corp)
  Administration (Excl
    Corporate)							

Capital Investment
  Matters (b)
  Approvals
    — To Be Capitalized
    — To Be Leased
  Expenditures (c)
    — Carryovers
    — Current
    — Total
  Depreciation and
    Amortization							

> Under Capital Investment Matters, the "Approvals" lines are separated between the values of property, plant, and equipment to be capitalized as compared to that which is to be leased. In both cases, the amounts to be shown represent purchase cost, and the separation should be in line with current philosophy and should have the concurrence of the treasurer's office.

(a) Current year estimate includes accounted period thru _____ .
(b) Include matters relating to building space and capital goods, irrespective of financing method, in accordance with definitions contained in finance manual section 25.2.
(c) Involving capitalizable property only.

PLANNING HIGHLIGHTS
(DOLLARS IN MILLIONS & TENTHS)

COMPANY PRIVATE
Page 2 of 2

DIVISION _____ DATE SUBMITTED _____

	LAST YR 19___	CUR. YR (a) 19___	BDGT YR 19___	19___	19___	19___	19___
Assets (End of Period)							
Current							
Noncurrent							
TOTAL							
Funding: INC (DEC) in Customer Advances							
(INC) DEC in Total Debt							
Miscellaneous							
Base for Corp. G&A Assessment							
Manpower (End of Period)							
Employees							
Contract Labor							
TOTAL							
Additions:							
Total Manpower							
For Replacement							
For Growth							
Engineering and Scientific							
For Replacement							
For Growth							
Royalty and Know-how Income (Pretax)							
Key Measures (End of Period)							
Accts Rec Weeks Wks							
Reg Inventory Weeks Wks							
Return on Sales (NS-T) %							
Asset Turnover X							
Return on Assets %							
NS-T Per Person (d)							

> In the Manpower section, provision has been made to display the expected annual manpower change for replacement as opposed to for greater workloads. The office of research and development and the office of engineering may ask for additional support in regard to engineering and scientific manpower additions.

(a) Current year estimate includes accounted period thru _____.
(d) Include contract labor; use average based on year-end positions.

BUSINESS – AREA SUMMARY – GOVERNMENT

COMPANY PRIVATE

DIVISION _____ DATE SUBMITTED _____

BUSINESS AREA _____

TOTAL ORDERS (NET) —

INTERNAL EFFORT SALES ☐

	LAST YR 19__	CUR. YR 19__	BDGT YR 19__	19__	19__	19__	19__

GOR (Outside)
 + IWR (In)
 − IWR (Out)
 	
 TOTAL ORDERS (NET)
 	
 Net Sales – Internal Effort
    − Outside
    − Interdivisional
    − Intradivisional
    TOTAL
 	
 Profit After Tax
    % On NS-IE   %
 IDP Expense
 Bid Proposal Expense							

OPERATION OR PRODUCT-LINE SUMMARY

COMPANY PRIVATE

DIVISION _____ DATE SUBMITTED _____

OPERATION OR PRODUCT LINE _____

SCALE (NET SALES)

SCALE (% SERVED MARKET)

The key measures shown below this chart are those thought to be of primary importance for the operation or product line. However, space is provided to add measures or indicators as may be deemed appropriate and important by the operation or product-line manager.

SALES AS % SERVED MARKET

NET SALES

	LAST YR 19__	CUR. YR 19__	BDGT YR 19__	19__	19__	19__	19__
GOR (Outside) + IWR (In) − IWR (Out) **TOTAL ORDERS (NET)**							
NET SALES − Outside − To Other Company Entities − Within Div. or Subs. Co. **TOTAL** Profit After Tax % on Net Sales % IDP Expense							
Memo: Estimated Share of Served Market							

PROJECT FUNDING SHEET – GOVERNMENT
(DOLLARS IN THOUSANDS)

COMPANY PRIVATE

PROJECT TITLE			PROJECT NO.	ISSUE NO. DATE
PREPARED BY	DATE	BUSINESS AREA	CUSTOMER	

DESCRIPTION OR CLARIFYING REMARKS

		BUDGET YEAR FUNDING										
FUNDS	TYPE	JAN	FEB	MAR	APR	MAY	JUNE	JULY	AUG	SEPT	OCT	NOV	DEC
CO	IDP												
	PROP												
GOR	STUDY												
	DEV												
	PROD												

MILESTONES:

INTERNAL ▼
EXTERNAL ▲

When the plans book is printed, this sheet is to be printed on a *left-hand* page; accompanying comments are to be shown on a right-hand facing page.

		LONG-RANGE FUNDING					
FUNDS	TYPE	TOTAL PRIOR*	BUDGET YR.	19___	19___	19___	19___	5-YEAR PERIOD
CO	IDP							
	PROP							
GOR	STUDY							
	DEV							
	PROD							
			GRAND TOTAL - 5-YEAR GOR					

MILESTONES:

INTERNAL ▼
EXTERNAL ▲

*TOTAL – ALL YEARS PRIOR TO BUDGET YEAR.

PROGRAM SUMMARY — GOVERNMENT
(DOLLARS IN MILLIONS AND TENTHS)

COMPANY
PRIVATE

DIVISION _____ BUSINESS AREA _____ DATE SUBMITTED _____

PROGRAM	CUSTOMER	FIVE-YEAR GOR SUMMARY					5-YEAR TOTAL
		BDGT YR 19___	19___	19___	19___	19___	
TOTAL POTENTIAL							
TOTAL PLANNED							

This is the only place in the plans book where program identification is made in support of the GOR summary throughout the five-year-plan period. The derivation of "Total Planned" is to be determined in conjunction with the views of division and business-area management, and would generally reflect the summation of factored GOR.

The GOR value, capture probability, and factored value should be shown year by year for each program. An example of the correct format is:

$$\text{GOR} \rightarrow \frac{2.0 \quad \text{.9} \leftarrow \text{capture probability}}{1.8} \leftarrow \text{factored GOR} (= 2.0 \times .9)$$

MANPOWER REQUIREMENTS (END OF PERIOD)

COMPANY PRIVATE

DIVISION _____ DATE SUBMITTED _____

LOCATIONS/OPERATIONS	LAST YR 19___	CUR. YR 19___	BDGT YR 19___	19___	19___	19___	19___
DIVISION HEADQUARTERS							
Administration							
Engineering and Scientific							
Manufacturing							
Marketing							
Finance							
Industrial Relations							
TOTAL							
CONTRACT LABOR							
Administration							
Engineering and Scientific							
Manufacturing							
TOTAL							
Administration							
Engineering and Scientific							
Manufacturing							
Marketing							
Finance							
Industrial Relations							
TOTAL							
Administration							
Engineering and Scientific							
Manufacturing							
Marketing							
Finance							
Industrial Relations							
TOTAL							
Administration							
Engineering and Scientific							
Manufacturing							
Marketing							
Finance							
Industrial Relations							
TOTAL							

Use one data set to display division totals.

SUMMARY OF FLOOR-SPACE REQUIREMENTS
BY MAJOR LOCATIONS
(SQUARE FEET IN THOUSANDS)

COMPANY PRIVATE
Page 1 of

DIVISION _____ COMPILED BY _____ DATE SUBMITTED _____

	TOTAL FLOOR SPACE OCCUPIED AT END OF YEAR							
	LAST YR 19___	CUR. YR 19___	BDGT YR 19___	19___	19___	19___	19___	19___
DIVISION TOTAL								

Leased Space
  – Long Term
  – Short Term
  – TOTAL
Company-Owned Space
Government-Owned Space
Total Space Occupied								

Commentary:

> This exhibit shows the actual and/or intended floor space to be occupied at the end of each of the specified years. Accordingly, it will follow the details of planned changes in facilities and will not necessarily reflect the exact amount of space that might be efficiently utilizable at any given point. Space is provided for appropriate commentary.

Leased Space
  – Long Term
  – Short Term
  – TOTAL
Company-Owned Space
Government-Owned Space
Total Space Occupied							

Commentary:

> Leased space is considered "long term" if commitment is for five years or more.

Leased Space
  – Long Term
  – Short Term
  – TOTAL
Company-Owned Space
Government-Owned Space
Total Space Occupied							

Commentary:

SUMMARY OF THE FLOOR SPACE/MANPOWER RELATIONSHIP

COMPANY PRIVATE

DIVISION _____ DATE SUBMITTED _____

LOCATION _____

MANPOWER
(IN THOUSANDS)

FLOOR SPACE OCCUPIED
(IN THOUSANDS OF SQUARE FEET)

LAST YR	CUR. YR	BDGT YR				
19___	19___	19___	19___	19___	19___	19___

SQUARE FEET/MAN (AVERAGE):

SUMMARY OF MACHINERY AND EQUIPMENT REQUIREMENTS
(EXCLUDING BUSINESS DATA PROCESSING EQUIPMENT)
(DOLLARS IN THOUSANDS)

COMPANY PRIVATE
Page 1 of __

DIVISION _____ DATE SUBMITTED _____

	ADDITIONS DURING THE CALENDAR YEAR						
	LAST YR 19__	CUR. YR 19__	BDGT YR 19__	19__	19__	19__	19__
DIVISION TOTAL • Contract Required • Replacement and Modernization • Increased Capacity • Other TOTAL							
• Contract Required • Replacement and Modernization • Increased Capacity • Other TOTAL	\multicolumn{7}{l}{This exhibit discusses additions only. Do not net out disposals. No business data processing equipment should be included in this exhibit.}
• Contract Required • Replacement and Modernization • Increased Capacity • Other TOTAL							
• Contract Required • Replacement and Modernization • Increased Capacity • Other TOTAL							
• Contract Required • Replacement and Modernization • Increased Capacity • Other TOTAL							

NOTE: The company intentionally leaves the next page of the actual form blank. -- Ed.

SUMMARY OF MANUFACTURING LOAD BY PROGRAM SERVED

COMPANY PRIVATE

(BASED ON EQUIVALENT INTERNAL EFFORT SALES LEVEL)
(DOLLARS IN MILLIONS AND TENTHS)

DIVISION _____

PLANT _____ DATE SUBMITTED _____

	LAST YR 19___	CUR. YR 19___	BDGT YR 19___	19___	19___	19___	19___
PROGRAM:							
OUTSIDE SALES (IE BASIS)							
PROGRAM:							
INTERDIVISIONAL SALES (IE BASIS)							
PROGRAM:							
INTRADIVISIONAL SALES (IE BASIS)							
TOTAL SALES (IE BASIS)							
MEMO: MANPOWER (END OF PERIOD)							

SUMMARY OF IWR [OUT] *
(DOLLARS IN THOUSANDS)

COMPANY PRIVATE

DIVISION _____ DATE SUBMITTED _____

	LAST YR 19__	CUR. YR 19__	BDGT YR 19__	19__	19__	19__	19__
• • • •							
• • • •							
• • •							
• • • •							
TOTAL IWR OUT							

This exhibit indicates the annual orders for products and services placed by the business area with other divisions or subsidiary companies within the corporation.

The execution of these orders in terms of interdivisional "sales" transfers is represented on Form entitled "Summary of Interdivisional Transfers-IN."

The spaces are for listing by business area, with a further delineation by major program.

*Interdivisional ORDERS placed.

SUMMARY OF IWR [IN] *
(DOLLARS IN THOUSANDS)

COMPANY PRIVATE

DIVISION _____ DATE SUBMITTED _____

	LAST YR 19___	CUR. YR 19___	BDGT YR 19___	19___	19___	19___	19___
• • • • •							
• • • • •							
• • • •							
• • • • •							
TOTAL IWR IN							

> This exhibit indicates the annual orders for products and services placed with the business area by other divisions or subsidiary companies within the corporation.
>
> The execution of these orders in terms of interdivisional "sales" transfers is represented on Form entitled "Summary of Interdivisional Transfers-OUT."
>
> The spaces are for listing by business area, with a further delination by major program.

* Interdivisional ORDERS received.

LONG-RANGE BALANCE SHEET AND FUNDING PLAN
(DOLLARS IN MILLIONS AND TENTHS)

COMPANY PRIVATE

DIVISION _____ DATE SUBMITTED _____

	LAST YR 19__	CUR. YR 19__	BDGT YR 19__	19__	19__	19__	19__
BALANCE SHEET							
Cash							
Receivables (Net):							
U.S. Govt Billed							
U.S. Govt Unbilled							
Other							
Inventories:							
FP Contracts Sales Value							
Other							
Other Current Assets							
Total Current Assets							
Long-Term Receivables							
Plant and Equipment							
— Gross							
(Reserve)							
Net							
Other Noncurrent Assets							
Total Assets							
Advances from Customers							
Other Current Liabilities Excl Debt							
Outside Debt							
Intercompany Loans							
Intercompany Account							
Capital Stock and Surplus							
Total Liabilities and Equity							
FUNDING							
Net Income (Loss)							
Depreciation and Amortization							
(Add) to Plant and Equipment							
(INCR) DECR in Receivables and Inventories							
INCR (DECR) in Customer Advances							
INCR (DECR) in Other Current Liab							
Other (Incl P&E Disposal)							
(INCR) DECR in Total Debt							

GOR AND PROGRAMMED EXPENDITURES
SUMMARY – GOVERNMENT
(BY BUSINESS AREA)
(DOLLARS IN THOUSANDS)

COMPANY PRIVATE

DIVISION _____ DATE SUBMITTED _____

	LAST YR 19__	CUR. YR 19__	BDGT YR 19__	19__	19__	19__	19__
GOR IDP (GOVT POOL) IDP (OTHER) PROPOSAL (GOVT POOL)							
GOR IDP (GOVT POOL) IDP (OTHER) PROPOSAL (GOVT POOL)							
GOR IDP (GOVT POOL) IDP (OTHER) PROPOSAL (GOVT POOL)							
GOR IDP (GOVT POOL) IDP (OTHER) PROPOSAL (GOVT POOL)							
DIVISION TOTAL							
IRP IDP (GOVT POOL) IDP (OTHER) PROPOSAL (GOVT POOL)							
TOTAL EXPENDITURES							

SUMMARY OF FLOOR-SPACE INVESTMENT PLANS
(DOLLARS IN THOUSANDS)

COMPANY PRIVATE

DIVISION _____ DATE SUBMITTED _____

	ADDITIONS DURING THE CALENDAR YEAR							
	LAST YR 19__	CUR. YR 19__	BDGT YR 19__	19__	19__	19__	19__
DIVISION TOTAL							
Total Cost of New Space Leasehold Improvements Less: New Space to Be Leased New Investment for Space							
Total Cost of New Space Leasehold Improvements Less: New Space to Be Leased New Investment for Space	Work out details of presentation in conjunction with treasurer's office.						
Total Cost of New Space Leasehold Improvements Less: New Space to Be Leased New Investment for Space							
Total Cost of New Space Leasehold Improvements Less: New Space to Be Leased New Investment for Space							
Total Cost of New Space Leasehold Improvements Less: New Space to Be Leased New Investment for Space							

SUMMARY OF INTERDIVISIONAL TRANSFERS OUT
(DOLLARS IN THOUSANDS)

COMPANY PRIVATE

DIVISION _____ DATE SUBMITTED _____

	LAST YR 19__	CUR. YR 19__	BDGT YR 19__	19__	19__	19__	19__
• • • •							
• • • •							
• • • •							
• • • •							
TOTAL TRANSFERS OUT							

> This exhibit indicates the annual amounts of products and services transferred by the business area to other divisions or subsidiary companies within the corporation. Inasmuch as these "sales" transfers reflect the execution of previously placed IWRs-IN, the designation of major programs should agree with that exhibit.

SUMMARY OF INTERDIVISIONAL TRANSFERS [IN]
(DOLLARS IN THOUSANDS)

COMPANY PRIVATE

DIVISION _____ DATE SUBMITTED _____

	LAST YR 19__	CUR. YR 19__	BDGT YR 19__	19__	19__	19__	19__
• _____ • • •							
• _____ • • • •	\multicolumn{7}{l}{This exhibit indicates the annual amounts of products and services transferred to the business area by other divisions or subsidiary companies within the corporation. Inasmuch as these "sales" transfers reflect the exception of previously placed IWRs-OUT, the designation of major programs should agree with that exhibit.}
• _____ • • •							
• _____ • • • •							
TOTAL TRANSFERS IN							

Exhibit 10. Preparation of Long-Range Plans, American Airlines, Inc. (Excerpts)

The *first step* is a review and forecast of the *external environment*. . . . This includes a social, political, and technological forecast and the state of the domestic economy, particularly indicators pertinent to air transportation. . . . We follow with a forecast of the total domestic trunkline transportation market, both passenger and cargo. . . . All pertinent sources of information are used.

Our *second step* is a review and forecast of our internal environment . . . including our individual segment traffic volume, services, and the expected fare structure. . . . One of the most difficult problems is the examining of alternative courses of action. . . . We depend less on straight historical projections and more on a real plan of taking specific steps to build to a desired end result. . . . Finally, we examine the impact on our previous year's plan of current trends in the economy, and of changed industry and company conditions. . . . The external and internal environmental forecasts summarized become the assumptions furnished to all departments for their common planning base. . . .

Our *third planning step* is the annual issuance of the president's planning letter, setting forth "constraints" which provide guidelines for all subsequent activities. These constraints include broad statements . . . and specific instructions. . . . The planning letter sets forth specific corporate problems to be attacked in this year's planning effort. . . . This is an opportunity to point out policy changes which should be made for future plan revisions.

Our *fourth planning step* is a *meeting with each department* participating in the development of the plan to ensure a full understanding of the immediate planning effort. . . .

Our *fifth planning step* is the development by the functional departments of *specific plans and action programs* to meet the requirements set forth in the president's letter. . . .

Our *sixth planning step* is the *analysis by the corporate planning department* of all functional department plans, questioning of assumptions, testing of decisions, and folding of these plans into our integrated plan. . . . In case of differences . . . which cannot be resolved, the president makes the decision.

As the *seventh* or *final planning* step the integrated plan is presented to the president and his advisory council for review and approval. . . . After approval the plan is issued as a guide to company management's detailed operating plans and decisions, as a timetable against which the company's progress is measured and as a starting point for future plan revisions. . . .

We feel that our greatest improvement efforts must be applied to sincere exploration of more alternatives and improved forecasting.

Short-term goals are sometimes confused with long-term objectives. Frequently, the desired end result is stated, not quantified; or where that is impossible, future deadlines are not set for implementing a program. Every functional program should fit into a specific supporting role in the overall plan. Before any action program is included in the plan, it must have some meaningful measurement applied to its impact on the desired final end results. . . .

Exhibit 11. *Position Description for Senior Vice-President—Economic Planning, United Air Lines, Inc.*

BASIC FUNCTION

Establishes and administers programs for companywide profit management. Develops and recommends long- and short-term economic objectives for the company. Administers companywide programs covering budgeting, fleet planning, economic research, industrial engineering, operations research and development, organization planning, regulatory proceedings, and route research and development. Provides management consulting services to company management in these fields of activity.

RESPONSIBILITIES

1. Establishes and administers programs for companywide profit planning, profit improvement, and budgetary control, including review of the performance of all company elements in meeting corporate profit objectives.
2. Develops and recommends long- and short-term economic objectives for the company.
3. Develops and maintains programs for the analysis and interpretation of national economic conditions, developments, and regional trends.
4. Establishes and assures the continuing development of an effective program of fleet planning and economic research for the company.
5. Establishes and administers programs for companywide industrial and management engineering and operations research and development.
6. Establishes and administers companywide programs for organization analysis and planning, job analysis, and evaluation.
7. Establishes and maintains programs and research for route development and for effective prosecution of route, rate, and economic regulatory proceedings. Fosters sound regulatory relationships and coordinates companywide activity concerning economic regulation.
8. Establishes and maintains an economic review of the company's sales objectives and quotas to insure consistency with company revenue goals.

BASIC RELATIONSHIPS

1. The senior vice-president—economic planning is administratively responsible to the executive vice-president and general manager for the performance of all responsibilities assigned to the office of the senior vice-president—economic planning.
2. All personnel within the office of the senior vice-president—economic planning are administratively responsible to the senior vice-president—economic planning, either directly or through subordinate supervisors.
3. The senior vice-president—economic planning is chairman of the budget committee and is a member of the schedule policy committee and the tariff policy committee.

Exhibit 12. *Statements of Basic Function for Economic Planning Positions, United Air Lines, Inc.*

Economic Research and Fleet Planning

Director: Develops recommendations with regard to fleet composition, including projected schedules and equipment, route structure, business conditions, and competition. Directs preparation of forecasts of general business conditions, industry capacity, and industry passenger and cargo traffic volumes. Directs the conduct of economic studies related to the development of company objectives and long-range plans. Develops long-range profit projections and economic forecast data. Coordinates the development and dissemination of planning data. Directs the conduct of other economic studies as requested.

Manager of Economic Research: Analyzes or directs the analyses of economic developments.

Economic Research and Development Planning

Manager: Identifies and defines long-range corporate objectives and recommends to management specific objectives together with appropriate policies and planning programs to achieve them. Directs the analysis and interpretation of business conditions, economic trends, and other environmental factors which affect the economic prospects of the company. Directs the preparation of forecasts of the economy and airline industry passenger and cargo traffic and capacity. Conducts economic studies related to corporate objectives, policies, and decisions, and in response to management requests for special analyses. Coordinates consulting relationships with economists and research organizations and maintains professional contacts with industry, academic, and government economists.

Staff Economist: Conducts research relating to general business conditions and its effects on United Air Lines. Prepares studies of current economic issues affecting the industry, such as those resulting from government policies on taxes, subsidies, and user charges. Establishes and maintains contacts with economists in industry and government. As directed, writes articles, makes speeches, and represents the company where airline economic problems are considered.

Manager of Economic Analysis: Directs or conducts economic studies of various elements of the company's operation to provide information to management and to develop recommendations for action. Analyzes costs and develops cost data for use in evaluating business decisions in such areas as airplane scheduling, charter and extra section operations, tariffs, and fleet planning. Maintains a continuing study of revenue performance and of revenue yield elements; provides forecasts of revenue and produces revenue yield data used for economic studies.

Staff Manager-Planning Statistics: Develops and recommends the nature of periodic economic planning data, establishes planning timetables, and assimilates input from other administrations. Develops planning data not supplied by other sources, such as forecasts of industry and United lift, and of station traffic and aircraft movement activity. Participates in definition and economic evaluation of alternate station activity levels. Produces related physical statistics and internal planning data; coordinates release of not regularly published economic planning material. Consolidates and develops planning data for presentation in management planning reviews and to interested outside parties. Maintains record of performance against planning statistics and keeps management informed of results.

PROFIT PLANNING DIVISION

Manager: Develops and coordinates the company's profit planning program. Establishes procedures and maintains regulations relating to this program. Conducts studies and develops new and improved techniques relating to profit planning and control. Develops alternative profit objectives and goals together with recommendations for management consideration. Develops and maintains a system of profit and cost analysis charts and reports portraying trends, projections, analyses,* comparisons with other airlines. Prepares revenue, expense, and profit projections for the guidance of management. Provides interline liaison for the exchange of cost performance data with other carriers. Maintains liaison with the accounting department regarding accounting procedures and the design and preparation of accounting reports.

Exhibit 13. *Position Description for Corporate Director of Development Planning*

SUMMARY

Provide staff assistance to the corporate management on problems of long-term planning, particularly as related to good order and effective programming in the development of new company products.

SPECIFIC RESPONSIBILITIES

1. Continually explore the state of art in science and engineering with a view to finding applications in which significant advances are likely to occur.
2. Continually study economic trends of the nation, of the military services and airlines, and of the aircraft and related industries to aid in forecasting the future growth of the corporation.
3. Continually appraise the future competitive position of the corporation, to aid in selecting the future product line and to aid in proposing areas for greater development emphasis.

---

* Comparisons with company profit objectives . . . and comparisons with other airlines.

4. Periodically coordinate, with the corporation and operating divisions' staffs, the preparation of corporate management plans (master plans), with the purpose of reviewing the overall corporate facility and financial requirements; continually collect background data in preparation for such management plans; and provide information and/or make recommendations to the policy committee of the long-term program of the company.

5. Provide any special technical assistance that may be requested by the policy committee or its members.

POLICIES AND PROCEDURES

1. Normally, presentations made by the policy committee will also be made to the rest of the corporation staff, including the division general managers.

2. Relations with planning or study groups in the operating divisions will be on a cooperative basis. Continual liaison will be maintained for this purpose.

3. Wherever possible, information compiled in the development planning department will be distributed to appropriate division personnel.

ORGANIZATION

1. The director of development planning will organize and maintain a combined technical, economic, and clerical staff to achieve the objective stated above in the Summary. He will also engage consultants or outside organizations as necessary and prudent to aid in accomplishing the various specific tasks.

2. The director of development planning reports to and is accountable to a senior vice-president in all respects of the foregoing functions and responsibilities.

Exhibit 14. Position Descriptions for Director–Planning and Business Development and Director of Financial Planning, Samsonite Corporation

---

Position Title: Director–Planning and Business Development

I. *Identifying Data*
   Division: Corporate Staff
   Department: Planning and Business Development
   Position Number:

II. *To Be Filled in by the Incumbent*

   A. Description of Duties

   Please describe the duties of your job as you perform them in practice. State how often (daily, weekly, monthly), and estimate the percentage of your time spent on these duties. Do not list more than six.

	Duties	% of Time
PLANNING	1. Foster the concept and process of professional management through planning.	35%
	2. Direct the development of the corporate plan and coordinate divisional planning including marketing, manufacturing, finance, and facilities.	
	3. Direct the development of economic forecasts for current and possible new business.	
	4. Develop an on-going planning system including the preparation and continual updating of a planning manual.	
	5. Assist the president in the development of corporate purpose, goals, and strategy.	
	6. Conduct specialized planning seminars.	
NEW BUSINESS DEVELOPMENT	1. Develop and continually update corporate criteria for evaluation of acquisitions and venture opportunities.	35%
	2. Develop an analytical framework for evaluating mergers, acquisitions, and ventures.	
	3. Develop plans for consummating and integrating an acquisition.	
ADMINISTRATIVE ASSISTANT	1. Provide the president with administrative follow-up and control.	10%
	2. Develop follow-up reporting tools for use by the president.	
FACILITIES PLANNING	1. Responsible for review and evaluation of current facilities.	20%
	2. Responsible for determining additional facilities requirements.	
	3. Responsible for the development of new facilities.	

B. Scope of Supervision:
 Two to three subordinates, maybe as many as ten. (There are a number of people in the facilities planning group.)

C. Position Reports to: (Title)
 President of Samsonite Corporation

D. Position Requirements
  1. Please identify that aspect of your job which, in your opinion, is the most complex. Give an illustration.
     The development of corporate strategy, the decisions with regard to acquisition, and getting the divisions to actively support the planning concept.

  2. What is the most important skill or personal quality required to successfully fulfill this most complex aspect? (*Ex.:* ability to work under pressure, outstanding interpersonal skills, etc.)
     Creativity and resourcefulness in developing programs, directing subordinates, and in working with the executive committee to get agreement.

E. Comments—is there anything else about your job which you feel is important for its proper evaluation?
   Ability to get results through people not under one's control, to insure assistance from outside contacts such as investment bankers and outside executives.

III. *To Be Filled in by the Supervisor*

  A. Referring to the description of duties as filled out by the position incumbent, rank each duty in order of importance.

     Is there any important duty that you would like eventually to be (1) performed on this job and/or (2) eventually removed from the job?

  B. Position Requirements
     1. Please estimate both the minimum and the maximum amount of education required to handle this job. Specify in connection with each entry the major areas of concentration.

Min. Max.

☐ ☐ High-school degree

☐ ☐ Some college. No. of years: _____
      Major area of concentration:

☐ ☐		College degree. Type (B.A._____ B.S._____ Other_____) Major area of concentration:
☐ ☐		Some postgraduate work. No. of years _____ Major area of concentration:
X ☐		Postgraduate degree. Type (M.A._____ M.S._____ Ph.D._____ Other_____) Major area of concentration: Economics, Finance, Marketing

2. Please estimate both the maximum and the minimum number of years of experience required to handle this job. Specify the area in which this experience is needed and whether experience should be direct or indirect.

		(Type of Experience—	
	Minimum	*Check One)*	
Area	*No. of Yrs.*	*Direct*	*Indirect*
Economics	3	X	
Finance	2	X	
Marketing	2	X	
Planning	3	X	

		(Type of Experience—	
	Maximum	*Check One)*	
Area	*No. of Yrs.*	*Direct*	*Indirect*
Economics	8	X	
Finance	4	X	
Marketing	3	X	
Planning	4	X	

3. What special skills are necessary or desirable to successfully perform this job?

Incumbent   Supervisor   Analyst
Date: Date: Date:

Position Title: Director of Financial Planning

I. *Identifying Data*
   Division: Corporate
   Department: Financial Planning
   Position Number:

II. *To Be Filled in by the Incumbent*
   A. Description of Duties

   Please describe the duties of your job as you perform them in practice. State how often (daily, weekly, monthly); estimate the percentage of your time spent on these duties. Do not list more than six.

Duties	% of Time
1. Issues annual and long-range operating plans for combined corporation including operating and capital budgets. Responsible for policies and procedures involving the relationship with the line management.	
2. Conducts periodic monthly reviews of operations with president and executive committee and board of directors. (Board reviews are done quarterly.)	
3. Is responsible for financial consulting to president on such matters as company and division targets, transfer pricing policy, price administration, reporting systems, etc.	
4. Issues other recurring reports, including the quarterly and annual stockholder's report (provides all narratives and charts).	
5. Develops and assists in development of such other special projects as pricing administrative procedure, management incentive compensation, and transfer pricing and management reporting relationship.	

   B. Scope of Supervision:
      Direct—7 Exempt, 3 Nonexempt
      Functional Responsibility *—14 Exempt, 4 Nonexempt
   C. Position Reports to: (Title)
      Corporate controller

---

* Includes luggage division profit planning, furniture division profit planning, toy division profit planning, Samsonite of Canada, Samsonite of Europe, Altro, S.A.

D. Position Requirements
   1. Please identify that aspect of your job which, in your opinion, is the most complex. Give an illustration.
   <u>Relationship with executive level and middle management and management of ten people reporting directly to manager.</u>

   2. What is the most important skill or personal quality required to successfully fulfill this most complex aspect? (*Ex.:* Ability to work under pressure, outstanding interpersonal skills, etc.)
   <u>Interpersonal skills combined with technical ability to recognize and solve complex financial problems.</u>

E. Comments—is there anything else about your job which you feel is important for its proper evaluation?
<u>The value that management, and indirectly the stockholders, can derive from using financial planning can have significant impact on earnings of corporation.</u>

III. *To Be Filled in by the Supervisor*
   A. Referring to the description of duties as filled out by the position incumbent, rank each duty in order of importance.
   <u>1, 2, 3, 4</u>

   Is there any important duty that you would like eventually to be (1) performed on this job and/or (2) eventually removed from the job?
   <u>(1) Merger and acquisition function</u>

   B. Position Requirements
   1. Please estimate both the minimum and the maximum amount of education required to handle this job. Specify in connection with each entry the major areas of concentration.

Min.   Max.

☐   ☐   High-school degree

☐   ☐   Some college. No. of years: _____
          Major area of concentration:

216

| [X] | [ ] | College degree. Type (B.A.____ B.S. __X__ Other____)
Major area of concentration:
Finance, Economics, Mkt. |

| [ ] | [ ] | Some postgraduate work. No. of years: ____
Major area of concentration: |

| [ ] | [X] | Postgraduate degree. Type (M.A.____ M.S. __X__
Ph.D.____ Other____)
Major area of concentration:
Finance, Economics, Mkt. |

2. Please estimate both the maximum and the minimum number of years of experience required to handle this job. Specify the area in which this experience is needed and whether experience should be direct or indirect.

Area	Minimum No. of Yrs.	(Type of Experience—Check One) Direct	Indirect
Finance (Acctg.)	5+	X	
Management Experience	2+	X	
Marketing	2		X
Mfg. & Engineering	2		X

Area	Maximum No. of Yrs.	(Type of Experience—Check One) Direct	Indirect

3. What special skills are necessary or desirable to successfully perform this job?
The experience and knowledge to be able to evaluate and integrate management information to all levels—ranging from peers and subordinates to regular participation in board of directors meetings.

Incumbent   Supervisor   Analyst
Date: Date: Date:

217

Exhibit 15. A Selection of 1968 Newspaper Display Advertisements for Planning Executives

VICE-PRESIDENT, CORPORATE PLANNING

An attractive career opportunity with a nationally known multidivisional manufacturer of machined products for an executive with comprehensive functional and administrative capabilities in the area of long-range corporate planning and evaluation of future growth potential.

A qualified candidate will have a college degree and will possess a minimum of 15 years' experience, which would reflect significant knowledge of analysis, evaluation, and planning necessary for a successful corporate development program.

DIRECTOR OF PROFIT PLANNING

A large growing investment organization has an opportunity for a senior profit planning executive. The successful candidate will be responsible for developing and implementing budgets and assisting top management in long-range planning, goal setting, and approaches to meeting objectives.

The director will have several years' experience in budget and profit planning in the securities and financial service industry and possess the ability to sell his ideas to management at all levels, as well as being capable of grasping an overview of our industry and national trends. A bachelor's degree in finance or accounting is required. M.B.A. or C.P.A. preferred.

CORPORATE PLANNING MANAGER

An excellent opportunity for an individual who wants to get totally involved in charting the path this billion-dollar, aggressive, diversified corporation should take in order to capitalize on its management, organization, computer hardware, and other resources.

He should have a professional understanding of modern management principles with a good knowledge of corporate finance . . . proven ability in analyzing and defining corporate problems. Be able to conduct industry studies . . . make recommendations and *sell* ideas through oral and written presentations to top management.

This is a fine management position which requires a man who is capable of working either on his own or in a management team approach and assuming major responsibility for projects dealing with growth, diversification, and long-term planning programs. Would like a minimum of five years' experience (consulting experience useful); M.B.A. helpful, but not an absolute requirement. Can you create, research, analyze, and *sell* your ideas? If so, talk to us.

Director of Corporate Planning

He will be responsible for the full range of corporate planning in a large multinational corporation, including complete development of annual plans for the corporation. His activities will include direct contact with the group president as well as all the major officers of the parent corporation.

The prime candidate has to have been involved with the business planning function of a major corporation and must have three to five years of solid financial planning background. Applicant should be thoroughly conversant with budget and accounting procedures and familiar with the overall concepts of data processing and the systems function. A broad basic knowledge of all business functions—i.e., marketing and production—is essential for this position.

Director of Corporate Planning

An aggressive individual to fill a new position at a diversified consumer-oriented company. This position reports directly to the vice-president–manpower and planning. The individual sought for this challenging position should ideally have an M.B.A. and three to five years' experience in one of the following areas: consulting, investment banking, accounting, or as an analyst. Responsible for development of corporate plans for expansion through internal growth and external acquisition.

Corporate Planner

An opportunity for an individual experienced in all phases of corporate planning—quantitative and qualitative—in a rapidly growing national organization. He will have primary responsibility for developing and maintaining an integrated planning system. He will be dealing directly with executives and divisional staff planning specialists in assisting them in making the planning process an integral part of the management function. He will help executives and managers define their goals, assign priorities to those goals, and utilize available resources in achieving them. In addition, he will coordinate planning activities between the various divisions and develop and conduct group seminars with executives and managers to continue their education in the use of the planning system.

The ideal candidate for this position will have an M.B.A. and seven to ten years' experience in corporate planning covering the full range of management functions.

Assistant to Manager of Profit Planning

Professional opportunity on the corporate finance staff of a major multidivisional manufacturing company. This position offers a significant opportunity at corporate level to coordinate and review profit plans, capital budgets, and manufacturing cost analyses of operating companies. Assignments will also include working with top management in special financial studies. Ideal candidate will have a minimum of two years' experience performing the specific responsibilities outlined (some supervisory experience helpful) and a minimum of seven years of progressively responsible overall experience. Applicant will also have a college degree (M.B.A. helpful) with undergraduate education in accounting.

Exhibit 16. Planning Committee Functions, Trans World Airlines Inc.

---

1. Establishes objectives and provides overall guidance for the corporation's planning program and process.
2. Establishes the specific responsibilities for operational and strategic planning in each area of the company.
3. Approves major business and technical planning premises, objectives, and strategy.
4. Approves environmental assumptions which serve as a frame of reference for other phases of corporate planning.
5. Reviews the major strategic plans and programs, objectives, and "missions" of each major area of TWA. These areas include, but are not limited to:

    - Marketing and resource allocation—including new route plans and total airline scheduling objectives.
    - Major facilities requirements and programs—aircraft, ground equipment, and facilities.
    - Manpower (nonunion and union) and management development.
    - Finance, including financing programs.
    - Data processing.
    - Methods, standards, and cost improvement.
    - Diversification, including merger objectives.

6. In furtherance of the foregoing, reviews the major strategic plans and programs of each major department or division on a regular basis.
7. Reviews progress against accepted objectives, plans, and programs.

The planning committee will be supported by a five-man staff which will report to the secretary of the committee. The staff will be composed of a director, a manager, and three analysts. Included will be individuals with a wide range of business know-how and competence in planning procedure. The staff will guide and coordinate the interdepartmental development of plans and prepare and maintain periodic reports on the status of strategic plans and programs for each major department. Additionally, this staff will undertake special planning studies, including those relating to computerized planning models.

Exhibit 17. *Duties of the Central Corporate Planning Staff at American Airlines, Inc.*

We established a central corporate planning staff to perform a central forecasting and strategic planning role and to coordinate the planning efforts of individual staffs. . . . Our planning staff pulls a final plan together, recommending it to the president to achieve the objectives top management has previously established. In this process the planning staff reconciles conflicts between interrelated functional plans. After plan approval the staff monitors the accomplishment of major short-term plans to insure that they are consistent with the long-range plan and that the required basic steps are being taken to make the approved long-range plan successful. The planning staff reviews each complete annual operating plan for consistency with the long-range plan, pointing up any detailed changes necessary to mesh the short-term actions with more distant objectives.

The corporate planning staff participates in the development of individual functional plans through the process of review, a challenging of questionable assumptions, and a resolving of conflicts between different interrelated functions, instead of criticism of individual plans after their development; there is a working with departments as plans are developed.

We have organized the central staff as a small group with varied talents. While the group requires a good operating and technical understanding of functional areas activities, it makes no effort to duplicate each functional skill. Such a move would be costly and would create conflicts between "experts."

We believe that in addition to handling its planning and special assignments, our planning staff can be an ideal training location for the assignment of management of particularly high potential.

The establishment of a central planning staff fixes the responsibility for the quality, timing, and integration of the plan and provides one unit whose sole purpose is to push the plan through successful development. This *avoids a committee approach,* which did not seem appropriate to us.

Exhibit 18. *Appropriation Requests, Corporate Procedure Manual, an Automobile Manufacturer*

INSTRUCTIONS:

1. *Request number.* Location preparing the request assigns a reference number. As a prefix to the number, the originating location's corporate location code number is indicated. Rejection or cancellation of a request permanently cancels the assigned number.

2. *Request.*
- *Title.* The title should indicate a brief but adequate description of the request. Omit part number, technical terms, and phrases that are self-evident. Following the title, indicate the applicable reason code description per current capital plan instructions.
- *Type.* Indicate one or more of the following types of requests: program appropriation request, program project appropriation request, project appropriation request, supplemental request, critical long-lead request, emergency request, deviation request, lease request, and disposal request.

Section B contains a definition of each of these requests and explains the application of each. [Section B is not included in this book.]

3. *Fund requirements.*
- Enter total program/project fund requirements detailed on Appropriation Request Data form. If funds have been previously approved, indicate as follows:

    $_____this request
    $_____total to date

- When related lease or disposal authorization is included on Appropriation Request Data form for simultaneous approval, indicate as follows:

    $_____facilities   or $_____facilities
    $(_____) disposal $_____lease

- When the request is for approval of a new lease and cancellation of an existing lease, indicate as follows:

    $_____new lease
    $(_____) existing lease

4. *Increase (decrease) in profits.*
- Enter the estimated increase (or decrease) in profits that will occur during the first 12 months starting with the month in which the proposal expenditures begin. This amount should be arrived at in the same manner that the "operating margin after taxes" is determined on the Financial Analysis Summary.
- Enter the average-year increase (or decrease) in profits after taxes from the Financial Analysis Summary.

5. *Financial measurements.*
- Enter the financial measurements after taxes from the Financial Analysis Summary.

6. *Description and purpose.*
- This information should explain the what, why, how, when, and where of the proposed action. Normally such an explanation can be made in less than 1,000 words. If necessary, indicate and continue narrative on a supplemental page.

Exhibit 19. Financial Analysis Summary, Appropriation Requests, Corporate Procedure Manual, an Automobile Manufacturer

	FINANCIAL ANALYSIS SUMMARY ☐ DOLLARS ☐ THOUSANDS OF DOLLARS								REQUEST NO.
DIVISION OR UNIT				PLANT				DATE	
ESTIMATED PRODUCTION	MODEL YEAR SAVINGS (LOSS)					AVERAGE YEAR			
DATE	19	19	19	19	19	PRESENT	PROPOSED	SAVINGS OR (LOSS)	
TOOLING VOLUME									
SALES									
C O S T S	DIRECT MAT'L. & INBOUND TRANS.								
	DIRECT LABOR								
	INDIRECT LABOR								
	FRINGE BENEFITS								
	MAINTENANCE MATERIAL								
	SUPPLIES								
	TAXES								
	RENTAL EXPENSE								
	OTHER EXPENSE								
	DEPRECIATION								
	PROJECT EXPENSE								
	PREPRODUCTION EXPENSE								
	LAUNCHING COSTS								
	TOOL AMORTIZATION								
	OUTBOUND TRANSPORTATION								
	GEN. & ADMIN. EXPENSE								
	OTHER INCOME & DEDUCTIONS								
	TOTAL COSTS								
OPERATING MARGIN BEFORE TAXES									
OPERATING MARGIN AFTER TAXES									
DEPRECIATION/AMORTIZATION									
TAX CREDIT ON NEW ASSETS									
CASH RETURN									

INVESTMENT	INITIAL AMOUNT	INVESTMENT FOR PAYOUT PERIOD	AV. INVESTMENT FOR RETURN
PROJECT ASSETS (INCL. SPECIAL TOOLS)			
EXPENSE			
CASH AND RECEIVABLES			
INVENTORY			
TOTALS			

PAYOUT PERIOD AFTER TAXES	AVERAGE RETURN ON AVERAGE INVESTMENT	
_____ YEARS _____ MONTHS	BEFORE TAXES	%
	AFTER TAXES	%

Exhibit 20. Request Justification, Corporate Procedure Manual, an Automobile Manufacturer

Factor	First Five Years	Average Year
Cost		
Project, preproduction, and launching costs	Write off in first year.	Use 20% of total for projects of five years' duration or more. For projects of less than five years' duration, use the average cost for number of years involved.
Depreciation	Use declining balance rates.	Use straight-line rate.
Tool amortization	Use amortization rates applicable to each year as per amortization cycle.	Show average—over product cycle. (Two-year cycle equals 50%, etc.)
Other "out-of-pocket" costs	Forecast cash differences at tooling volume for each year.	Forecast cash differences at average tooling volume for a five-year period.
Investment		
Project expense	Not applicable, since the rate of return is computed for an average year only.	Exclude from investment base.
Fixed assets—new	As above.	Use 50% of cost of depreciable and amortizable assets. 100% for all others.
Special tools	As above.	Use 50% of cost.
Fixed assets—transferred	As above.	Exclude from investment base.
Working capital and inventory	As above.	Forecast requirements at average tooling volume for a five-year period.
Facilities Being Replaced		
Depreciation and taxes	Net against depreciation and taxes on new assets.	Exclude from consideration.
Investment base	Not applicable.	Not applicable.

Exhibit 21. Postproject Evaluation (Projected and Actual Accomplishments), Corporate Procedure Manual, an Automobile Manufacturer

INSTRUCTIONS

1. *Increase (decrease) in profits—after tax.*

    - *First Three Months—Projected.* Enter the operating margin change after taxes from the "project for period" column.
    - *First Three Months—Actual.* Enter the operating margin change after taxes from the "actual for period" column.
    - *Average Year—Projected.* Enter the operating margin change after taxes shown on the original Financial Analysis Summary.
    - *Average Year—Actual.* Enter the operating margin change after taxes shown on the revised Financial Analysis Summary.

2. *Financial measurements—after tax.*

    - *Percent Return and Payout Period—Projected.* Enter this information from the "project" column of the payout and return section.
    - *Percent Return and Payout Period—Actual.* Enter this information from the "actual" column of the payout and return section.

3. *Comments.* The information in this section is presented in narrative form and should summarize the findings of the postproject evaluation. Basically, the following questions should be answered as completely as possible:

    - What were the objectives of the original proposal and were the objectives achieved? If not, why not?
    - Was the project completed in substantially the same form as it was approved?
    - What is the reason for any variance from the original proposal? All significant variances shown on the Postproject Evaluation—Comparison of Projected and Actual Financial Data should be explained in detail.
    - Was the timing of expenditures, production dates, etc., substantially as presented in the original proposal? Explain any significant variance.
    - Were any unusual conditions encountered during the period of review and what effect, if any, did they have on the overall progress of the proposal?
    - What are the future prospects of the project?

Exhibit 22. Project Appropriation Request, Appropriations Manual, Ford Motor Company

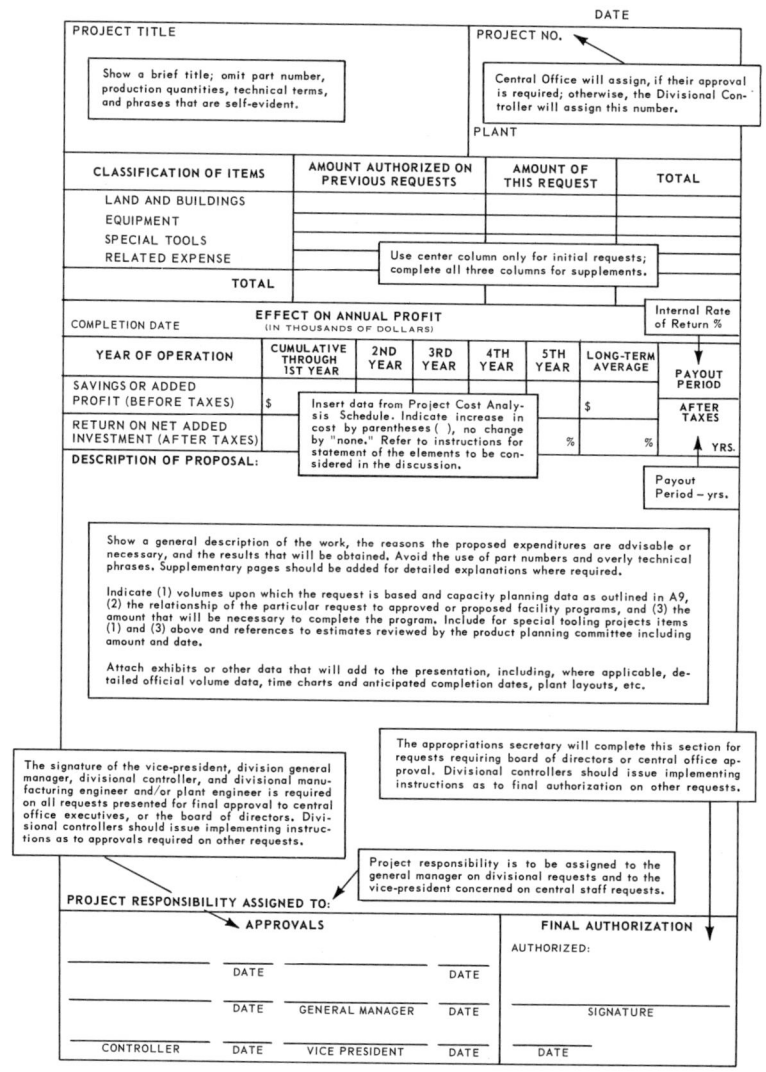

Exhibit 23. Project Worksheet, St. Regis Paper Company

LRP PHASE II PROJECT WORKSHEET
(SUBMIT 1 FORM FOR EACH PROJECT)

TITLE: _____

DESCRIPTION OF PROJECT:

REPORTING UNIT: _____

LIFE OF PROJECT (GUIDELINE OR ECONOMIC)
_____ YEARS

IF START-UP COSTS ARE INCLUDED, STATE AMOUNT AND YEAR
$ _____   19 ____

($000 OMITTED)	1969	1970	1971	1972	1973
UNITS SOLD (SPECIFY)					
NET SALES – TRADE	$	$	$	$	$
– INTERCOMPANY					
TOTAL NET SALES	$	$	$	$	$
COST OF GOODS SOLD – DEPREC. (STRAIGHT-LINE)	$	$	$	$	$
– OTHER FIXED					
– LABOR INCREASES					
– VARIABLE					
TOTAL COST OF GOODS SOLD	$	$	$	$	$
GROSS PROFIT	$	$	$	$	$
SELLING EXPENSES					
ADMIN. & GENERAL EXPENSES					
TOTAL SELLING & ADMIN.	$	$	$	$	$
OPERATING INCOME	$	$	$	$	$
ADDITIONAL WORKING CAPITAL – ACCTS. REC.	$	$	$	$	$
– INVENTORY					
TOTAL WORKING CAPITAL	$	$	$	$	$
CAPITAL EXPENDITURES: PROJECT	$	$	$	$	$
MAINTAINING PROJECT					
PROPERTY RETIREMENTS: BOOK VALUE	$	$	$	$	$
CASH VALUE	$	$	$	$	$

APPROVED BY: _____   DATE _____

PROJECTED CASH FLOW

YEARS	CAPITAL EXPENDITURES (INCL. WORKING CAPITAL)	OPERATING INCOME AT 50% PLUS DEPRECIATION
1ST		
2ND		
3RD		
4TH		
5TH		
6TH		
7TH		
8TH		
9TH		
10TH		
11TH		
12TH		
13TH		
14TH		
15TH		
16TH		
17TH		
18TH		
19TH		
20TH		
21ST		
22ND		
23RD		
24TH		
TOTAL	$	$

DISCOUNTED CASH FLOW
PROFITABILITY INDEX _____ % AFTER TAX

COMMITTED ☐   (INCL. IN PHASE I)

Exhibit 24. Checklists for Market Positions and Market Developments, Continental Can Company, Inc.

Checklist 1—Market Positions

The following checklist is to assist in preparing an appraisal of the division's strengths and weaknesses in the broad area of contact with its markets.

1. How do our reputation and customer relationships compare with those of our competitors? Are there any aspects of our reputation and relationships which might be applicable to business activities in which we do not now participate?

2. Have we been successful in identifying the factors of greatest importance in influencing the purchase decisions of our customers and prospects? Have we oriented our product lines, sales, promotions, and service programs properly in view of these factors?

3. Is our business broadly based, or are we overly dependent upon a small number of customers? Does a disproportionately large share of our profit derive from a single product or a single class of customer?

4. Is our product line too narrow or too broad? Are the products truly complementary?

5. Are we selling effectively to all the geographic markets which are economically accessible? Are we selling to all the customer classes that should be logical prospects for our products? What limiting factors inhibit or prevent us from selling into additional markets?

6. Is our distribution system well suited to the needs of our customers? Would this system be capable of distributing efficiently any product lines which we do not now sell? Are there wasteful or otherwise undesirable overlaps between our distribution system and that of other Continental divisions?

Checklist 5—Market Developments

The following checklist is to assist in identifying market developments likely to be of importance to the division during the long-range planning period.

1. Who and where are our most important customers for the future? What are their major marketing and business problems which will have an impact on us as suppliers?

2. What factors will influence our customers' attitudes toward self-manufacture?

3. What average annual rate of growth or decline do we expect in industry demand for each major product line in which we now compete?

    a) What has been the recent historical trend in industry sales volume?
    b) Is the end-use served by the product mature or approaching maturity?
    c) Will our type of product make inroads on other products which serve a closely related customer need—e.g., cans vs. glass bottles for beer and beverages? In what end-uses is this most likely to occur?

d) Will our type of product be subject to inroads by competitive products? In what end-uses is this most likely to occur?

4. What new products recently introduced or likely to be introduced during the planning period will compete to fill customer needs that we now serve?
   a) What suppliers (or types of suppliers) have introduced or are likely to introduce each new product?
   b) Will this new product grow at the expense of existing products which Continental currently produces?
   c) Would this be an attractive new product for Continental? What would be our comparative advantages vs. existing or potential competitors? What would be our disadvantages?
   d) If Continental were to produce this new product, to what extent would the product replace sales of (1) our division's existing product lines or (2) products of other Continental divisions?

5. What geographical shifts will take place in our potential market which might affect our sales and profit opportunities?

6. Are industry pricing practices likely to become more orderly or less orderly during the planning period?

7. What new consumer products will be introduced during the planning period which should be candidates for packaging by our division?

Exhibit 25. Checklist for Technological Developments, Continental Can Company, Inc.

Checklist 6—Technological Developments

The following checklist is to assist in identifying technological developments likely to be of importance to the division during the long-range planning period.

1. What recent developments by Continental may have substantial impact on the division during the planning period?
   a) New manufacturing processes or equipment?
   b) New packaging systems or products?
   c) New materials?

2. What recent developments by others may have substantial impact on the division during the planning period?

3. To what extent will the developments described in items (1) and (2) above make obsolete the division's present equipment, products, and/or packaging systems?

4. What development programs relevant to the division's business are known to be under way by competition, by the government, or by other outside agencies? Do any of these programs seem close to fulfillment? What might be their impact?

5. What apparent needs of our customers and prospects are not well satisfied by today's technology? Is there any likelihood that such needs may be filled during the planning period as a result of our own or our competitors' technological developments?

Exhibit 26. Form for Division Cash Plan, a Food Company

DIVISION	FISCAL 1968		FISCAL 1969				FISCAL 1970
DOMESTIC UNITS	MARCH QTR.	TOTAL YEAR	JUNE QTR.	SEPT. QTR.	DEC. QTR.	MARCH QTR.	TOTAL YEAR	TOTAL YEAR

DOMESTIC UNITS

OPENING BALANCE
CASH SOURCE OR (USE) [1]
  PROFIT BEFORE TAXES
  DEPRECIATION EXPENSE
  NET BOOK VALUE OF
    FIXED ASSET DISPOSALS
  WORKING CAPITAL (INCR)/DECR. [2]

  CAPITAL ADDITIONS
  OTHER ASSETS (INCR)/DECR.
  OTHER LIABILITIES INCR/(DECR)

NET CASH INCREASE (DECREASE)
CASH (NEEDED) AVAILABLE

CLOSING BALANCE

  GROSS SALES
  NET SALES
  COST OF GOODS SOLD

FOREIGN UNITS – U.S. DOLLARS

CASH FLOW TO CORP. [3]
  DIVIDENDS – INTERCO
  ROYALTIES – INTERCO
  INTERCO CURRENT ACCT - INCR/(DECR)

  TOTAL

CASH DRAIN ON CORP. [3]
  EQUITY CONTRIBUTIONS
  ACQUISITION CONTRIBUTIONS
  OTHER (IDENTIFY)

  TOTAL

CASH & MARKETABLE SECURITIES - CLOSING BALANCE

  CAPITAL ADDITIONS
  DEPRECIATION
  GROSS SALES
  NET SALES
  COST OF GOODS SOLD

[1] (use) – Indicates increase in assets and decrease in liabilities.
[2] Less cash and state and federal income tax payable (per balance sheet)
[3] Attach explanatory comments

Exhibit 27. Form for Projection of Sales, Income, and Return on Employed Capital for Divisions' Long-Range Plans, Continental Can Company, Inc.

Long-Range Plan _____ Division, Schedule 1
Projection of Sales, Income, and Return on Employed Capital for 1971

	1966 Current Estimate				Forecast of Average Annual Sales Changes 1966–1971			1971 Forecast			
	Gross Sales Trade	B/F Sales	Pretax Net Income	Average Employed Capital	Pretax Return on Employed Capital	Total Industry Unit Basis	Total Industry Dollar Basis	CCC (Dollar Basis)	Gross Sales Trade	B/F Sales	Pretax Net Income	Average Employed Capital	Pretax Return on Employed Capital
	$000	$000	$000	$000	%	%	%	%	$000	$000	$000	$000	%
Total Division													
Product Group A													
Product Group B													
Product Group C													

"Sales," "net income," and "employed capital" are those reflected at division level in monthly management control reports. Employed capital includes rented and leased-back plants; all newly acquired assets are assumed to be owned outright. Breakdown of employed capital is provided on schedule 1B.

Exhibit 28. Form for Sales and Net Income by Year for Divisions' Long-Range Plans, Continental Can Company, Inc.

Long-Range Plan _____ Division _____
Sales and Net Income by Year Through 1971   Schedule 1A

	1966 Current Est.		1967 Forecast		1968 Forecast		1969 Forecast		1970 Forecast		1971 Forecast	
	Gross Sales Trade	Pretax Net Income	Gross Sales Trade	Pretax Net Income	Gross Sales Trade	Pretax Net Income	Gross Sales Trade	Pretax Net Income	Gross Sales Trade	Pretax Net Income	Gross Sales Trade	Pretax Net Income
Total Division	=====	=====	=====	=====	=====	=====	=====	=====	=====	=====	=====	=====
Product Group A												
Product Group B												
Product Group C												

Employed Capital by Year Through 1971   Schedule 1B

	1966	1967	1968	1969	1970	1971
Total Fixed Assets—Jan. 1						
Fixed Assets Acquired						
Depreciation	( )	( )	( )	( )	( )	( )
Retirements, Write-offs and Abandonments	( )	( )	( )	( )	( )	( )
Total Fixed Assets—Dec. 31						
Average Fixed Assets						
Average Inventory (Month-End)						
Average Receivables (Month-End)						
Average Employed Capital						

Fixed assets should be computed at unrecovered cost. Rented and leased-back plants should be included; assume for purposes of

Exhibit 29. Instructions for Preparing Financial Summary of Long-Range Plan, Continental Can Company, Inc.

1. The format to be employed is illustrated by Schedule 1, Projection of Sales, Income, and Return on Employed Capital for 1971. Supporting Schedules 1A and 1B detail the year-by-year transition from 1966 to 1971.

2. Although Schedule 1 indicates a breakdown by product groups, the division's operations may be broken down by end-use markets, plant locations, or other criteria if such breakdown is more meaningful. For most divisions the breakdown should be on the same basis used for annual budget presentations, with additional or fewer categories as appropriate to the longer time span. If it is anticipated that new product groups will be added by 1971, for example, such product groups should be identified and shown separately from current product groups.

3. Schedule 1 should display the logical financial implications of business strategies and plans of action proposed by the division. If two or more substantially different strategies are under active consideration, a separate Schedule 1 should be provided for each such strategy.

4. Guidelines with respect to *overall* U.S. prices and labor costs should be as follows:

   a. The consumer price index will rise by 2% per annum.
   b. Industrial prices on average will increase by 2% per annum.
   c. Average hourly labor costs, including fringe benefits, will increase by 4% per annum.

Projections of sales and income should *not* assume automatically that selling prices and costs relevant for the division will conform to the overall guidelines above. On the contrary, the relationship between price levels and cost factors which affect the division should be forecast on the basis of demand, supply, and competitive factors specific to your division's situation.

5. It is essential that the forecast of new capital requirements be all-inclusive, not merely the sum of known projects. In other words, sufficient capital must be provided to support the projected sales and income levels, regardless of whether or not the division knows specifically how and where the capital will be employed.

Exhibit 30. Form for Consolidated Long-Range Financial Plan, St. Regis Paper Company

LONG-RANGE FINANCIAL PLAN

REPORTING UNIT:

	HISTORICAL		BUDGET	PLANNED			
(THOUSANDS OF DOLLARS)	1966	1967	1968	1969	1970	1971	1972	1973
PHASE I								
NET SALES	100.0 %	100.0 %	100.0 %	100.0 %	100.0 %	100.0 %	100.0 %	100.0 %
COST OF SALES								
GROSS PROFIT								
EXPENSES:								
SELLING								
ADMIN. & GENERAL								
TOTAL								
OPERATING INCOME								
PHASE II (DESCRIPTION OF SPECIFIC PROJECTS LISTED BELOW)								
NET SALES				100.0 %	100.0 %	100.0 %	100.0 %	100.0 %
COST OF SALES								
GROSS PROFIT								
EXPENSES:								
SELLING								
ADMIN. & GENERAL								
TOTAL								
OPERATING INCOME								
CONSOLIDATED								
NET SALES			100.0 %	100.0 %	100.0 %	100.0 %	100.0 %	100.0 %
COST OF SALES								
GROSS PROFIT								
EXPENSES:								
SELLING								
ADMIN. & GENERAL								
TOTAL								
OPERATING INCOME								
INTERCOMPANY SALES			%	%	%	%	%	%
CAPACITY USED (UNIT:								
CAPACITY AT 100.0%			100.0	100.0	100.0	100.0	100.0	100.0

DESCRIPTION OF PROJECTS:

DATE:

Exhibit 31. Form for Cash Flow and Ratios for Long-Range Financial Plan, St. Regis Paper Company

REPORTING UNIT:

LONG-RANGE FINANCIAL PLAN

(THOUSANDS OF DOLLARS)	*HISTORICAL 1966	1967	BUDGET 1968	1969	PLANNED 1970	1971	1972	1973
CASH FLOW OPERATING INCOME								
ADD: − DEPRECIATION								
− AMORTIZATION								
LESS WORKING CAPITAL − RECEIVABLES								
− INVENTORY								
TOTAL								
CASH FLOW								
LESS CAPITAL EXPENDITURES: − MAJOR PROJECTS								
− MAINTAINING								
TOTAL								
NET CASH FLOW								
* PER BALANCE SHEET								
TOTAL ASSETS (RECEIVABLES, INVENTORIES, AND NET FIXED ASSETS OTHER THAN TIMBERLANDS)								
RATIOS FOR REPORTING UNIT ANNUAL SALES GROWTH (%) GOAL								
LRP HEREON								
OPERATING INCOME TO NET SALES (%) GOAL								
LRP HEREON								
RETURN ON TOTAL ASSETS (%) GOAL								
LRP HEREON								

COMMENTS:

APPROVED BY:
DATE:

Exhibit 32. Long-Range Plan, Phase I, Operating Income Worksheet, St. Regis Paper Company

LRP PHASE I OPERATING INCOME WORKSHEET

REPORTING UNIT: _____

(THOUSANDS OF DOLLARS)	1968	(1)	1969	%	1970	%	1971	%	1972	%	1973	%
UNITS SOLD												
NET SALES: TRADE		%										
INTERCOMPANY												
TOTAL												
COST OF GOODS SOLD:												
DEPRECIATION												
OTHER FIXED												
LABOR INCREASES (2)												
OTHER (VARIABLE)												
TOTAL												
GROSS PROFIT												
SA&G EXPENSES: SELLING												
ADMIN. & GENERAL												
TOTAL												
OPERATING INCOME												

(1) – ORIGINAL BUDGET
(2) – LABOR INCREASES ARE INSERTED FOR THE REASON THAT THESE MUST BE RECOUPED BY SPECIFIC PHASE II PROJECTS (SELLING PRICE INCREASES OR COST REDUCTIONS) IN ORDER NOT TO INFLUENCE PROFITS.

WORKING CAPITAL INCREASE: RECEIVABLES												
INVENTORY												
CASH INFLOW												
CAPITAL EXPENDITURES FOR MAINTAINING OPER. FACILITIES												
NET CASH FLOW												

DATE: _____

Exhibit 33. *Instructions for Completing Long-Range Financial Planning Forms, St. Regis Paper Company*

Forms to Be Completed:

1. Phase I Operating Income Worksheet.
2. Phase II Project Worksheet.
3. Consolidated Sheet (Summary of Phases I and II operating income).
4. Cash-Flow and Ratios Sheet.
5. Calculation of Profitability Index Worksheet. [Not included here.]
6. Interpolation of Profitability Index Worksheet. [Not included here.]

Procedures for Completing Forms:

Phase I Operating Income Worksheet

The Nonproject Worksheet represents planned results without capital expenditures above that necessary to maintain facilities. (For maintaining capital expenditure projects which exceed $250,000 see Phase II Worksheet.) One sheet is to be completed for each location and one summary sheet for each division.

Sales should be forecast at normal growth rate for present facilities, with no allowances for changes in selling prices. (It is assumed that selling price changes will be offset by changes in raw-material prices. Should this assumption be unreasonable then a Phase II Project Sheet should be completed for the price changes.)

Depreciation is straight-line, with estimated annual adjustments for maintaining capital expenditures and fully depreciated assets. With respect to the deletion of fully depreciated assets from the depreciation base, please be guided by the policies set forth in the SPM, Office of the Comptroller, Section 10-5, Revised 12/1/65.

Other fixed is the sum of the figures shown on lines 12 and 13 of the current budget's Analysis of Changes in Budget Profit (Form 10-232 Schedule B) less depreciation and SA&G expenses. Divisions that do not prepare a Schedule B should use what they consider a realistic figure.

Labor increases are based on a study by the corporate industrial relations department and include Social Security increases. (See attached schedule for details.)

Other variable is based on the current budget's percentage of sales.

SA&G expenses are projected based upon historical trends.

Working-capital increases are incremental and should be based on current ratios to sales.

Cash inflow is operating income, plus depreciation and less working-capital increases.

Capital expenditures for maintaining operating facilities are estimates that should have some bearing on the current capital budget amount and prior years' actual expenditures.

Phase II Project Worksheet

The Project Worksheet represents planned results with income producing capital expenditures for either expansion or cost reduction, and those maintaining capital expenditures exceeding $250,000 that normally would be included in Phase I.

Generally, a separate worksheet should be prepared for each project over $250,000. Those projects under $250,000 should be treated as maintaining capital expenditures and included in Phase I. The worksheets, for the most part, will be developed from the data in the five-year capital budget.

Divisions with total assets (receivables, inventory, and net fixed assets) of less than $5 million should prepare a separate worksheet for all projects over $100,000 and treat projects of less than $100,000 as maintaining capital expenditures to be included in Phase I.

If labor increases for a project are significant, they should be included on worksheet.

Capital expenditures and working capital should be shown incrementally.

Where a project does not involve a significant capital expenditure but has major income potential a project sheet should be submitted. If further clarification is desired, please contact the budget department.

Forms for the calculation of profitability index are attached. Procedures are covered in the SPM, Office of the Comptroller, Section 10-9.

Consolidated Sheet (Summary of Phase I and Phase II)

Phase I is the consolidation of the Phase I Operating Income Worksheet and those Phase II sheets, if any, which have been "committed"—e.g., approved JOPA's.

Phase II is the total of all "noncommitted" Phase II sheets.

Consolidated is the total of Phases I and II.

Intercompany sales is total intercompany in consolidated net sales.

Capacity used is total volume for consolidated net sales. "Capacity at 100%" should be increased/decreased in future years by all Phase II projects which affect volume.

Description of projects: Titles, stated briefly, of all Phase II projects included in plan.

Cash-Flow Sheet

Operating income is consolidated figure on Consolidated Sheet.

Depreciation, working capital, and capital expenditures are the total of amounts appearing on Phase I Worksheet and Phase II Project Worksheets.

Divisions with amortization (including excess cost) should refer to appropriate schedules for annual amounts.

Total assets for historical years are December 31 balance sheet figures (receivables, line 15; inventory, line 21; and net fixed assets, line 40) plus, where applicable, receivables, notes, and excess cost on New York ledgers.

Future years' total assets are computed by subtracting depreciation and amortization, and adding working capital and capital expenditures to the last actual total assets figure.

(It should be noted that Timberland's figures are not included in divisional data.)

Ratios: *Divisional goals* are presently under consideration by the corporate long-range planning and policy committee.

Annual sales growth is the percent growth of consolidated net sales.

Operating income to net sales is the percentage shown for consolidated operating income.

Return on total assets is consolidated operating income (*not* net cash flow) as a percentage of total assets.

Exhibit 34. Illustrative Planning Strategies, a Food Company

Company Planning Strategies

Purpose	Function	Action to Be Taken	Goals	Controls	Assigned to
Improve organization	General management	1. Reassign executive responsibilities through new organization structure to more effectively manage the company, giving added attention to improvement and growth areas.	New organization chart by 8/1/67	Review as necessary	
	General management	2. Develop new job descriptions to clarify responsibilities and authority.	Complete by 1/1/68	Review annually	
	General management	3. Establish salary administration committee to evaluate and modify as necessary salary ranges and salary adjustment program to insure equitable pay for all employees.	Establish committee by 12/1/67	Review annually	
	General management	4. Establish specific set of objectives and analyses needed in each division and department to identify threats and opportunities and to reduce to writing as plan of action and assignment of responsibilities.	Prepare annually by 1/31/68	Semiannual review by department managers and president	Department managers

240

General management	5. To accommodate new tenant, move data processing and print shop to warehouse building; remodel and move headquarters office to second floor of office building.	Accomplish by 9/1/67	Constant review Warehouse Office
Sales	6. Train and develop assignments for merchandising manager.	Complete by 10/1/67	Review monthly
Controller	7. In view of _____'s liquidation, review current and future staff needs and develop manning table for five-year period.	Complete by 10/1/67	Review annually
Increase efficiency Controller	8. Determine EDP needs for future business incorporating central billing and inventory controls for all sales division. Explore feasibility of electronic inventory control depending on capabilities of recommended equipment.	Submit plan by 1/1/68	To be established after plan adopted

241

Exhibit 35. *Form for Summary of Major Product Program Analysis, an Electronics Manufacturer*

Group _____
Division _____
Program Number _____

Major Product Program
Analysis
Schedule 1-1

Summary of Major Product Program Analysis

PROGRAM MANAGER:

PRODUCT DESCRIPTION:

MAJOR MILESTONE COMPLETION DATES

    Design
    Prototype
    Release for Tooling
    Tooling
    Pilot
    Release to Manufacture
    First Production Lot
    Market Availability

FINANCIAL DATA

    Estimated Unit Cost
    Estimated Unit Gross Profit
    Estimated Total Development Cost
    Cumulative Return on Sales
    Cumulative Return on Assets
    Present Project Work
    Project Desirability Index

APPROVALS: _____ _____
                 _____ _____

Exhibit 36. Form for Reporting Commercial Potential for Major New Products

Group _____
Division _____
Program Number _____

**New Product Program
Analysis
Schedule 1-2**

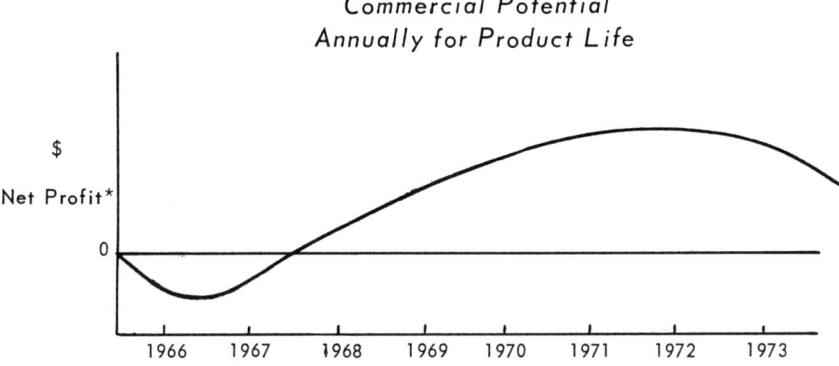

Commercial Potential
Annually for Product Life

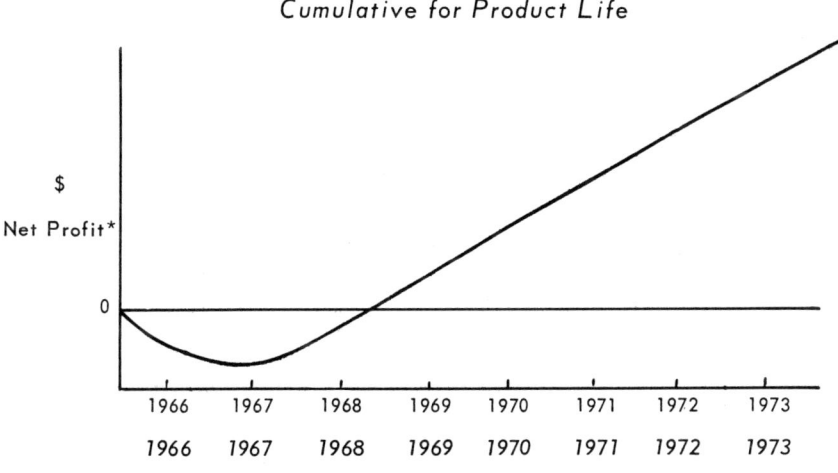

Cumulative for Product Life

Estimated
Percentage of
Division
Net Profit

* Line 7, Schedule 1-5

243

Exhibit 37. *Outline of Analysis of Product Objectives and Description for Major New Product, an Electronics Manufacturer*

Group _____   Major Product Program
Division _____   Analysis
Program Number _____   Schedule 1-3

Product Objectives and Description

1. *Product Description Including Major Features or Characteristics*
   Attach complete specification sheet if available.
2. *Cost and Price Targets*
   What range of unit cost targets do you feel 90% confident of achieving?
3. *Basic Business Proposition—The Differential Advantage*
   What justifies your confidence that we have something important and unique to offer in this product?
4. *Patent or Other Proprietary Implications*
5. *Major Risks of This Program*
   What could go wrong?
6. *Major Technical Problems*
7. *Technical Relationship to Other Products*
8. *Unusual Requirements in Manufacturing or Marketing Skills, Facilities, or Strategies*
9. *Key Personnel Required*
   Who will be responsible for meeting objectives and solving major problems?

Exhibit 38. *Outline of Analysis of Market Opportunity for Major New Product, an Electronics Manufacturer*

Group _____   Major Product Program
Division _____   Analysis
Program Number _____   Schedule 1-4

Market Opportunity

1. *Particular Market Aimed at*
   Identify that portion of the total market for which the product is technically adequate and economically competitive.
2. *Projected Size of Market and Company's Projected Share of It*
   Give basis for these estimates. What range of sales volume do you feel 90% confident of achieving?
3. *Best Estimate of How Volume Varies with Price*
   Give reason for selecting target price.
4. *Specific Competitive Advantages of This Product*
5. *Evidence of Value Added vs. Cost of Significant Features*

6. *Anticipated Developments and Reaction of Competitors*
   Indicate anticipated competitive developments prior to the introduction of the product and reaction to the product when introduced.
7. *Effect Product Will Have on Existing Products in the Line*

Exhibit 39. *Form for Calculating Effect on Annual Profit of a Major New Product, an Electronics Manufacturer*

Group _____   Major Product Program
Division _____   Analysis
Program Number _____   Schedule 1-5

Effect on Annual Profit

| | | | | | | Cum. |
| | 1967 | 1968 | 1969 | 1970 | 1971 | After | Total |

1. Sales of New Product $
                               Units
   Less Sales Taken from $
      Existing Product   Units
2. Net Additional Sales $
3. Net Additional Gross Profit
      (*incremental*)
4. Less Other Expenses
      (*incremental*):
   Project expense prior to commercialization
   General and Administrative
   Advertising and Sales Promotion
   Other Selling Expense
   Other Divisional Expense
   Group Expense
5. Incremental Profit (Before P/S, Taxes)
   Return on Sales
   Return on Net Added Assets
6. Incremental Profit (After P/S, Taxes)
   Return on Sales
   Return on Net Added Assets
7. Net Additional Gross Profit
      (*full cost*)
8. Less Other Expenses (*full cost*):
   Project expense prior to commercialization

245

General and Administrative
Advertising and Sales Promotion
Other Selling Expense
Other Divisional Expense
Group Expense
9. Profit (Before Corporate Allocations, P/S, Taxes)
Return on Sales
Return on Net Added Assets
Return on Total Investment
10. Profit (After Corp., P/S, Tax, Interest, etc.)
Return on Sales
Return on Net Added Assets
Return on Total Investment

Investment Base

	1967	1968	1969	1970	1971	Cum. After	Total

11. Net Added Facilities
12. Net Added Equipment
13. Working Capital
14. Inventories
15. Other Capital Requirements
16. NET ADDED ASSETS
17. Unrecovered Project Expense
18. Allocation of Existing Fixed Assets
19. Cash inflow (after tax) from
    —Investment credit
    —Depreciation
20. *Total investment*

Exhibit 40. Form for Reporting Allocation of Manpower and Detail of Development Costs for a Major New Product, an Electronics Manufacturer

---

Group _____   Major Product Program
Division _____   Analysis
Program Number _____   Schedule 1-6

Allocation of Manpower and Detail of Development Costs

ALLOCATION OF MANPOWER

Program Manager
Responsibility for Major Functional Activities
Responsibility for Support Activities

DETAIL OF DEVELOPMENT COSTS

Added Facilities
Added Equipment
Project Expense Before Commercialization:
- Advanced Development
- Development
- Design
- Production Engineering
- Tooling
- Manufacturing Start-Up
- Marketing Start-Up
- Other
- Total Project Expense

Total Development Cost

Exhibit 41. *Form for Reporting Unit Costs and Profitability for a Major New Product, an Electronics Manufacturer*

Group _____   Major Product Program
Division _____   Analysis
Program Number _____   Schedule 1-7

UNIT COSTS AND PROFITABILITY

Unit Manufacturing Cost

	Labor Min.	Labor $	Mfg. Ovhd. $	Mat'l $	Mat'l Ovhd. $	Total
Major Parts / Components						
a						
b						
c						
d						
e						
f						
g						
Assembly						
Total						

UNIT PRICING

Unit Cost from Above
Other Costs Associated with Product
  Warranty
  Service
  Selling and Distribution
  General and Administrative
  Development

247

Total Cost Before Corporate Allocations, Capital Gains or Losses, Interest, Profit Sharing, and Federal Income Taxes
Selling Price Required to Attain _____% Profit
Average Discount from List
List Price

UNIT PROFIT

Gross Profit
% to Sales
Net Profit
% to Sales

Exhibit 42. *President's Letter Announcing Start of a Formal Long-Range Planning Process, Continental Can Company, Inc.*

To: Division Vice-Presidents and General Managers

Subject: Long-Range Planning

The current pace and diversity of our business demand that we institute a more formal long-range planning procedure than has been necessary in the past. Accordingly, each operating division will prepare and submit a divisional long-range plan to the corporate planning department by July 1, 1965. It is expected that each plan will be discussed subsequently by the division general manager with his group executive vice-president and the president.

Long-range planning is an important responsibility of division management; no one can do your planning for you. The corporate planning department is available, however, to help develop techniques and formats appropriate to your particular situation. It also should be called upon freely to review your progress and to discuss any problems encountered in the course of planning.

There is no single formula by which to specify the content for a useful long-range plan. In almost every case, however, plans should include the following:

1. A statement of the current situation, including (a) an outline of the "franchise" or "mission" of your division as you see it, (b) an analysis of your competitive strengths and weaknesses, and (c) an evaluation of profitability of your operations in relation to resources employed.

2. A forecast of the environment in which your division will operate during the planning period, which should extend at least through 1970. Trends in markets, technology, competition, labor, and other cost factors should be taken into account. (To help you with this, the corporate marketing department will release a five-year forecast of market trends on about May 1. Start of plan preparation should not await this document, but its contents should be considered prior to submission of your plan.)

3. A brief description of the problems, opportunities, and alternative strategies which are suggested by your forecast of the environment in which

you will be operating, followed by a thorough analysis of the strategic plan which you select.

4. Based upon the anticipated environment and the strategic plan which you select, realistic profit goals should be established and stated. If a suitable return on employed capital cannot be obtained, you should outline strategies for converting undesirable segments of the business into capital for employment elsewhere.

5. The resulting plan of operations should be expressed in summary form in terms of sales, income, and employed capital for each year 1966 through 1970. (A standardized format for this financial summary will be provided by the corporate planning department.) The support required to achieve the plan, such as research results, management requirements, and major capital projects, should be summarized briefly.

Effective planning is a continuous process, and changing conditions may make obsolete any written document in a short time. Therefore, while it is expected that the formal submission of plans will be required only once annually, major changes in your thinking should be reported by amendments to your plan as appropriate.

Carefully prepared divisional long-range plans are essential if group and corporate management are to evaluate properly the many demands for research and capital funds. Moreover, the thought process necessary in preparing a long-range plan, the material developed, and the timing of submission should prove helpful to your normal sales, income, and capital budgeting effort. Finally, and most important, your plan should be valuable as a guide to you and your associates in operating your division.

E. L. Hazard

cc: [Heads of corporate staff departments]

Exhibit 43. Introduction to "Guide for Preparing a Divisional Long-Range Plan," Continental Can Company, Inc.

Certain common steps have been found in the planning processes of most highly successful executives, both within Continental and in other companies. Carrying out all of these steps systematically usually enables a manager to make efficient use of time devoted to planning. More important, touching all the bases greatly increases the likelihood that the ultimate plan of operations will be sound.

In this guide the essential steps of planning are described in a logical sequence. This does not imply that one "chapter" of a plan can be written down with finality before the next is begun. Quite the contrary, efficient planning is a circular (and unending) process of continuous refinement. In writing out a long-range plan, therefore, you probably will want to schedule several drafts, allowing sufficient time between drafts to fill the information gaps which each draft is likely to uncover.

In this guide several of the steps of long-range planning are illustrated by checklists which are applicable to most Continental divisions. These checklists are arranged to facilitate subdividing the task of developing information. The entire planning process, however, will require continuous participation of the division general manager.

Exhibit 44. Table of Contents for "Guide for Preparing a Divisional Long-Range Plan," Continental Can Company, Inc.

INTRODUCTION

SECTION I. *Stating the Current Situation*

   A. Defining Scope of the Division
   B. Evaluating Profitability
   C. Appraising Strengths and Weaknesses
      Checklist 1: Market positions
      Checklist 2: Development capabilities
      Checklist 3: Manufacturing facilities and know-how
      Checklist 4: People

SECTION II. *Specifying the Future Environment*

      Checklist 5: Market developments
      Checklist 6: Technological developments
      Checklist 7: Cost factors
      Checklist 8: Competitive activities

SECTION III. *Formulating Strategy and Objectives*

SECTION IV. *Developing a Plan of Action*

SECTION V. *Establishing Specific Goals*

SECTION VI. *Summaries for Corporate Purposes*

Exhibit 45. Form for Forecast of Annual Capital Requirements for Divisions' Long-Range Plans, Continental Can Company, Inc.

Long-Range Plan _____ Division, Schedule 1A

Forecast of Annual Capital Requirements Through 1970

	1965	1966	1967	1968	1969	1970
Total Employed Capital, Jan. 1						
Fixed Assets						
Inventory						
Receivables						
Net Change in Employed Capital During Year						
New Fixed Assets						
Depreciation	( )	( )	( )	( )	( )	( )
Retirements, Write-offs, and Abandonments	( )	( )	( )	( )	( )	( )
Changes in Amount of Inventory						
Changes in Amount of Receivables						
Total Employed Capital, Dec. 31						
Fixed Assets						
Inventory						
Receivables						
Average Employed Capital During Year (Mean of Total Employed Capital Jan. 1 and Dec. 31)						

Fixed assets should be computed at unrecovered cost. Rented and leased-back plants should be included; assume for purposes of this schedule that all new fixed assets will be owned outright.

Exhibit 46. Memorandum from Director of Planning and Research, Outlining Contents and Approach to the Preparation of Divisions' Long-Range Plans for 1969–1973, Miehle-Goss-Dexter, Inc.

[In the spring of 1969 the company signed a merger agreement with the North American Rockwell Corporation. It was stated then that the merger should mark a new era in the graphic arts industries with the combining of North American's aerospace technology and Miehle-Goss-Dexter's extensive experience in printing systems.]

To: Division and Subsidiary Presidents   Date: February 6, 1968
Copy to: [Heads of Corporate Staff Departments]

From: R. L. Peterson
Subject: Long-Range Plan for 1969–1973

This cover letter and the attached document outlining the specific content and pertinent instructions are intended as the basis for each division's preparation of the 1969–73 Long-Range Plan. We are instituting a number of changes and additions to increase the usefulness of this effort, recognizing that they will add to the complexity and extent of the plan.

OBJECTIVES OF THE LONG-RANGE PLAN

1. It is our objective to have the LRP sufficiently well prepared that it will be an active document throughout the year. Also, it is our intent that the report which represents your long-range plan will be *as much a "plan"* as it is a forecast of operating results. To this end we have included a number of instructions concerning descriptive material which is to be submitted with your forecasts.

2. Heavy emphasis will be placed on presenting the rationale and documentation of the plans which lie behind the actual financial forecasts included in the plan. We feel this will be to everyone's benefit and if done properly, will eliminate problems during or after the review sessions.

3. A major objective in building a good plan, thoroughly reviewed and accepted by both division and corporate management, is to develop a set of long-term targets and programs such that the divisions can be generally autonomous in accomplishing the programs and results from that point forward.

Corporate management and staff can then devote more of their attention to: (1) those problems in any division which have been mutually identified in this plan; (2) giving a great deal more of their attention to the future of the corporation.

4. As a part of our overall financial planning, the 1969 figures included in the LRP will be considered an accurate forecast of the 1969 profit plan which is to be officially submitted by August 15, 1968. This will pertain to both the operating statements and the capital budgets which will be part of this plan. These figures are to be developed on a quarterly basis for all of 1969 and the first two quarters of 1970.

5. The corporate staff groups will also be asked to prepare an appropriate plan and forecast to be included as a section in the overall corporate long-range plan.

6. Subsequent to the completion and presentation of division and staff LRP's, work will be undertaken to outline any expansion and/or acquisition objectives which will be required to meet the corporate overall growth and performance objectives. This will be delayed until the division and staff LRP's have been completed, to allow time for assisting in plan preparation and review. Also, a better job can be done having the benefit of these plans and forecasts before determining our needs in this area.

TIMING OF PLANNING ACTIVITIES

The timing for long-range plans this year is being altered to facilitate adequate preparation and review. Various divisional plans are submitted on April 1, April 15, May 1, and May 15.

April 1	*April 15*	*May 1*	*May 15*
Goss Div.	Miehle Div.	MGD Limited	Dexter Div.
	MGD Canada	European Sales	Lawson Div.
	MGD Pneumatics	Subs.	
		Fincor	

This schedule permits a minimum of approximately two full months for the preparation of the forecasts and the outlining of your current or any newly developed plans which underlie these forecasts.

PROCEDURAL ITEMS

Although a number of changes will be made, reference should be made to the Long-Range Planning Practices bulletin dated March 31, 1967, for certain procedural items not covered herein. You will note that there are several changes already outlined in this letter and the attached document. The following should be noted:

1. A liaison man should be appointed, through whom we can obtain any necessary information. It is our intention to make, as appropriate, in-process reviews as to the progress and direction of the respective planning efforts and thereby be of any assistance possible before the plan's completion, rather than asking for a lot of rework or additional information after the plan is originally submitted.

2. We fully expect the extent and complexity of the planning effort to be documented in the long-range plan must be adjusted to suit the respective divisions because of their varying size and nature of their business. After you have had an opportunity to review this material, please contact the writer so we may discuss the specifics which are to be included and your choice of a liaison man.

3. Information exchange—please bear in mind that it will still be necessary to exchange information at the earliest practical date concerning the requirements for, or availability of, capacity to be used in interdivision subcontracting.

Also, as regards Eastern and Western Hemisphere marketing, the "selling unit" is to provide the appropriate manufacturing unit with forecasts by product line of the export volume of new orders.

The attached paper outlines the specific content and instructions which should form the framework for your long-range plan. Our purpose in detailing this to this degree is to indicate the thoroughness of planning which we look forward to, and to assist in the understanding and analysis of the plans at the corporate office. We are interested to a degree in the common format, such that the plans will be similar, but are not interested in forced conformity.

As mentioned earlier, we will be in touch with you concerning any questions you may have as to what is to be included in this year's plan.

Bibliography

Alderson, Wroe, and Green, Paul E. *Planning and Problem Solving in Marketing.* Homewood, Ill.: Richard D. Irwin, 1964.
Ansoff, H. Igor. *Corporate Strategy.* New York: McGraw-Hill, 1965.
Anthony, Robert N. *Planning and Control Systems.* Boston: Harvard University Press, 1965.
Appraising the Market for New Industrial Products. Studies in Business Policy, 123. New York: National Industrial Conference Board, 1967.
Argenti, John. *Corporate Planning.* New York: Dow-Jones-Irwin, 1968.
Bell, Daniel, ed. *Toward the Year 2000: Work in Progress.* Boston: Houghton Mifflin Co., 1968.
Bennis, Warren G.; Benne, Kenneth D.; and Chin, Robert. *Planning of Change.* New York: Holt, Rinehart and Winston, 1961.
Berg, Thomas L., and Shuchman, Abe, ed. *Product Strategy and Management.* New York: Holt, Rinehart and Winston, 1963.
Bierman, Harold, Jr., and Snidt, Seymour. *The Capital Budgeting Decision.* New York: Macmillan Co., 1960.
Bobbe, Richard A., and Schaffer, Robert A. *Mastering Change,* AMA Management Bulletin 120, 1968.
Bowman, Donald M., and Fillerup, Francis M. *Management Organization and Planning.* New York: McGraw-Hill, 1963.
Branch, Melville C. *The Corporate Planning Process,* AMA, 1962.
———. *Planning: Aspects and Applications.* New York: John Wiley & Sons, 1966.
Bright, James R. *Technological Planning on the Corporate Level.* Cambridge: Harvard University Press, 1962.

———. *Research Development and Technological Innovation.* Homewood, Ill.: Richard D. Irwin, 1964.
Brion, John M. *Corporate Marketing Planning.* New York: John Wiley & Sons, 1967.
Bunge, Walter R. *Managerial Budgeting and Profit Improvement.* New York: McGraw-Hill, 1968.
Burns, Thomas, and Stalker, G. M. *Management of Innovation.* Chicago: Quadrangle Books, 1961.
Bursk, Edward C., and Fenn, Dan H., Jr., ed. *Planning the Future Strategy of Your Business.* New York: McGraw-Hill, 1956.
Cannon, J. Thomas. *Business Strategy and Policy.* New York: Harcourt, Brace and World, 1968.
Capital Expenditure Control Program. Accounting Practice Report 7. New York: National Association of Accountants, 1957.
Cash Flow Analysis for Managerial Control. Research Report 38. New York: National Association of Accountants, 1961.
Cetron, Marvin J. *Technological Forecasting.* New York: Technological Forecasting Institute, 1969.
Chamberlain, Neil W. *The Firm Micro-Economic Planning and Action.* New York: McGraw-Hill, 1962.
Crisp, Richard D. *Sales Planning and Control.* New York: McGraw-Hill, 1961.
Dean, Joel. *Capital Budgeting.* New York: Columbia University Press, 1951.
Dearden, John. *Cost and Budget Analysis.* Englewood Cliffs, N.J.: Prentice-Hall, 1962.
Ewing, David, ed. *Long-Range Planning for Management.* New York: Harper & Row, 1964.
———. *The Human Side of Planning.* New York: Macmillan Co., 1969.
Faulhaber, Thomas A. *Manufacturing: Strategy for Growth and Change,* AMA, 1967.
Financial Analysis to Guide Capital Expenditure Decisions. Research Report 43. New York: National Association of Accountants, 1967.
Forrester, Jay W. *Industrial Dynamics.* Cambridge: M.I.T. Press, 1961.
Gershefki, George W. *The Sun Oil Company Corporate Model.* Oxford, Ohio: Planning Executives Institute, 1969.
Goetz, Billy E. *Management Planning and Control.* New York: McGraw-Hill, 1949.
Haas, Raymond M.; Hartman, Richard I.; James, John H.; and Milroy, Robert R. *Long Range Planning for Small Business.* Bloomington: Bureau of Research, Graduate School of Business, Indiana University, 1964.
Hackney, John W. *Control and Management of Capital Projects.* New York: John Wiley & Sons, 1965.
Hart, Albert G. *Anticipations, Uncertainty, and Dynamic Planning.* New York: Augustus M. Kelley, 1951.
Heckert, J. B., and Wilson, J. D. *Business Budgeting and Control.* New York: Ronald Press Co., 1967.

Heiser, Herman C. *Budgeting Principles and Practice.* New York: Ronald Press Co., 1959.
Hempel, Edward H. *Top Management Planning.* New York: Harper & Row, 1945.
Henry, Harold W. *Long Range Planning in 45 Industrial Companies.* Englewood Cliffs, N.J.: Prentice-Hall, 1967.
Holt, Charles C.; Modigliani, F.; Muth, J.; and Simon, H. A. *Planning Production, Inventories and Work Force.* Englewood Cliffs, N.J.: Prentice-Hall, 1960.
Humble, Thomas N. *Standards in Strategic Planning and Control.* Austin: University of Texas Press, 1966.
Istvan, Donald F. *Capital Expenditure Decisions.* Bloomington: Bureau of Business Research, Graduate School of Business, Indiana University, 1961.
Jallow, Ray. *Development and Contribution of an Asset Management Methodology to the Long Range Planning Function in the Banking Industry.* Los Angeles: Graduate School of Business Administration, University of California at Los Angeles, 1966.
Jantsch, Erich. *Technological Forecasting in Perspective.* Paris: Organization for Economic Cooperation and Development, 1967.
Jones, Reginald L., and Trentin, George. *Budgeting: Key to Planning and Control,* AMA, 1966; revised edition, 1971.
Kahn, Herman, and Wiener, Anthony J. *The Year 2000: A Framework for Speculation on the Next 33 Years.* New York: Macmillan Co., 1967.
Knight, W. D., and Weinwurm, E. H. *Managerial Budgeting.* New York: Macmillan Co., 1964.
Le Breton, Preston P., and Henning, Dale A. *Planning Theory.* Englewood Cliffs, N.J.: Prentice-Hall, 1961.
Lesser, Arthur, Jr., ed. "Decision Making Criteria for Capital Expenditures," *The Engineering Economist.* Hoboken, N.J.: Stevens Institute of Technology, 1966.
Lewis, R. B. *Profit Planning for Management.* Englewood Cliffs, N.J.: Prentice-Hall, 1960.
Lippitt, Vernon G. *Statistical Sales Forecasting.* New York: Financial Executives Research Foundation, 1961.
Mainer, Robert. "Impact of Strategic Planning on Executive Behavior." Boston Safe Deposit and Trust Company, 1965.
"Management of New Products." New York: Booz, Allen & Hamilton, 1960.
Managing Company Cash, Studies in Business Policy 99. New York: National Industrial Conference Board, 1961.
Mansfield, Edwin. *The Economics of Technological Change.* New York: W. W. Norton, 1968.
Margolin, Stephen A. *Approaches to Dynamic Investment Planning.* Amsterdam: North Holland Publishing Co., 1963.
Maw, J. Gordon. *Return on Investment Concept and Application,* AMA Management Bulletin 122, 1968.

Miley, Arthur L. "Directory of Planning, Budgeting and Control Information." Oxford, Ohio: Planning Executives Institute, 1969.

Miller, Ernest C. *Objectives and Standards—An Approach to Planning and Control,* AMA Research Study 74, 1966.

———. *Objectives and Standards of Performance in Financial Management,* AMA Research Study 87, 1968.

Moore, G. H., and Shiskin, J. *Indicators of Business Expansions and Contractions.* New York: Columbia University Press, 1966.

Morse, Dean, and Warner, Aaron W. *Technological Innovation and Society.* New York: Columbia University Press, 1966.

National Industrial Conference Board. *Forecasting Sales.* Studies in Business Policy No. 106. New York: 1961.

Novick, David, ed. *Program Budgeting.* Cambridge: Harvard University Press, 1965.

O'Brien, M. P. *Technological Planning and Misplanning.* Cambridge: Harvard University Press, 1962.

Oxenfeldt, Alfred R. *Developing a Product Strategy,* AMA, 1959.

Payne, Bruce. *Planning for Company Growth—Executives' Guide to Effective Long Range Planning.* New York: McGraw-Hill, 1963.

Pegram, Roger M., and Bailey, Earl L. *The New Product Race: The Market Executive Looks Ahead.* New York: National Industrial Conference Board, 1967.

Pessemier, Edgar A. *New Product Decision.* New York: McGraw-Hill, 1966.

Pflomm, Norman E. *Financial Committees,* Studies in Business Policy 105. New York: National Industrial Conference Board, 1963.

———. *Managing Capital Expenditures,* Studies in Business Policy 107. New York: National Industrial Conference Board, 1963.

Planning in Business. Menlo Park, Calif.: Stanford Research Institute, 1963.

Prehoda, Robert W. *Designing the Future—The Role of Technological Forecasting.* Philadelphia: Chilton Book Co., 1966.

Prince, Thomas R. *Information Systems for Management Planning and Control.* Homewood, Ill.: Richard D. Irwin, 1966.

Ringback, Kjell Arne. *Organized Corporate Planning Systems.* Madison: Graduate School of Business, University of Wisconsin, 1968.

Rose, T. G., and Farr, D. E. *Planning for Corporate Growth.* New York: McGraw-Hill, 1957.

St. Thomas, Charles E. *Practical Business Planning.* New York: American Management Association, 1965.

Scott, Brian W. *Long Range Planning in American Industry.* New York: American Management Association, 1965.

Shriver, Richard H., and White, Russell C. *Distribution Planning and Control: Effective Use of Computer Systems and Models,* Research Study No. 96. New York: American Management Association, 1969.

Silk, Leonard. *Forecasting Business Trends.* New York: McGraw-Hill, 1963.

Solomon, Martin B., Jr. *Investment Decisions in Small Business.* Lexington: University of Kentucky Press, 1963.

Sord, Burnard H., and Welsch, Glenn A. *Business Budgeting.* New York: Controllership Foundation, 1958.

Stedry, Andrew C. *Budget Control and Cost Behavior.* Englewood Cliffs, N.J.: Prentice-Hall, 1960.

Steiner, George A. *Top Management Planning.* New York: Macmillan Co., 1969.

Steiner, George A., ed. *Managerial Long Range Planning.* New York: McGraw-Hill, 1963.

———, ed. *Strategic Factors in Business Success.* New York: Financial Executives Research Foundation, 1968.

Steiner, George A., and Cannon, Warren M., eds. *Multinational Corporate Planning.* New York: Crowell, Collier and Macmillan Co., 1966.

Stewart, Robert F. "Framework of Business Planning," Stanford Research Institute Long Range Planning Service Report No. 162. Menlo Park, Calif.: 1963.

———. "Summary Tabulation of Responses to 1966 Survey of Business Planning." Menlo Park, Calif.: Stanford Research Institute Long Range Planning Service, 1967.

Stewart, Robert F., and Doscher, Marion O. "The Corporate Development Plan," Industrial Economic Division Report 183. Menlo Park, Calif.: Stanford Research Institute, 1963.

Stewart, Robert F.; Knight, Allen J.; and Morse, Cavender J. "The Strategic Plan," Long Range Planning Service Report 168. Menlo Park, Calif.: Stanford Research Institute, 1963.

Sweet, Franklin H. *Strategic Planning.* Austin: Bureau of Business Research, University of Texas, 1964.

Technological Innovation—Its Environment and Management. Washington, D.C.: U.S. Department of Commerce, 1967.

Terborgh, George. *Business Investment Policy.* Washington, D.C.: Machinery and Allied Products Institute, 1958.

Thompson, Stewart. *How Companies Plan,* AMA Research Study 54, 1962.

———. *Management Creeds and Philosophies,* AMA Research Study 32, 1958.

Tietjen, Karl H. *Organizing the Product Planning Function,* AMA Research Study 59, 1963.

Tse, John Y. D. *Profit Planning Through Volume-Cost Analysis.* New York: Macmillan Co., 1960.

Usry, Milton F. *Capital Expenditure Planning and Control.* Austin: Bureau of Business Research, University of Texas, 1966.

Villers, Raymond. *Research and Development Planning and Control.* New York: Financial Executives Research Foundation, 1964.

Walker, Ernest W., and Baughn, William H. *Financial Policy and Planning.* New York: Harper & Row, 1961.

Warner, Aaron W.; Morse, Dean; and Connely, Thomas E., eds. *The Environment of Change*. New York: Columbia University Press, 1968.

Warren, E. Kirby. *Long Range Planning—The Executive Viewpoint*. Englewood Cliffs, N.J.: Prentice-Hall, 1966.

Waterston, Albert. *Development Planning—Lessons of Experience*. Baltimore: Johns Hopkins Press, 1965.

Welsch, Glen A. *Budgeting Profit Planning and Control*. Englewood Cliffs, N.J.: Prentice-Hall, 1957.

Zarnowitz, Victor. *Appraisal of Short Term Economic Forecasts*. New York: Columbia University Press, 1966.